True to You

Living our Faith in our Multi-minded World

◆ Donald C. Posterski ◆

Editing: Michael Schwartzentruber
Design: Michael Schwartzentruber
Cover design: Lois Huey-Heck
Hand-marbled paper: Elizabeth Nachwey

Canadian Cataloguing in Publication Data

Posterski, Donald C., 1942-
True to You

Includes bibliographical references.
ISBN 1-55145-058-5

1. Multiculturalism-Religious aspects-Protestant churches. 2. Pluralism (Social sciences)
3. Ethics. I. Title.
BX4817.P67 1995 261'.1 C95-910189-6

Published by
Wood Lake Books Inc.
10162 Newene Rd., Winfield, BC
Canada V4V 1R2

Printed in Canada by
Hignell Printing Ltd.
Winnipeg, MB, R3G 2B4

◆ Contents ◆

◆ Foreword ◆

Canadian Christians need this book. Canada itself needs this book. But first, here's what we don't need.

We don't need another book that takes a simplistic, hard line on the complex issues of our times. We don't need a book that has hold of only one side of an idea and has the interests of only one group at heart. We don't need a book that drives a wedge into the joints of both church and country, that wrenches wider the fissures of misunderstanding and mistrust that already fracture common life.

We also don't need a book of vague musings and wistful dreams. We don't need a book of sugary sentiments that pays no attention to the deeply-rooted problems involved in racism, sexism, multiculturalism, regionalism, separatism, nationalism, and chauvinism of all stripes. We don't need a superficial analysis of our dilemmas followed by a prescription of warm fuzzies.

Finally, we don't need a book of facts and figures crammed into unintelligible charts and indigestible prose. We don't need 14 propositions divided into 35 categories laden with hundreds of statistics. We don't need complicated sentences that throw up qualification after qualification so that a sense of the forest is utterly lost as the reader tries to dodge tree after tree.

Instead, what we need is a tract for the times, and we have one here. We have a careful analysis of a number of layers of contemporary Canadian culture, buttressed by serious analysis but never bogged down in minutiae. We have a thoughtful consideration of various points of view that is yet committed to its own conclusions. We have a map of the present, and a prospectus for the future.

"The best lack all conviction, while the worst are full of passionate intensity," wrote poet William Butler Yeats. But here Don Posterski writes with passionate intensity on behalf of moderate convictions. We need a book like this primarily because we need more people like its author: passionate moderates, committed moderates, active moderates, persuasive moderates.

Canada was built by moderates. It has enjoyed and suffered its flamboyant extremists, but the politicians and businesspeople and soldiers and parents and clergy and professionals and farmers and tradespeople who constructed this nation and who make it up today have been moderate in temperament and manner. In the present raucous political debates, in the sensationalistic press, in the sound-bites of television, as well as in school board meetings, community clubs, and houses of faith—who will speak for moderates? Who will help moderates find their voices and listen well to the voices of others? Who will stand in the gaps between estranged Canadians of differing colors and sexes and regions and religions?

Don Posterski offers a way for moderate Canadians to moderate our sometimes overheated public life—and our private arguments! This book can help shape and motivate moderate minds and hearts to help Canada negotiate the difficulties already upon us and those that surely lie ahead.

We need help on how to think before we can decide what to think and what to do. Don Posterski's book concentrates on attitudes first, and that's good, I think, at least partly because I myself don't agree with every opinion in these pages! And one doesn't have to agree with this or that view of the author to benefit from the encouragement, elucidation, and equipment this book provides.

More can be helpfully read, of course. Canadian history, current sociology, and cultural criticism from a variety of viewpoints will complement the quick sketches of this volume. The notes of this book itself will guide the reader also to important theological reflections upon what it means to be a responsible citizen of both the City of God and the City of Humanity. This book, then, is a helpful way in to many of the salient issues and an orientation toward the further thought and action that the to help make the world a more just place, dealing with diversity is inescapable.

The book is framed in seven chapters. Chapter one documents the ascendancy of secular pluralism in modern society and identifies five ways today's Canadians respond to the emerging diversity. The second chapter defines and illustrates the different forms of pluralism that coexist in our modern world. While ideological pluralism is deemed to be an enemy of the faith, cultural pluralism is affirmed as a friend of the faith. Chapter three proposes that a culture cannot be built on diversity alone and calls everyone to relinquish rights and embrace common values. Chapters four, five, and six wrestle with specific ways to deal with diversity and map a strategy for pursuing "principled pluralism." Chapter seven affirms again that the Christian faith not only belongs in today's society, but that it can continue to make a critical contribution to how we all believe and behave. Current issues illustrating the forms of diversity that so often disrupt us are used throughout the book to keep the ideas connected to the realities of everyday life.

This book is more about how to think than what to think. The intent is to reveal why we respond as we do. The aim is also to deepen the legitimacy of diversity and cultivate an appreciation for life that extends beyond our personal borders. I hope readers will walk away with a model for understanding the dynamics of diversity and an awareness that when yet another batch of differences invades life, there are defined ways to respond.

I also want to warn readers that the content of the chapters often moves back and forth between personal and organizational categories. There are times when the material applies specifically to church life and other times when the broader culture is addressed. This may seem to be inconsistent, but it is how we live. We start the day at the personal level, often with members of our families. If the workplace is a part of what we do, we move into the organizational realm. Both our personal and organizational realms are framed within the culture that surrounds us. Increasingly, our immediate culture is connected to and influenced by global realities. Hopefully, our faith is a part of who we are regardless of what we are doing.

Writing a book is especially demanding when the work of writing must happen around the edges of life. I'm blessed with supportive people around me. My colleague Chuck Ferguson served well by offering candid feedback and insightful suggestions. In your words Chuck, thanks for helping "comb knots out of the tangled hair." Joan Morin extended herself way beyond the responsibilities of being a competent and caring administrative assistant. Dr. Ken MacMillan and Marla Stewart Konrad scrutinized the final text. Friend and former research colleague Irwin Barker helped develop several ideas. My daughter, Brenda Melles, sharpened my understanding of some of the controversial subject matter from her generation's point of view. My wife, Beth, cheered and critiqued me through yet "another book" with graciousness. Andrew Grenville and Rob Burbach from The Angus Reid Group enthusiastically contributed their research design and analytical skills to the project. Editors Mike Schwartzentruber and Jim Taylor at Wood Lake Books also deserve special acknowledgment for collaborating on this project. They have been ready to put their imprint on some perspectives that are outside their preferences. To other friends and colleagues, Ed Neufeld, John Wilkinson, Glenn Smith, and Chuck Hoffman, who both cheered and chided, I'm grateful.

Although issues remain unresolved in my mind about how to live as serious Christians in our emerging pluralistic society, my spirit resonates with Jacques Ellul. We must plunge into the social, political and spiritual problems of the world, "not in the hope of making it a paradise but with the hope of making it a little bit better."[2]

Blue Heron
Lake Rosseau, Ontario

legislation, while others cry "foul" and "discrimination" and call for "justice for all."

- The same scenario characterizes the abortion debate. Obviously, abortion is an issue that is not restricted to just those people who take faith seriously, but religion is a primary predictor of how people view the matter. Still, in some communities where churches exist across the street from each other, the Sunday morning sermon in one church will endorse the "pro-choice" view, while on the other side of the street, parishioners will hear a case defending the "pro-life" position. Inside both of those churches, parishioners could well be sitting in the same pew next to each other, quietly or openly, holding contradictory views.

No thoughtful person would ever argue that we should simply accept all of our past assumptions. After all, people who pulled the strings of power in the past didn't always use good judgment. But somehow, life seemed more stable. Isn't there any solid ground to stand on? Even the Bible is being subjected to new levels of scrutiny.

What are we to think when international scholars gather to vote on which sayings of Jesus are genuine and which should be discarded? After acknowledging and confessing that the historic faith has been patriarchal, is it really progress to proclaim that God transcends gender and then reimage God as Sophia?

Sometimes it seems as though our society is having a nervous breakdown and that our churches are contributing to the illness.

And it's not just a matter of having undefined feelings about what is happening around us; when we **do** take time to reflect carefully, we become even more troubled. We start asking questions such as,

- Why is being politically correct more fashionable than telling the truth?
- Is it really better to turn tolerance into a virtue than it is to set limits and call for shared community standards?
- Why is being inclusive of everyone else's views more compelling than self defining and taking a stand?

As Leszek Kolakowski says in his book *Modernity on Endless*

Trial, "Sometimes it seems as if all the words and signs that make up our conceptual framework and provide us with our basic system of distinctions are dissolving before our eyes."[1]

Obviously, the issues are not simple. We **do** understand that the feelings and tensions are generated because we live in a society with people who are different from us. We recognize that we are faced with the task of reconciling our views with the views of others, our rights with the rights of others. On one side, we know that in order to live with ourselves we have to be true to ourselves. But on the other side, we also know that other people need room to express their opinions and live out their choices too.

So what are the issues to be addressed and resolved? Succinctly stated may I pose three dilemmas?

1. How can we live peaceably and productively with our increasing diversity?
2. How can we construct a society that allows us to live with strong convictions while giving others the prerogative to do the same?
3. As God's people, active in our different denominations and religious traditions, are there ways for us to understand and even appreciate our differences so that we can celebrate our common faith commitments?

The alternatives

Some people seem predisposed to deny the beauty of diversity. They live like artists who paint pictures with only one color on their palette. They create monochrome worlds. Accordingly, one way of thinking is the only way to think. One way of believing is the only way to believe. One way of behaving is the only way to behave.

But just as there are people who reduce life down to their own size, there are other people who embrace the opposite extreme. They live with a mentality which holds that if all ways are not beautiful, they are at least permissible. As long as no one breaks the law and people don't get hurt along the way, they are ready to champion diversity as an ultimate virtue. They are like artists who mix many colors of paint in a single container and then move toward the canvas. In the author's view, the pictures they paint are passionless and bland.

Portraying God as the master artist of the universe gives us direction. From the beginning, God etched color into creation. One-color rainbows had no place in the Creator's original design. Painting a one-color world would insult God's creativity. And for us, what would life be like in a one-color world? Combinations of colors in any form would be inconceivable. The beauty of diversity in any category of life would be impossible.

At the same time, the world God created is much more than a random splash of colors. Creation is choreographed with order and design. The sun edges into the morning sky and fades into the darkening night. Spring is followed by summer and the fall gives way to winter. The laws of physics depend on predictability. We could not have landed on the moon if the moon had suddenly decided to veer off its orbit to visit another planet.

Celebrating diversity and making room for everyone's point of view sounds compelling; but unfettered it leads to random confusion, especially in a society where people have no choice but to live together.

Somehow we need to find a balance between encouraging diversity and putting limits on diversity. We will need to acknowledge other people's prerogatives to color code their world as they wish, while we continue to decide on our own favorite colors. But if we live solely with a mentality that says, "You paint with your colors" and "I'll paint with my colors" we will produce collective chaos. If we are to create a socially viable future, we will also have to stand side-by-side and use some common colors from the same palette as we paint portraits of our shared community life.

The proposal

The mindset of this book is to live in the modern world with our eyes wide open to the issues of the age. The aim is to find order in an increasingly unpredictable world. The hope is to do so by offering a framework for being true to ourselves, while at the same time, extending proper regard for the prerogatives of others. The goal is to move beyond just acknowledging differences.

Accordingly, the invitation is to both appreciate and celebrate the richness of diversity. But also, the pages that follow will press us to decide what we are going to believe and how we are going to behave in the midst of the diversity swirling around us. The challenge will be to decide what flags we will fly in the pluralism parade.

On the one hand, the following chapters will frustrate people who look for simple answers to complex problems. On the other hand, the following chapters are intended to help those who want to live with coherence in the muddle of escalating social, moral, and religious diversity. Ultimately, a pivotal conviction drives the book. As we make progress in our ability to deal with our diversity, we will not only be able to live more peaceably and productively together, we will be able to relate to each other with increasing integrity.

I choose to stand alongside journalist and fellow Canadian Jeffrey Simpson, who longingly wrote, "I hope with all my heart... that my children will inherit a country more secure in its identity and more capable of demonstrating that the challenge of diversity need not lead to division."[2]

◆ Pondering the Options ◆

Chapter One

Introduction

As Canadians growing up in our home and native land, we learned the rules of social etiquette. Our mothers and fathers communicated those rules clearly: "keep your elbows off the table," and "don't talk with your mouth full." Being told not to interrupt when someone else was already talking was as basic as having breakfast.

But today, on the cultural etiquette front, the rules are not as clear. We are many peoples with many differences living in one nation. As such, we struggle to find everyday approaches for making modern Canadianism work. In particular, we need to refine the manner in which we relate to each other's differences. Our challenge is to learn new rules for proper cultural etiquette.

Part of our problem is that we have never been here before. And in real life, there are no rehearsals as we set about the task of making history. The first time through is performance time. Every interval is a unique weaving in the frame of life. But in our journey through this particular measure in time, we are having our difficulties.

◆ A. Remember when ◆

While a significant segment of the population is somewhat uneasy about the future, many have fond memories of the past. We remember when children, in public schools from coast to coast, began their days by reciting the Lord's Prayer. When our federal politicians followed the same practice in parliament, we took pride in the public acknowledgment of the country's Christian roots. We readily recall when, without argument, a family was a man and a woman living in a home with one or more children. We remember when people got married and then moved in with each other, when having sex outside of a marriage covenant was considered morally wrong. We have recent memories of Sundays when shopping centers were closed and the majority of people attended church. We didn't have to argue with our children about whether or not they would play in hockey tournaments or go to Sunday school because hockey wasn't scheduled on Sabbath mornings. We remember when life had fewer loose ends, when tomorrow was predictable, and we felt more secure. Certainly, there were lots of imperfections. But back then, questions had clearer answers and problems had less complicated solutions.

Whether a rational case can be made for it or not, many of us live with a sense of loss. And even though we know that living together in a society is not like sitting at a computer where you press the delete button to get rid of script you no longer want, we still long nostalgically for the past. On occasion, we live in the present with a sense of despair, and sometimes we look to the future with fear. As Michel Foucault has written, we live with a sense of increasing vulnerability, "a certain fragility has been discovered in the very bedrock of existence...even in those aspects that are most familiar, most solid and most intimately related...to our everyday behavior."[1]

Change is certain

If you have the opportunity to visit the nation's capital and tour the parliament buildings, you will be reminded that the patterns of yesterday are not automatically transferred into today's designs for life.

Housed in the third floor of the Peace Tower is the "Memorial Chamber" which pays tribute to Canadians who laid down their lives in honor of their country and for the sake of freedom and peace. The memorial was officially opened in 1928.

The names of each of the 65,000 Canadians who died in World

War I and those of the 45,000 who were killed in the battles of World War II are carefully inscribed on page after page and bound together in massive leather-covered books.

Inscribed in the marble walls are various dates and inscriptions including an excerpt from Psalm 139:

> Whither shall I go from thy Spirit? or whither shall I flee from thy presence?
>
> If I ascend up into heaven, thou art there: if I make my bed in hell, behold, thou art there. If I take the wings of the morning, and dwell in the uttermost parts of the sea; even there shall thy hand lead me, and thy right hand shall hold me.
>
> (Psalm 139:7–10, KJV)[2]

As I stood reading the inscription, a number of thoughts flooded into my mind. One thought was that if the memorial had been erected in the 1990s instead of 1928, the biblical citation would not be chiseled into the marble. Change is one certainty that marks the modern world.

Acknowledging change as a certainty need not be interpreted as a judgment against change. Neither is remembering and appreciating patterns from the past synonymous with resisting change in the future. Obviously, many changes usher in positive results. But change doesn't necessarily translate into progress and improvement. Clearly, there are issues to be raised and resolved.

As today's history writers standing at the intersection between yesterday and tomorrow, what direction should we face? Do we attempt to go back and reclaim the past? Or do we assess the cultural rules and regulations governing the present and simply pursue the future? As God's people, do we seek to restore some of the formal Christian presence in society? Do we press our points of view as God's point of view for Canada as a nation? What are our best options? And along the way, can we understand what happened to push the church to the sidelines of society?

◆ B. Decline of formal religion ◆

The historical role of religion in Canada parallels the experience of most nations. "Throughout human history, religion has been the most decisive way of defining a cosmos or a world...

Human identity is recognized and known within this [religious] context,"[3] writes Charles Long in *Pushing the Faith*. In Canada, French-speaking Quebec was deeded to the Catholics and the Anglican church flew the Protestant flag for the English most everywhere else.

Religion continues to be a dominant identifier of people in the nation. Asking the question, "What is your religious background?" is almost as inclusive as inquiring, "What is your family background?" Close to nine out of 10 Canadians will respond, "I am Catholic, I am Protestant, I am Sikh, or I am Hindu."

Although the Canadian calendar continues to be structured around Judeo-Christian events, with Christmas and Easter as statutory holidays, the status of religion has been demoted. While the vast majority of modern Canadians continue to identify with religious organizations, they are less prepared to participate with regularity or to apply their religious faith to matters in their day-to-day lives. The data detail the current situation.

High on God—low on church

In a survey of 1502 Canadians conducted by the Angus Reid Group in the summer of 1994, 412 or 27% claimed to have regular contact with a church. These participants either attend weekly or at least once a month. Of the group of 412 church participants, 74% attend regularly and are formal members of their church, 17% attend a particular congregation without being formal members, and 9% attend regularly but tend to roam from church to church.[4]

The patterns of involvement of these people of God sort themselves into two categories: committed participants and conditional participants.[5] The committed participants are more avid weekly attenders than the conditional types (72% compared to 60%). Conditional participants are more likely to be monthly attenders (40% compared to 28%). In other words, the committed participants are more frequently involved but the conditional are very active too.

Committed participants are characterized by frequent participation and high commitment. They are the card carrying, formal membership people who form the core of local congregational life. They identify with both their local church and the affiliated denomi-

Fig. 1.1
Comparisons of committed and conditional participants

	Committed Participants	Conditional Participants
	Percent who "Strongly Agree"	
I feel close to the church I attend	38	25
I think you need to go to church to be a good Christian	31	22
I am involved in a small group (e.g., Bible study, ministry service, discussion group	47	13

Source: Angus Reid Group: July 1994.

nation or religious tradition. Members of the clergy love the committed participants. They are weekly attenders, feel close to the church they attend, and are inclined to think that one needs to actively participate in church life in order to be a good Christian. A total of 47% of the committed participants also make the choice to be involved in a small group, such as a Bible study, ministry service, or discussion group.

Conditional participants attend church regularly but they participate without the commitment marked by formal membership. They also have other reservations. One category of conditional participants (17%) clearly identify with the local church they attend but are not attached to the church's associated denomination. The other category of conditional participants (9%) are even reticent to commit themselves to a local parish or congregation. They are roamers. They go from church to church like some people go from store to store shopping for specials.

Conditional participants have quite likely switched denominations. Compared to the 47% of committed participants, only 13%

are active in a small group of some kind. They attend less frequently, feel more distanced from the church they attend, and are less inclined to think one has to go to church to be a good Christian. *(See Fig. 1.1)* They certainly do not attend church business meetings. Because they have probably switched churches already, unless their local church situation is positive and continues to meet their spiritual needs, their staying power is suspect.

Committed and conditional participants are the "visible" Christians in the culture. They are the ones who can be seen getting into their cars or waiting for a bus to head off to church on Sunday morning. Because approximately only one out of four Canadians attend church regularly, they experience some of the same feelings other "visible minorities" encounter in modern society.

Cultural Christians form the majority of the society. Approximately two out of three Canadians fit the definition. They continue to identify themselves as Catholics or Protestants but they do not attend church on any regular basis. Ironically, they may hold formal membership and be counted on a church roll but they do not participate. Still, they have a user-friendly attitude toward the church of their affiliation. Particularly when it is time for the sacred rites of passage related to birth, marriage, and death, cultural Christians expect to use the services of the church. But using the church does not make them likely prospects as regular attenders. Because 86% of cultural Christians also believe that "you do not need to go to church in order to be a good Christian," they are content to view the church strictly as a provider of these rites of passage. The tongue-in-cheek comment of Anglican Rector, The Reverend Harold Percy is accurate: "Cultural Christians wouldn't come to church regularly if you offered them frequent flyer points."

The picture of the religious scene in the country painted by the latest information from Statistics Canada adds clarity. When the 27% of regular attenders are subtracted from the 82% of the population who identify as Catholics or Protestants, we are left with 55% who fit into the cultural Christian category. (*See Fig. 1.2*)

Other world religions are embraced by no more than one million who live in Canada. Still, the country's larger cities have significant numbers of Muslims, Hindus, Buddhists, and Sikhs. The construction of new temples and mosques indicates the presence of

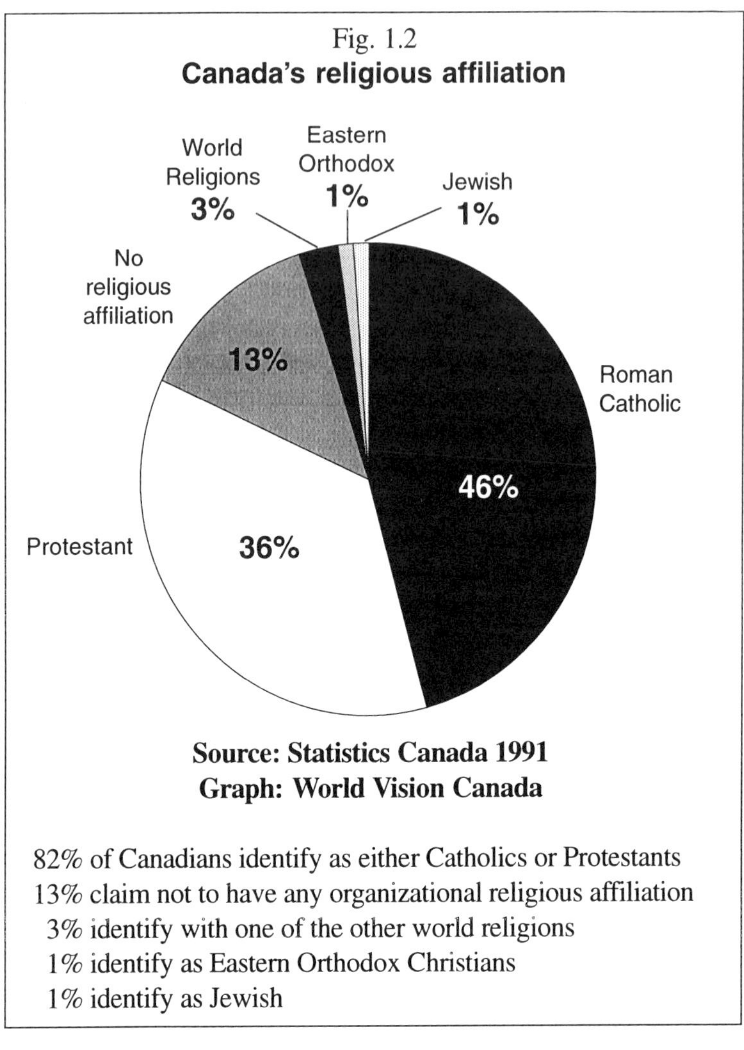

Fig. 1.2
Canada's religious affiliation

Source: Statistics Canada 1991
Graph: World Vision Canada

82% of Canadians identify as either Catholics or Protestants
13% claim not to have any organizational religious affiliation
3% identify with one of the other world religions
1% identify as Eastern Orthodox Christians
1% identify as Jewish

people worshiping in ways that are consistent with their beliefs and convictions. Immigration has always resulted in the importing of religion into Canada and current patterns are diversifying the religious landscape. What is sometimes overlooked, however, is that two out of three immigrants who come to Canada identify themselves as Christians—either Catholic or Protestant.[6]

Religious nones (Canadians stating "no religious affiliation") are not as irreligious as their designation implies. What is consistent

Fig. 1.3
Religiosity of religious nones

	Percent who "Agree Strongly" or "Moderately"
In my view, Jesus Christ was not son of God	46
I feel God is the source and sustainer of everything	36
I believe the Bible is the inspired word of God	26
I have an intense, personal relationship with God	21
As far as I am concerned, I am a Christian	32

Source: Angus Reid Group: July 1994 N = 204

about their beliefs is that they have disengaged from any organizational religious attachment. However, a significant segment of those who resist identifying with organized religion continue to hold on to conventional religious beliefs and claim a personal relationship with God. *(See Fig. 1.3)*

Based on 1991 census data, Statistics Canada estimates that out of a population of approximately 27 million people there are 21,970 agnostics and 13,510 atheists in the land. Whether or not the majority of modern Canadians are spiritually lost or not remains a matter for debate. But one thing is certain. Religiosity and spirituality is seeded in the soil of the land and rests in the souls of today's Canadians.

The religious demographics are too complex to synthesize in a single statement. However, if we look visually at how Canadians view God and then respond to the church, a case can be made to contend that, in general, the majority of Canadians are "high on God" but "low on the church." *(See Fig. 1.4)*

Testing faith claims

The minority status of the "committed" and "conditional"

Fig. 1.4
Comparison of Commitment to God and Church

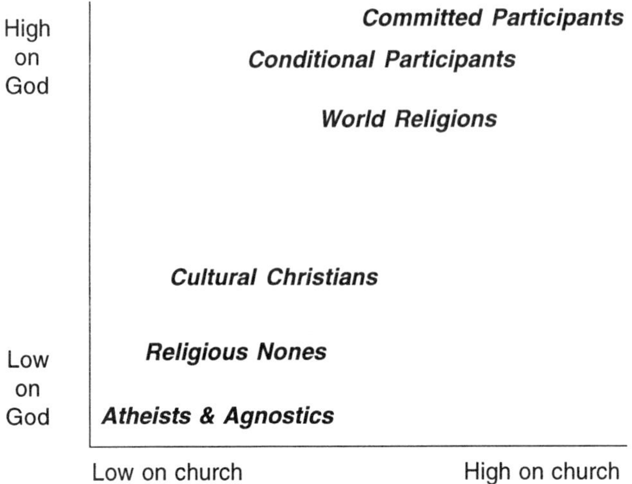

participants alongside the dominance of "cultural Christians" and "religious nones" in contemporary Canadian society raises a number of issues. Has the time come for the church to develop new liturgies that simply celebrate past accomplishments? Is visible Christianity outmoded except for those who want to keep the old ways alive? "Is religion like building model airplanes, just another hobby: something quiet, something private, something trivial—and not really a fit activity for intelligent, public-spirited adults?" as Stephen L. Carter asks in his book *The Culture of Disbelief.*[7]

Whatever the case, as the historical integrator of the nation's morality and view of existence, organized religion is no longer considered necessary to sustain today's social order. The church has been relegated to a more restricted social role but is still available for those who choose to be personally involved.[8]

Psychologist Gordon Allport divides religious claims into two categories—the extrinsic and the intrinsic. In doing so, he distinguishes between those who absent themselves from active participation in church life and those who are active churchgoers.

> The extrinsic type...have no true association with the religious function of the church and neither feel obligated to

> attend church regularly nor to integrate religion into their way of life... Religion is strictly utilitarian: useful for the self in granting safety, social standing, solace, and endorsement of one's chosen way of life.
>
> The intrinsic form of religious sentiment regards faith as a supreme value in its own right. It is oriented toward a unification of being, takes seriously the commandment of brotherhood [sic], and strives to transcend all self-centered needs.[9]

Allport's criteria supports the author's view that all expressions of belief and religious faith should not be considered equally valid. Just as we readily evaluate the quality of health care and education, so we should test the validity of various faith claims.

Personalized faith compared to socialized faith

Faith in God is still part of the Canadian inheritance. Just as values get passed on, so faith is transmitted from one generation to the next. Children almost automatically embrace the religious affiliation of their parents. For the majority, being a Catholic or being a Protestant is the socialized norm. The result is that when both young and older Canadians are asked, "Do you believe that God exists?" approximately 80% respond positively.[10] In Allport's terms, extrinsic faith remains entrenched in the culture.

Inherited faith and belief in God provide a sound spiritual foundation from which to pursue full-fledged faith. However, family faith is not autonomous faith and neither is socialized faith equivalent to personalized faith. One of the reasons we have such an abundance of cultural Christians in Canada is that people have not translated their socialized faith into personalized faith. Many people are left believing in God, but they do not personally know the God they believe in.

Active faith compared to passive faith

Christian faith is often described as a relationship. God is conceived as the Creator of the universe but is still accessible to all who are created. Jesus Christ is the redeemer of life who invites people into a restored relationship with himself. Prayer is the communication that nurtures the relationship. The sacrament of the Lord's Supper may be mysterious, but the experience engenders life. Worship in the presence of others confirms the reality of faith.

Obviously, people can have faith in God without prayer, the sacrament of communion, and shared worship. But that kind of faith is like a relationship with a friend who lives hundreds of miles away, a relationship with no telephone calls, letters, or contact. There may be occasional fleeting thoughts and memories of experiences from the past, but it is a dormant friendship. The relationship is more historical than current, more hypothetical than real, more passive than active. Dormant relationships and dormant faith have limited value.

Public faith compared to private faith

The New Testament envisions the people of God gathering together. The clarion call is, "Do not forsake the assembling of yourselves together." (Hebrews 10:25) Accordingly, testing people's faith claims on the "active—passive" and "public—private" axis is legitimate. However, using church attendance alone as a checklist for valid faith is inadequate. Attending Saturday evening mass or parading to church on Sunday without deliberate attempts to apply one's faith to Monday's agenda is fraudulent.

Documented horror stories and too many personal experiences leave little defense against the accusation that far too many public faith church attenders are committed hypocrites. It is also true that people who value their private faith, or for that matter, people who make no faith claims at all, are fully capable of living commendable lives. Still, affirming church participation as a norm for God's people remains desirable.

The point to affirm, however, is that full-fledged faith is both valued in private and observable in public. Privatized faith is better than no faith at all. But privatized faith that is practiced in public has more integrity. There is a qualitative difference between belief that is held as an attitude and belief that is expressed in behavior. So there is a qualitative difference between anonymous faith and faith that is confessed publicly in word and deed.

Privatized faith is hidden faith. It can be more theoretical than practical. Most often, it is also undeveloped faith. Public faith is observable faith. It is shared with others and also embraces a readiness to enjoy God, to taste and see that the Lord is good.

People who are relaxed with God in private and comfortable about being identified with God in public can move in the direction of full-fledged faith.

One of my assumptions, then, is that some level of active participation in spiritual worship and learning with other Christians is one mark of a fully faithful Christian. The involvement may not always take place in a formal church setting, but at the very least, the participation includes meeting together with other followers of Jesus for the purpose of affirming faith and pursuing service to God.

Religious philosopher Elton Trueblood notes the role of religious faith in society:

> The terrible danger of our time consists in the fact that ours is a cut-flower civilization. Beautiful as cut flowers may be, and much as we may use our ingenuity to keep them looking fresh for a while, they will eventually die, and they die because they are severed from their sustaining roots.[11]

To this point in Canada's history, the church has been a sustaining presence in the culture. It has nurtured values, cultivated ethics, instilled morals, and channeled the spiritual hunger of people toward the God of the universe. If the church is no longer able or allowed to serve society and her citizens as it has in the past, who or what will take its place?

◆ C. Ascendancy of secular pluralism ◆

There are different ways to interpret Canada's history, but if we peer at our past through a religious lens, the "two solitudes" description brings focus. French-speaking Canadians were positioned on one side of the cultural divide and those who spoke English stood on the other side. It was simply assumed that the French were Catholic and the English were Protestants. Accordingly, language and religion were the major identity indicators for the entire population. Although history provides instances of harsh judgment and open hostility between Catholics and Protestants, it could be argued that worship of the same God and the embrace of the same faith bestowed a Christian soul upon the whole nation.

People may disagree over Catholic and Protestant theology and the various worship styles they practice, but the common core of the commitments they shared shaped the norms of Canadian life. Christianity defined our cultural consensus. Until the arrival of the turbulent 1960s, the assumptions of the Christian faith were the assumptions of Canadian society. But for the past three decades organized religion has failed to meet adequately the demands of a new day.

Societies are like people. When they stop believing and behaving in one way, they start believing and behaving in other ways. The marginalization of formal religion and the accompanying decline in church attendance is a symbol of both stopping and starting for today's Canadians. Increasingly, Canadians are stopping the practice of constructing their lives with God at the center. The ways of the world are pushing aside the ways of God. The earthly and the temporal are progressively sovereign over the eternal and the spiritual. The secular realm is invading and overwhelming the sacred realm. Dependence on the Divine is being exchanged for independence. Repentance and confession are still valid, but only for those who hang on to the old ways. Values are not taught as virtues for everyone. Values are a personal matter, subject to one's own clarification. Connecting purpose in life to glorifying God just doesn't ring right to the majority of Canadians.

God is unnecessary

For the majority of Canadians, the emerging and prevailing cultural consensus is best described by the term **secular pluralism**. Sociologist Bryan Wilson has insightfully defined secularization as "that process by which religious institutions, actions and consciousness, lose their social significance."[12] Canadian culture is "secular" in that most people believe, either consciously or unconsciously, that God is unnecessary for making sense out of life. And society is "pluralistic" in that people put their lives together accepting the assumption that many ways of believing and behaving are equally valid.

Clearly, the process of secularization, resulting in society "becoming more secular," has characterized the Canadian way of life for a very long time. This progressive shift from religious dominance toward secular control has not only demoted the social standing of our churches, it has also pushed God to the edges of people's lives. When translated into a cultural creed, secularism creates a world where God is unnecessary. Days and nights come and go without any practical need for God's intervention or assistance. God may exist as a hypothesis for modern Canadians, but God's active role in the daily events of life is superfluous. For all practical purposes, with God out of the picture, says Philip E. Johnson in *First Things*, "every human becomes a 'godlet'—with as much authority to set standards as any other godlet or combination of godlets."[13]

There are two qualifiers regarding Canadian-style secularism that merit clarification. Because our Christian roots are still embedded in present-day culture, Canadian-style secularism is more a matter of practice than it is an articulated ideology. In other words, Canadians have not consciously voted God out of business by formally altering what they say they believe. Rather, they have **practically** pushed God to the outskirts of society and the margins of their personal lives by simply ignoring God's will and ways. The qualification is that, while currently most Canadians are well on the way to being genuinely secular, they are still only "semi-secularized." On the one hand, modern Canadians remain in touch with and linked to their religious roots. On the other hand, they are distanced and detached from living God-centered lives.

The second qualifier worth restating about Canadian secularism is that it is still socially friendly toward religion. Canadians are not anti-Christian. There is very little religious animosity in the mainstream of our society. Those who contend there is an anti-Christian conspiracy in the land undoubtedly feel coerced by the culture. They may so be subscribing to their own propaganda or behaving in ways that are culturally offensive.[14]

Pluralism is persuasive

Sociologist Peter Berger believes that the embrace of pluralism in North American has been even more consequential than the effects of secularism. Like many others, Berger points his finger at "science and technology as secularizing factors." While acknowledging that many scientists have been religious persons, the more influential fact, says Berger, is that "modern science fosters a mindset that is impatient of mystery and that seeks rational explanations in place of supernatural causalities."[15] But from Berger's perspective, it is the "pluralization of the modern social environment" that has undermined the possibility of establishing religious certitudes.[16]

Berger reasons that "pluralism is not just a lot of people of different colors, languages, religions, and lifestyles bumping into each other and somehow coming to terms under conditions of civic peace. It is not merely a fact of the external social environment. Pluralism also impinges on human consciousness, on what takes place within our minds."[17] And what takes place inside our collective minds either makes something plausible or implausible—believable or unbelievable. "When virtually everyone supports a particular belief, this belief, no matter what it is will attain the status of taken-for-granted truth."[18]

It is precisely because the attitudes and assumptions of pluralism have moved inside the minds of the majority of modern Canadians that truth claims have been reduced to a matter of personal opinion. Believing in the validity of many views thwarts the claim that one particular viewpoint can have absolute authority. Consequently, in the realm of beliefs and ethics, morals and values, it becomes exceedingly difficult to achieve any sense of certainty. In the end, pluralism wins the day for relativism. Truth is downsized to the prerogative of personal views and the last word in any debate about what is right or wrong is, "Well, that's your opinion." In the aftermath, people who have held to the maxim that "You shall know the truth and the truth will make you free" (John 8:32) are left struggling with the "erosion of our continuities."[19]

◆ D. Embracing postmodernism ◆

Secular pluralism alongside rampant relativism has lead to what scholars and academics call "postmodernism." This term is used to explain a cultural shift in the western world which, if it does not already define the present state of social affairs, is a prediction of what is just around the corner.

A review of western world history in capsule form is helpful at this point.

The **Renaissance** formally affirmed human life as the focal point of reality. Beginning in the 14th century and extending into the 17th century, it provided the transition from medieval times into the modern world. Inspiring the revival of art and literature, the Renaissance reawakened the human pursuit of knowledge.

The **Enlightenment** period emerged in the 17th and 18th centuries and nurtured new levels of admiration for the power of reason. Stressing the autonomous abilities of the individual, the Enlightenment spawned the scientific method that launched the world into exhilarating levels of self-determination. Albert Borgmann says that the Enlightenment was the "original liberation movement of our time, and what it promised, through science, technology, and a dynamic new economy, was to bring the forces of nature and culture under control, liberate us from misery and toil and enrich our lives."[20]

Twentieth century **Modernism** increasingly oriented itself toward humanism and technology. Still connected to religious roots and traditional views of morality, but assuming the principle of progress, the spirit of modernism both encouraged and endorsed human endeavor. The modern age fueled enthusiasm for the human potential and envisioned a world without limits.

Postmodernism enters the current landscape questioning the assumptions of modernism and the previous ways of conceiving of life. The belief that reason and the scientific method can provide a reliable or universal foundation for knowledge is specifically questioned. For postmodernism, life is a limitless expression of human pursuits, reality is a question of personal perception, and truth is a matter of personal preference. In *Pushing the Faith*, Benton Johnson says that "More and more matters are treated as changeable and negotiable rather than as unalterable matters of custom or morality."[21]

No right answers—no clear boundaries

Secularism and pluralism both complement and accelerate postmodern premises. For postmodernists, there are no right answers. Nothing is really final or conclusive. There are no clear boundaries for right and wrong, truth and error, goodness and evil. Life is filled with potential and prerogative, but it is also unpredictable and unmanageable. In the postmodern paradigm, "Personal preference is principle" and "Principle is personal preference."

There are no fixed points of reference except those one sets for oneself. Feelings can be the final arbitrators in determining what is right and wrong; or one may conclude that there is no right and wrong. The point is that in postmodernism there are no rules, there are no boundaries. Paradox, diversity, limitless alternatives, and plural possibilities all prevail. In its pure form, postmodernism creates a context for chaos and can lead to lawlessness. Even in a moderate form, postmodernism hampers our ability to develop a clear cultural consensus.

Postmodernism directly challenges Christian assumptions.[22] Attempts to systematize human experience break the rules. The search for universals is considered futile. The polarization of life into right and wrong or black and white categories is untenable. Accordingly, there is no trustworthy, grand narrative to explain human existence. The Creation-Redemption story, or for that matter Marxist thought, are simply unacceptable and invalid explanations for understanding how to believe and behave. As leading post-modernist thinker Michel Foucault observes, there is a sense of increasing vulnerability in the mood of the age, particularly "those who have been in positions of power feel vulnerable and fragile."[23]

Life within the postmodern frame is susceptible to fragmentation and to the unpredictable. Many rock videos are examples of what postmodernism can produce. As an array of disconnected images, they fragment and scramble life. They also invite patchwork personalities such as Madonna to enter the forum. As a postmodern icon, Madonna is entitled to be sometimes a blond and sometimes a redhead, sometimes to wear her underwear inside and sometimes to wear it outside, sometimes to be decent and sometimes to be indecent. When life is limitless and you have both the resources and stimulus to do so, the opportunity exists to invent and reinvent, to experiment and to try something that has not been tried before.

At the end of a sometimes decent and sometimes indecent appearance on *Late Night with David Letterman*, Madonna chided Letterman before she left the stage because, "You didn't ask about me!" One might pause to reflect and ask, "Who is the real Madonna?"

Playwright and former dissident Vaclav Havel, now president

of the Czechoslovakia Republic, said the following in a speech he gave in Philadelphia in the summer of 1994:

> We live in a postmodern world where everything is possible and almost nothing is certain...all consistent value systems (are) collapsing and cultures distant in time and space are (being) rediscovered.

Accordingly, whether it is life in Czechoslovakia or Bosnia or Rwanda or Quebec,

> the fewer answers the era of rational knowledge provides to the basic questions of human beings, the more deeply people, behind its back as it were, cling to the ancient certainties of the tribe.[24]

For people living with a commitment to the Christian faith, postmodernism can easily be perceived as a threat. Denying the validity of grand narratives, reducing truth to personal preference, and exchanging certitudes for randomness is hardly inviting to people who have staked their lives on "the way, the truth. and the life." (John 14:6) Still, it will also be important to look for the positive things that postmodernism can contribute.

For example, while postmodernism will be "too open" a system for most, some forms of Christianity may be "too closed" to be effective in this age. Grand narratives can become exclusive narratives. People who live with the mentality that "My way is the only way" to believe and behave are not only vulnerable to close-mindedness, they are susceptible to arrogance. Living with a sense of reasonable certainty is one thing; propagating unexamined religious rhetoric is another.

Fixed ways of thinking and doing things can stifle and restrain people and organizations. People who are locked into the supremacy of their own ways seldom value the ways of others. They can become little people living in small worlds. The mood of postmodernism invites exploration, welcomes intrigue, and celebrates surprises. Organizations that pull down the blinds on innovation and experimentation not only block out learning, they downsize their futures. Approaching life without one's mind already made up about everything can release creativity and generate newness. Many churches and their members would benefit from an encounter with both creativity and newness.

Postmodernism can also open doors of opportunity for the gospel. Setting aside old ways of making sense out of what God desires for creation and what Christ has done on the cross can stimulate new ways of making meaning for people in the modern world. Instead of just reflecting past messages and metaphors, the temperament of the times invites fresh images of God and the gospel.

There is another aspect worth considering. The inadequacies of postmodernism could well motivate people to look for something more. For some people, fragmentation will prompt a desire for coherence. Randomness will instill a longing for order. Uncertainty will create a craving for certainty.

If it seems too far a reach to look for the positive possibilities in postmodernism, we should remember that new ways of perceiving life usually emerge when past ways prove to be inadequate.

◆ E. Responding to diversity ◆

Long before postmodernism made a cultural appearance, sea captains needed navigational charts to steer their way through rocky channels. Even today, trappers in the north require compasses to plot their paths on overcast days. And certainly in the future we will all need charts and compasses to navigate our way through the increasing disarray and diversity that confronts and sometimes confuses us in modern Canada. What is our best approach as we steer into the future? Do we attempt to go back to the past and reclaim what used to be? Do we turn away from the change and confusion of the modern world and, as much as possible, live with those who see life as we see it? Or do we enter into the fray and collaborate with those who are different from ourselves, seeking all the while to create a desirable future? I propose that there are five different ways for Christians and those who believe otherwise to respond to present and future forms of diversity.

1. RECLAIM and Convert

There are a sizable number of Christian Canadians who would unabashedly like to "turn back the clock." They would like to return to what their memories tell them was a "more Christian Canada."

The majority of the people of God who qualify as "reclaimers" would like to reinstate the Lord's Prayer and to return to compulsory Christian education in public schools. They lament the fact that Canada is the only nation in the western world without abortion legislation, and they point to increasing access to pornography as a symbol of moral decay. They represent many Canadians who fear that family values are in jeopardy, and consequently, they resist any attempt to grant workplace rights to homosexuals. The mission drive in the inner spirit of these followers of Jesus is propelled by their strong faith commitment. Reclaimers are ruled by their convictions. They intentionally and prayerfully desire to convert people around them to their own views. They resist any change that stands in opposition to their clear principles.

But the harsh reality is that looking back with nostalgia and pining for life as it used to be is simply not an option for those who want to be taken seriously in the future. Arguing for a return to the past is like offering inadmissible evidence before a judge in a court of law. As well as being inappropriate, it becomes counterproductive.

When we listen to those in society who yearn for yesterday, we are able to distinguish certain themes.

"We were here first!" Faced with unwanted change and an influx of people with different religions and invasive cultural symbols, reclaimers appeal to cultural seniority. "We were here first," and if you want to be a part of Canada, "you should be like us" is the unstated rationale. Confronted with the presence of other world religions reclaimers exclaim, "Don't these people know that Canada is a Christian country."

If reclaimers are ready to appeal to cultural seniority, they should also confess to having a short-term memory. Except for aboriginal Canadians, all Canadians are immigrants.

"My way is the right way!" Confronted by alternative lifestyles and the erosion of their cherished values in society, reclaimers also champion cultural superiority. Instead of reaching out to be inclusive of people who are different from themselves, reclaimers seek to convert people to their ways and to construct an exclusive world. They protest against cultural shifts that would extend the boundaries of their lives beyond their own self-described limits. They seek to convince all people that they should live within the lines they prescribe for themselves.

Although the intent of reclaimers is most often noble, these people of God and the churches they represent will fail. We cannot go back to the glory days of Christendom any more than aboriginal peoples can go back to living off the land. As Lesslie Newbigin states in *Truth to Tell*, "Nostalgia for Christendom is very understandable but it is futile."[25]

Whether the yearning of reclaimers is understandable or not, the better alternative is to square one's shoulders into the future and find constructive ways to go forward.

In a democratic society, reclaimers should never be pressed to surrender their deeply held convictions. However, those who realize that life cannot go back to what it used to be will find new ways to be faithful to the God they love and desire to serve.

2. TRIBALIZE and Confront

On the surface, "tribalizers" are markedly similar to reclaimers. But when you look closely, there are differences. The tribalizers' first motivation is to make sure there is room in society for their views and their choices. They want to be certain they can have life on their terms. They can be blinded by their biases and boundaries. If necessary, tribalizers are prepared to be confrontational to get their way. They consistently champion their own views but their compassion toward the views of others is almost non-existent.

Their essential goal is not to convert others to their point of view. Tribalizers may attempt to withhold prerogatives from others who disagree with them, but that should not be confused with the reclaimers' drive to convert people. The abortion debate provides an example of how both "pro-life" and "pro-choice" advocates behave as tribalizers. Both sides look at life through their own window and are completely convinced that the other side is wrong.

Confrontation is a basic tactic for tribalizers. They live with harsh edges. They are aggressive. They are motivated by dissent. People who disagree with them are deemed to be the opposition. They are committed solely to their vested interests. Whether the issue is economic, political, educational, religious, or sexual in nature, tribalizers have one point of view. They are not really interested in understanding other people's perspectives, or for that matter, their rights. They are like defense lawyers who are committed to win at all costs. Tribalizers are ready to regionalize, fracture, isolate, segregate, and if necessary, shred society to get their way.

Challenged by change and convinced that their way is really the only way, tribalizers set up life so that it is necessary to take sides. Because right and wrong are so clear, it is relatively easy to inculcate "us against them" mentalities. Self-defining over against an enemy makes it natural to project life into "win—lose" scenarios. The "good" is then poised to confront the "bad." Almost any effort, whether noble or distasteful, is justified in order to defeat the enemy.

In contemporary Canadian society, the pendulum is definitely swinging toward the tribalizers. The present makeup of the federal parliament is an eloquent statement of tribalized politics and a regionalized nation. The official opposition is made up of a party that formally exists to fracture the country. After swearing allegiance to the Queen, Lucien Bouchard of the Bloc Quebecois and his 53 provincial partners proceeded to declare their agenda to pursue Quebec's separation from the same federation that pays their salaries. Although Preston Manning and his 52 Reform Party members do not represent the same degree of balkanization, their constituency support requires them to espouse the interests of Western Canadians. Without the prevailing dissenting spirit that feeds tribalization, neither the Bloc Quebecois nor the Reform Party would be in a position to parade their power on behalf of their parochial interests.

The religious realm has its form of tribalization too. Compared to the overt aggressiveness of the political world, church-style tribalism is more placid. The manner is not usually as obtrusive, but it still fosters isolation.

During the past few years I have hosted numerous breakfasts with ministers. The intent has been to seek their counsel regarding the development of research proposals. The practice has been to invite people from various denominations representing both mainline churches and evangelical congregations. Without exception, well-established ministers from the same city meet each other for the first time. During the table talk, these same members of the clergy are both surprised and impressed by the ministries their colleagues are engaged in. By the time the last cup of coffee is poured and the discussion ends, people not only look at each other with friendlier eyes, they inevitably confess they should have met before.

On more than one occasion around those breakfast tables, ministers from the same city have shared what their denominations project for the future. They have been affronted to learn that, without any communication between them or from the leadership of their denomination, plans are well in motion to enter the same expanding neighborhoods in order to plant new churches. What inevitably follows is the mutual confession, "We can't keep doing it this way."

Many readers may disagree, but whether the form of tribalization is passive or aggressive, tribalizers cannot lead us into a healthy future.

3. ACCOMMODATE and Include

Representing another alternative, some people believe that the best way to approach the future is to accommodate their ways to the ways of the modern world. "Accommodators" are predisposed to expand the boundaries of their previous views and to reach out to include people. In their attitudes and actions, Christians who seek to accommodate belong in the "Christ of Culture" category that Richard Niebuhr described in his classic book, *Christ and Culture.*[26] Rather than being exclusive, accommodators are inclusive. Acknowledging and valuing diversity is only a beginning for accommodators. In their enthusiasm for inclusiveness, they are ready to cherish and embrace divergence.

Accommodators see and celebrate the beauty of God's creation in almost everything. Their confidence in the goodness of the human spirit brings a buoyancy to relationships and the hope for a better future. In contrast, they give limited attention to the darkness of sin. Accommodators focus more on a theology that extols the benefits that flow from God as Creator than on the need to encounter Christ as Redeemer. Because they are more attracted to love than to truth, they are more drawn to the Great Command than to the Great Commission. (Matthew 22:36–40 and 28:18–20) These people of God would not likely attend a conference based on the theme "Biblical Directives for Being Different."

Accommodators appeal to people who believe in the inclusiveness of God's love for all creation. Their love for God motivates a concern for people. When it comes to compassion for others, they rate exceptionally high. Their conviction soars when other people's rights get trampled.

Accommodators are also in tune with social sensitivities. Being politically correct is at least as important as being biblically correct. Accommodators are cultural trendsetters. Whether the issue relates to justice for aboriginal peoples, emerging sexual norms, immigration policy, or environmental concerns, politicians can count on accommodators to support their progressive social legislation. Like reclaimers and tribalizers, many accommodators possess the ability to be profoundly indignant when people do not see life from their particular point of view.

One difficulty for "Christian accommodators" is that they not only distinguish themselves as "cultural trendsetters," but they run the risk of contributing to "cultural blending." In their zeal to embrace the next cultural cause, they can also pull life down to the lowest common denominator. Instead of prophetically bringing the eternal ways of God into the here and now, they run the risk of simply being assimilated into the prevailing social norms.

Whether we seek to shape a nation with political might, forge ahead to establish new churches, or search for a positive way to live alongside people who are different from ourselves, we need to find a more balanced way.

4. COCOON and Disengage

Almost ignoring the circumstances that swirl around them, significant numbers of Canadians take the "cocooning" approach to life.[27] "Cocooners" disengage from any real involvement with concerns that affect public life. They will only turn off the television and think about the broader issues of their existence when their personal interests are directly jeopardized.

The cocooner lifestyle produces a "live and let live" attitude in people. The "I'll live my way—you live your way" outlook fosters a form of social coexistence that drags collective life down to a state of indifference. Unless "my interests" are at stake, I have little cause for concern. The attitude says simply, "Let's live together, but let's stay out of each other's way." Cocooners are content to coexist. Beyond care for their personal concerns, they have limited capacity for either conviction or compassion.

Cocooners are not bad people. They get out of bed in the morning, eat breakfast, send their kids to school, and head off to work. In the main, they are responsible people. They keep their houses in good repair, plant flowers, exchange pleasantries with their neighbors, and make regular payments on their credit cards.

Cocooners who attend church do so on their own terms. They worship more than they work in church. They show up when it is convenient to do so. They do not serve on committees. Still, cocooners obey the law and pay their taxes. However, only a small percentage of them will have accumulated any charitable donation receipts during the year.

Cocooners look after themselves. They shovel the snow off the sidewalk in front of their homes, but they know exactly where their property line ends. In apartment building elevators, they say "good morning," but they don't know each other by name. They have little sense of responsibility for the people who live next door.

Cocooners are not extra-mile people. They let controversy and public debate belong to others. They are not motivated to run for public office or to get involved in their community league. Still, cocooners stay in touch with the times. They are comfortable with computers and travel with ease on the information highway. They are VCR people. They live life on their own timetable, with the people they like having close to them. But when it comes to life beyond the boundaries of their family and friends, they disassociate.

One could reason that if "cocooner types" were the only people in society, then society would not be a bad place to live. Yet when people scale down life to their own size, neither is society an especially good place to live.

5. COLLABORATE and Re-create

Perhaps our best chance to create a positive future arises as we attempt to become "collaborators." The invitation is to live in the modern world with a commitment to cooperation.

Obviously, we need to acknowledge that the term itself sometimes holds a negative connotation, especially in the shadow of past world wars, when to be a "collaborator" was to be a traitor. In that context, collaboration meant being in collusion with the enemy. However, it is time to recover the positive meaning of the word.

In a proper sense, collaborators are people who believe in mutuality. They live by a code which says they should treat other people the way they would like to be treated themselves. They expect reciprocity. Although collaborators live with strong convictions, they don't fall victim to the "My way is the only way" mentality. Instead, they believe that "Our ways are the only way" to find a positive future.

Collaborators are not easy marks for other people's agendas. Rather, they are "give and take" people. They are quite prepared to give people room to be true to themselves. But at the same time, they take the prerogative to be true to their own convictions. While they are compassionate toward others and readily acknowledge other people's perspectives, they are ready to own and champion their own perspectives too. As they strive for a balance between affirming their own positions while accepting the positions of others, collaborators are controlled by a simple commitment; they sell out to cooperation. Their mandate says, "We will live together; we will work together." Collaborators are "us" people.

Whenever I leave my office at regular closing time, rush hour is in full form. Just before I can get onto the main freeway, I face the obstacle of making a left-hand turn at a busy intersection. To complicate matters, about 100 meters from the intersection where I have to turn left, there is a large hotel that sends a steady stream of cars attempting to cross the street and cut into the lane of traffic waiting for the light to change. Each day I must decide whether or not to let a car or two cross in front of me and delay my own journey home. It strikes me that the practice of safe driving, and particularly driving with consideration for others, is an example of collaboration.

Every day, millions of Canadians leave their homes and slide behind the wheels of their automobiles. They steer their way into traffic and head for their destinations. Along the way, they do the normal, legal things. They stop at red lights and crosswalks, signal to make lane changes, and yield to oncoming traffic. As long as everyone obeys the rules of the road and keeps alert, there are very few accidents. We collaborate. We do the legal thing, the traffic keeps flowing and we arrive safely at our destinations.

But there is another level of collaboration that we can reach for as we drive our vehicles. It's not complicated. It simply involves extending a measure of courtesy to others. For example, when someone wants to change lanes, courtesy gives space to that person to cut in front. When a pedestrian steps off the curb to jaywalk, collaboration with a touch of courtesy pushes on the brake pedal. When another car wants to pass, instead of speeding up, we slow down a little. When cars get on the freeway, we let them into the flow of traffic. Who would argue? When it comes to driving, life works a lot better when we add a good dose of courtesy to the baseline standard of legal collaboration.

At a much more profound level, in his leadership of the civil rights struggle, Martin Luther King Jr. embraced both a collaborative and morally complicated posture. In the beginning, King was able to steer those involved in the civil rights movement toward change without violence. In the heat of the Montgomery, Alabama, bus boycott, he told one correspondent, "What we are preaching is best described by the Greek word *agapé*." In the "light and darkness" battle with racist evil, King was able to hang on to a redemptive vision. As a black man, instead of aiming to get even, he took the higher road and said of the white man, "While I will fight him to get out from under his subjugation, I will also try to understand him and I will not try to defeat him."[28] History records that both injustice and anger were so deep that violence could not be contained. Still contending for a non-violent resolve, King died from an assassin's bullet.

Martin Luther King's ideal standard remains as a lofty aspiration for us today. If there is a baseline for those of us who claim to be serious Christians, surely it involves the pursuit of a redemptive vision. Remaining passive in the face of injustice is unacceptable for people committed to God's redemptive ways. Pursuing a future that reforms and renews represents the way forward for those who identify themselves as followers of Jesus.

Within the modern maze of diversity, the people of God who

see themselves as collaborators live with a clear definition of who they are. Accordingly, they are ready to draw lines between what is right and what is wrong. They are people with limits and boundaries. They believe truth exists to be discerned. They believe that sin should still be named. But collaborators are also compelled by compassion. The prayer of St. Francis, "Grant that I may not so much seek to be understood as to understand" is part of a collaborator's creed.

The double commitment to themselves and to others can create tension for collaborators. Although they desire to include people compassionately, collaborators are ready to exclude people when genuine moral and spiritual differences exist.

Collaborators who live with a redemptive vision pull away from "win—lose" scenarios. Whether the debate centers on racist or gender issues, while making their own case clear, collaborators take the views of others seriously. They are not parochial people. Narrow-mindedness distresses them. Whether the concerns to be resolved are moral or ethical, sexual or social, instead of aiming to defeat the enemy, collaborators keep their balance. They unapologetically carve out their own cultural space while making sure there is also room for others. Without being weak or naive, they make space for others while reserving room for themselves.

Freedom to move

The five categories are not meant to pigeonhole people or to create group stereotypes. Because people behave as reclaimers or accommodators on one particular issue, that is not to say they would fit into the same category on all issues. For example, reclaimers could well function as tribalizers, and in some situations accommodators could behave as collaborators. However, it is probable that, as individuals, our temperaments and group associations define a dominant direction for us. And as churches and denominations, our doctrines and our methods undoubtedly result in a primary pull toward one of the five types. At the beginning of this book, the most important question is not, "Am I a cocooner, a tribalizer, or a collaborator?" Rather, the more crucial issue is, "To be true to my convictions, what do I believe I should become?"

◆ F. The case of religion in public schools ◆

A specific issue that has generated debate and tension in recent years has been the role of religion in the country's public schools. In the past, religious education was mandated as a formal part of the school curriculum. In practice, that meant students received compulsory religious education that was essentially Christian. In many communities, the "Bible Club" movement existed to supply Christians to be the school instructors.

Two court rulings had a dramatic effect on the long-standing inclusion of religious education in public schools. In one instance, the court declared that it was unconstitutional to start the school day by reciting the Lord's Prayer. In the other instance, the court interpreted compulsory religious education as a violation of the rights of those in society who were not self-confessed Christians. In the context of the court rulings, the Province of Ontario established the Watson Commission to develop a set of recommendations regarding the future of religion in public schools.

One step in the process was to invite the citizens of the province to send their opinions and recommendations to the commission. Over 1,000 submissions were sent, the vast majority from people who explicitly identified themselves as Christians. Only a small percentage of the total thought religion should be removed from the formal curriculum. Claiming that "Canada has always been a Christian nation," over half of those who said "yes" to keeping religion in the curriculum also contended that "Christianity should be the only option" taught in the course of studies.

Hundreds of Christians not only positioned Canada as a Christian country, they went on to make statements like, "If newcomers don't like it, tell them to go back where they came from," and "the trouble with Canada is that we are too open to other people's religions." You can imagine how the members of the commission viewed the incitements. In my own view, the comments are not only unacceptable, they are both un-Christian and un-Canadian.

The court ruling making mandatory religious education illegal in public schools resulted in the document containing the recommendations being shelved. If the conclusions were dusted off and implemented, they could provide a constructive way to proceed into the future.

Respect for religion

Calling for religion to be retained, Dr. Watson and the members of the commission recommended that the traditional "religious education" be changed to "religious studies," and that programs in public schools be based on a multi-faith curriculum. Watson rightly called for clarification between "teaching about religion" and "religious indoctrination."[29] The report went on to endorse the following guidelines for teaching religion in public schools:

- the school's approach to religion is academic, not devotional;
- the school may strive for student awareness of religions, but should not press for student acceptance of any one religion;
- the school may sponsor study about religion but may not sponsor the practice of religion;
- the school may expose students to a diversity of religious views, but may not impose any particular view;
- the school may educate about all religions, but may not promote or denigrate any religion;
- the school may inform the student about various beliefs, but should not seek to conform him or her to any particular belief.[30]

The summary conclusions acknowledged that "Christianity has been and continues to be the predominant religion in Ontario [Canada]," but that "we do live in a pluralistic society," and "many other religions are represented. They too need to be recognized, accepted, and respected in the same way as they are expected to respect Christianity." Acknowledging Canada's religious make-up while still aiming for balance, Watson recommended that a minimum of one-third of the time be based on Christianity, a minimum of one-third on other religions, and the remaining one-third determined at local school board levels.[31]

In summary, the inquiry recommended a compulsory Religious Studies program which would be multi-faith and nondenominational. "It should be an educational program averaging 60 minutes per week and focus on major world religions. Its purpose should not be to indoctrinate or instruct in any particular faith, but rather to learn about religion and to develop an awareness and understanding of the beliefs, attitudes, and behaviors of those who are followers of major living religions.[32]

The report further recommended that teachers be expected "to inculcate, by precept and example, respect for religion and those principles of morality underlying all major world religions and the highest regard for truth, justice, loyalty, love of country, humanity, benevolence, sobriety, industry, frugality, purity, temperance and all other virtues."[33]

The commission's recommendations may not be comprehensive but they are wise counsel for our shared future. The affirmation of faith and the call for our education and social decision-makers to make room for religion in the public forum deserves applause.

There is no benefit in arguing about what has already been decided. Given Canada's current secular and pluralistic society, the only way to include religion in the public school curriculum is to require that the content be multi-faith. Furthermore, in a society that tends to censor much of religious life out of the public forum, is it not better that religion be affirmed as a normal part of life? Surely including the realm of the spiritual in the everyday life of our schools is preferred to the implicit denial of spirituality if it is absent from the curriculum.

Similar issues are played out in the recent decision to discontinue the recitation of a long and archaic prayer, which included the Lord's Prayer, at the beginning of each day the House of Commons is in session. Is it better to have no prayer at all, or the following prayer as our parliamentarians turn to their decision-making?

> Almighty God, we give thanks for the great blessings which have been bestowed on Canada and its citizens, including the gifts of freedom, opportunity, and peace that we enjoy.
>
> We pray for our sovereign, Queen Elizabeth, and the Governor-General.
>
> Guide us in our deliberations as Members of Parliament and strengthen us in our awareness of our duties and responsibilities as members.
>
> Grant us wisdom, knowledge and understanding to preserve the blessings of this country for the benefit of all and to make good laws and wise decisions.[34]

Earlier in this chapter, issues certain were raised. As we approach the 21st century, in some senses straddling both yesterday and tomorrow, what stance should we take? In our attitudes and actions, do we attempt to "go back" and reclaim the past? Should we "pull out" of the mainstream and tribalize with like-minded people? Or is it better to "enter in" and seek to collaborate with others, whether we agree with them or not? It is my deep conviction that we can best respond to the changes and complexities of life that swirl around us by "entering in." Our best hope is to keep learning how to live together by collaborating—by cooperating as we pursue our future together.

◆ Pursuing a positive future ◆

Let me offer a word of caution. In order to pursue this finer future, there is one particular attitude that must be embraced. If we have any hope of collaborating constructively, we all must believe that diversity enhances the existence of everyone. Deep in our inner spirits, we will release ourselves to the assumption that understanding and appreciating each other expands and enriches us all.

Reflect on a few scenarios for a moment. Imagine life in an elegant restaurant with just one choice on a dinner menu. Think about a symphony orchestra with only a violin section. Picture a one-color world, where everything is grey or even green. To think that we can live well without diversity would be like expecting a painter to create a masterpiece with only one color.

The better alternative is to make room for more than one way. It is to expect to learn from each other, to celebrate a multi-cultural Canada, to better understand our multi-faith Canada, and to collaborate in our multi-minded Canada.

A few months ago, I received a birthday card that expresses my feelings more eloquently than I can write myself.

Here's to the man who knows
who he is and where he stands,
the man with enough confidence in his
own beliefs
that he isn't afraid to let others
express theirs...[35]

◆ Clearing Away the Confusion ◆

Chapter Two

Introduction

Canadian culture is in a confused state. Like a day in the Rockies when the weather can't decide what to do, one wonders what will happen next? In the morning there is sun, but the winds blow in the storm clouds. In the afternoon, after the rain and hail descend, the sun returns only to be consumed again by more clouds along with ominous lightning and menacing thunder. In the darkness of night, a gentle breeze blows, and one can't help but wonder what will happen tomorrow.

Some days I feel confused too. It's as though I'm traveling through strange terrain with a map that is out of date. I know where I would like to go, but the roads that I think I should take often lead me on detours.

Sometimes the road I'm on seems so narrow that there isn't even room for the oncoming traffic. Other times there are so many lanes there appears to be ample room to pass on either side or even turn around and go in the other direction. There are occasions when I would like to head for the exit ramp, and I become alarmed when I realize the people I'm used to traveling with have no intention of exiting.

I grew up believing what I was told. In a simplistic way, I accepted what I was taught. Preachers told me that "All things work together for good for those that love God." Sunday school teachers invited me to simply "Trust in the Lord."

Along the way I started to ask more questions. As a young adult, I often resisted what others around me accepted. Well-intentioned confidants suggested that some of my doubts and skepticism might be rooted in lack of spiritual commitment. Professors seemed to deflect my unresolved questions by contending that "the Bible is God's truth for all times and all cultures."

A long time ago, simplistic thinking lost its appeal. Pointless accidents that trigger premature death and leave widows and orphans, refugees, famine, holocaust-like mass genocide and incessant injustice, abuse, questions that don't have answers alongside problems that defy solutions—all these things keep me unfolding the map. My confession to those reading this book is that writing *True to You* is part of my continuing attempt to "work out my own salvation"—sometimes with "fear and trembling," but more often with enthusiasm for the task of exploring life.

In the 1960s, I remember being drawn, at the same time, to what appeared to be two polarizing and contradictory positions. On the one hand, there were the rationally compelling arguments of Francis Schaeffer. On the other hand, there was the emotive and intellectual appeal articulated by Joseph Fletcher. Schaeffer was the "truth" man. Fletcher was the "love" man.

Schaeffer argued eloquently and biblically that truth existed as an objective reality and that it could be both known and practiced. He coined the expression "true truth" and cautioned his devout followers to watch out for encroaching relativism.

Fletcher's strong appeal was to do the "loving thing." He reminded his followers that the Great Commandment was the highest calling for all God's creation. The human challenge was to figure out what was the most loving thing to do in any given situation.

Both Schaeffer and Fletcher continue to appeal to me. Even though they enter their commitment to faith from different doors, I am intellectually and behaviorally predisposed to embrace both their views. But making room for both views can be a perplexing task.

In order to think clearly and live coherently in the 1990s, there are also other issues to be addressed and resolved. There are terms to be defined and interpretations to be clarified.

◆ A. Secularism—an enemy of faith ◆

The current CTV advertising slogan, "Making Your World Make Sense," is more than just a symbol of the power of the media. It is a reminder that today is not like yesterday. Twenty years ago, such a claim would have been discarded by advertising executives as too blatant. But in today's world, the implicit claim that newscasters and political analysts can be the source of meaning and purpose is perceived to be an advantage. It is evidence that the power of the pulpit has been replaced by the potent influence of television.[1] The shift also indicates that our society has succumbed to the dominance of secularism.

In the previous chapter, we recognized that Canadians continue to be influenced by their religious roots. At the same time, we acknowledged that, especially during the last few decades, Canadian society has been pulled toward the assumptions of secularism. Even taking into account privatized spirituality, the data still supports the conclusion that the majority of Canadians are "semisecularized."

In practical terms, not only has the social standing of the church been demoted, but God has progressively been pushed to the edges of people's lives. Because secularism, by its very nature, proposes that we can put life together without any need for God, it inevitably preempts the role of God in people's lives. Instead of dependence on the Divine, secularism feeds a spirit of human independence.

Pervasive presence of unstated belief

Secularism is a belief system. It is an ideology. According to Webster's dictionary, secularism is a conceptual view of life that promotes "indifference to or rejection or exclusion of religion and religious consideration."[2] In its pure form, secularism not only marginalizes God, it eliminates any need for God.

There can be no other conclusion. Secularism is an enemy of the Christian faith. Any belief system that invites people to construct their existence without a place for the Creator and Redeemer of the world is more than just a competitor. Secularism challenges the faith. It is a rival, and in that sense, an opponent. And clearly, secularism is gaining the upper hand.

While secularism as a formal belief system is an enemy of the Christian faith, it will be important not to view secular people as enemies. The continuing secularization of life, or what we might call the "secular shift," is not a planned take-over by a group of calculating secularists. Christianity is not being conquered by a personalized adversarial foe. Rather, Christianity is being preempted by a quiet but unrelenting **process**.

Increasing numbers of people let the gravitational pull of their lives distance them from God. Instead of being God-focused and spiritually responsive to God's influence in their lives, they design their existence on their own terms. Step by step and stage by stage, they become less Christian and more secular. Without announcing a conversion to secularism, week after week and month after month, the majority of Canadians behave as secularists. The direction of their lives takes them further and further away from God.

Think about how Canadians act culturally and spiritually. Only rarely do Canadians act compulsively or make radical decisions. The total number of Canadians who, on a given day in the past 30 years, have suddenly announced that they no longer believe in God could probably hold a convention in a small business board room. But the pull away from God results in the pervasive presence of the unstated belief that God is unnecessary.

Life is not static. We do travel. However it is chronicled, the secular journey distances people from God. Instead of centering one's thoughts and affections on the pursuit of God, secularization pulls us toward self-determination. Rather than consciously seeking God's preferences in our decision-making, the role of human responsibility takes over. As secularism seeps deeper into one's inner spirit, the orientation toward God weakens. Increasingly, response to God only happens on special occasions or when a crisis suddenly invades. Eventually, spiritual indifference devolves into the absence of any awareness that God both deserves and desires a place in day-to-day living. It isn't that most people plan to distance themselves from God; somehow, it just happens.

Canadian secularists are not godless foes. They are people who have either consciously or unconsciously allowed God's influence to erode in their lives. They have demoted God and promoted other interests. As people, they are not enemies of the faith. Only a few act antagonistically. The vast majority have simply left the faith and gone on to other pursuits.

There is another quiet phenomenon that accompanies secularization. The focus for life shifts from an external orientation toward an internal orientation. Instead of being called to relate outside oneself, the secular journey almost inevitably pulls one inward. By contrast, when we consciously acknowledge God, we are pulled in the outward direction. For example, true worship reaches for transcendence. When prayer is more than a personal shopping list, one's attention is lifted toward the Creator and out to people and the calamities that scar the world. Giving time and money in response to people in need prevents an excessive preoccupation with oneself. Seeking the mind of Christ on complicated decisions or discerning God's truth so one can think through a complex social policy counters narcissism. Left on our own, we are more likely to be contained by the size of our self-constructed worlds.

For many good reasons, secularism is an enemy of the faith. But secularism doesn't exist as a single force in modern society. Elusive phenomena such as relativism are also grafted into the spirit of the age. When secularism is compared to relativism it is difficult to determine which comes first. One might argue that secularism and relativism are like writers and their ideas—fused together in an inseparable alliance. But regardless of exactly how the two social forces converge or interact, today's society is set up for rampant relativism.

◆ B. Relativism—an enemy of faith ◆

Coming to grips with the complexities of relativism is much more difficult than understanding secularism. It would be easy to lash out at relativism and categorically declare that it is an unequivocal enemy of the Christian faith. After all, relativism reduces God's revelation to a matter of personal opinion. In the realm of morals and ethics, in the arena of values and personal lifestyle choices, when it comes to beliefs and behaviors relativism decrees that there are no universals. Where relativism rules, there cannot be ultimate supremacy for any particular position. Accordingly, all aspects of life in the personal sphere are negotiable. There are no absolutes and all of life is up for grabs. Surely such an antitruth position is an enemy of the faith.

Intellectual integrity demands a measure of caution, however. Before we fall into ranting and raving about the demise of truth and the loss of absolutes and certitudes, we should pause and reflect.

Overclaiming and underclaiming

There are many religious people, as well as many scientists, who translate their views into certitudes. These people are usually comfortable with authoritative answers and closed responses to complicated questions. The truth is that many of these well-intentioned people would do well to get down on their knees and confess that when it comes to making truth claims, they are excessively zealous. They are guilty of overclaiming. And in doing so, they are prone to be too clear about too many things.

But just as there are overclaimers, there are also underclaimers. Other members of God's family go to the opposite extreme. They are just as adamant that when it comes to values, morals, and personal beliefs, it is impossible to be certain about anything. The underclaimers are content with loose ends and ambiguities. They are more relaxed with unanswered questions and unresolved doubts. But in the end, underclaimers are not clear enough about enough matters of faith and life.

Isn't it more honest to suggest that weather forecasters and truth claimers share a lot in common? Today's professionally trained weather forecasters have access to sophisticated technology and extensive networks of information which help them make their projections. On any given day, we might hear them confidently declare that "tomorrow will be sunny and warm." But in the next breath, when it comes to stating exactly how warm it will be, we are apt to hear the words, "the **expected** high should reach...." If precipitation is part of the forecast, the best estimate can only be stated as a probability. Even though the projection is calculated on hard evidence and clear criteria, the forecaster is limited to stating a probability of precipitation.

Discerning God's truth is a lot like making weather forecasts. There are many aspects of God's truth that can be confidently declared. There is no need for reticence when it comes to affirming the historical Jesus and the fact of the cross. The scriptures are a unique revelation from the Creator to the created.

Evil is destructive. The beauty of the life of love is a certainty on which to stake one's life. But on many matters of theology and doctrine, we cannot be as certain. Knowing the full mind of Christ on complex social issues and lifestyle choices is more difficult. Even after careful scholarship and a full measure of prayer, sometimes the most honest thing we can do is project probabilities and express personal convictions.

In my opinion, the truth about truth is that although truth exists as an external and eternal certainty, the human ability to discern God's truth is severely limited. Just as weather exists, so truth exists. But just as forecasting the weather with certainty has its limits, so does determining the full scope of God's truth.

Leaning in the direction of overclaiming, systematic theologian J. I. Packer, invites God's people to a high view of the scriptures and articulates lofty aspirations when it comes to knowing God's truth. He states that the theologian's role is "to detect and eliminate intellectual pollution, and to ensure, as far as man [sic] can, that God's life-giving truth flows pure and unpoisoned into Christian hearts."[3] Like-minded seminary professor David Wells contends, "We must recognize that truth is not subjective but is based on objective reality and truth as revealed in the scriptures... It is truth for the open market, truth for the nation, truth for other nations."[4]

In contrast, writer Frederick Buechner leans in the direction of underclaiming. An author of both fiction and nonfiction works, Buechner is almost apologetic about discerning God's will and ways. He creatively, but cautiously, suggests, "I like to believe that once or twice... I have bumbled my way into at least the outermost suburbs of the Truth that can never be told but only come upon, that can never be proved but only lived for and loved."[5]

Surely, somewhere between boldly claiming to know almost everything about God's revelation to creation and apologetically confessing to know almost nothing, there is a place for God's people to stand with confidence.

Missiologist Lesslie Newbigin holds a mediating position. He acknowledges the tension between knowing and not knowing. He confesses that "there is a proper place for Christian agnosticism... Christians are—or should be—learners to the end of their days."[6] Still, Newbigin speaks confidently: "The effort to know the truth involves struggle, groping, feeling one's way. It is true that there are also moments of sudden illumination, but these come only to those who have accepted the discipline of patient groping, of trying out different possibilities, of sustained reflection."[7]

Beyond the query that wonders why the search for truth is so arduous, the question that begs for an answer is, "Can we find ground to stand on where we are neither overclaiming nor underclaiming?" Particularly in a world that disconnects itself from the very idea that truth exists to inform one's personal beliefs and morals, how can we keep our balance?

Although it is not a comprehensive answer, one way to keep your balance, or one way to find that elusive ground to stand on, is to be true to your light while also being true to your darkness.

True to your light— true to your darkness

The Christian life is a journey of faith. Even on the question of the existence of God, it has long been accepted that believing in the reality of God is a matter of faith. Although there is more evidence to support the position that God exists than there is to refute the claim, the scriptures remind us that "faith is the assurance of things hoped for, the conviction of things not seen." (Hebrews 11:1)

Acknowledging a faith bias is no reason to become defensive or apologetic. Everyone else lives by faith too. Humanists and hedonists, materialists and Marxists, nihilists and existentialists, agnostics and atheists all live by their particular assumptions of faith. In fact, it takes more faith to believe that God doesn't exist than it does to affirm divine reality.

For centuries, philosophers and theologians have articulated criteria for knowing what is real and true. Claims about knowledge have long been tested against reason, experience, tradition, and the Bible. As reliable as it may be for Christians to screen carefully various truth claims through this fourfold grid, it is obvious that we can be more certain of some matters of faith than we can be about others.

Followers of Jesus can confidently believe that the God who exists created the world. That is our light. But on the questions of when and how the Creator fashioned creation, we are faced with darkness. We simply do not know. The declaration that God created the world in seven 24-hour days in the year 4004 B.C. is not only shoddy scholarship, it is preposterous.

The historical existence of Jesus is a fact. His miraculous intervention in the world as the long-promised Messiah is certain. The uniqueness of Jesus is a critical point to retain and the realities of his death and resurrection are nonnegotiables to preserve. We have bright light shining on those claims. But the question of when Jesus will return to establish the next stage of history is open for debate. We simply don't know. Neither do we have the full mind of Christ on cherished doctrinal details concerning baptism, heaven, hell, purgatory, the inspiration of scripture, the sacraments, tithing, conversion, birth control, sexuality, grace, mercy and retribution.

Fuller Seminary President, Richard Mouw, contends that there are two distances that separate us from a complete knowledge of the absolutes that could guide our lives.

> The first is the distance between creature and Creator. This is an eternal distance. It will never go away. Since God is infinite and we are finite, we will never know as God knows. This means that there may very well be dimensions of God's moral standards that we will never fully understand.
>
> The second distance separates the way we are now from the way we will someday be. "We shall be changed." We will never know as God knows, but we will someday understand things much better than we do now: "For now we see in a mirror dimly, but then face to face. Now I know in part; then I shall understand fully, even as I have been fully understood." (1 Corinthians 13:12)[8]

Lesslie Newbigin seems to agree, to a point. There is "admirable humility about the statement that the truth is much greater than any one person or any one religious tradition can grasp. The statement is no doubt true but it can be used against truth when it is used to neutralize any affirmation of the truth."[9] This double-edged reality pulls us back to the need for balance.

On the one hand, the drive must be toward being true to the light in one's life. Especially in the current mood of escalating relativism, the first call is to hold fast to one's convictions. The posture is to embrace the certainty that both God and truth exist. It is to live with a commitment to pursue a deeper understanding of God's revealed truth in order to practice his will and ways. More than just seeing the Christian faith as one belief option among many, people of light will also be convinced that those who believe as they do will be gifted with both life after birth, and life after death.

On the other hand, in order to protect themselves from the dangers of overclaiming, the people of light will also be true to their darkness. Rather than absolutizing their positions, they will confess their subjectivity. A humble hermeneutic will accompany their pursuit and practice of truth. While confidently pursuing and diligently searching for what is true and right and good, they will also be comfortable confessing, "As far as I can tell, God hasn't communicated the final word on that yet."

Relativism in Canadian society

If relativism has the final word, "true" and "false" questions on examinations will be eliminated. Journalists and police detectives will no longer see any value in searching for facts. The courts in the land will set aside the absurdity of asking witnesses to take oaths obligating them to tell the truth. And teachers, theologians, and preachers will have no basis, other than their own opinion, upon which to make a case for whatever they want to communicate. The successful people in a world ruled by relativism will be those individuals who best develop the art form of making room for various views.

Whether or not "true" and "false" questions will continue to instill anxiety in students at exam time, and whether or not journalists and detectives persist in searching for facts, relativism will continue to invade our world.

The data is conclusive. The majority of Canadians have already embraced the conclusion that "what's right and wrong is a matter of personal opinion." (*See Fig. 2.1*)

The younger generation, women, Quebecers, and those who have abandoned their religious connections lead the way. But even evangelical conservatives, those who attend church weekly, and surprisingly, those who identify with the United Church, rate just slightly less than 50% on the issue.

The prevailing mood of the age is clear. When the private side

Fig. 2.1
"What's right and wrong is a matter of personal opinion"
Percent who "Agree strongly" or "Moderately agree"

By Region

National	B.C.	Alta.	Sask. Man.	Ont.	Que.	Atlantic
57	54	53	59	54	65	54

By Age

18–34	35–54	55+
65	52	54

By Gender

Female	Male
61	54

By Church Attendance

National	Weekly	Monthly	Occasional	Never
57	49	52	63	59

By Denomination

R.C.	Angl.	United	Luth. Presby.	Conserv.	World Rel.	No Rel.
60	51	49	60	46	59	64

Angus Reid Group: July '94. N = 1502

of life is the frame of reference, when morals and values and beliefs are the focus of attention, no one can claim to possess "the truth." It is all a question of perspective. "All claims to truth are equally valid; there is no universal or privileged vantage point which allows anyone to decide what is right and what is wrong."[10]

But why do we moderns find relativism so attractive? After all, relativism accelerates individualism, fuels uncertainty, and fragments life. In the end, relativism is a dead-end street. It is not only unlivable, it sets society up for overreaction. When relativism reaches a certain intensity, "absolutism becomes very attractive again." Relativism liberates, but the resulting liberty can produce painful impermanence and uncertainty. People then "seek liberation from relativism."[11]

The answer is not complete, but there are both philosophical and sociological reasons. S. D. Gaede suggests that, "We have lost both the grounds for believing in truth and the communities necessary to cultivate and transmit truth from one generation to the next."[12]

For God's concerned and committed people, the quandaries are troubling. How can Christianity's claims to truth be taken seriously when there are so many rival alternatives, and when "truth" itself has become a devalued notion? Were we unwise to have pursued certitude? Would we have done better to have developed a view of life that only called for the formation of personal convictions and organizational distinctives?

After all the qualifications and questions, if we are to be clearly Christian, we must also take the position that relativism is an enemy of the faith. While we must not overclaim what we can know about God's ways, without a framework of truth to support its claims, the Christian faith will be put out of business by the spirit of the age.

◆ C. Cultural pluralism—a friend of the faith ◆

Although "pluralism" is not as complicated as is relativism, there are still issues to clarify. The first question to ask is, "What does pluralism mean?"

"Plural" simply means "more than one." When applied to the realm of beliefs, plural means there is more than one ultimate source from which to formulate one's beliefs. When used to describe a society, we say that "we live in a pluralistic society." What we are doing is defining society so that different people can believe and behave in different ways while still living alongside each other. For God and the Christian church in Canadian society, it means that increasing numbers of cultural competitors have arrived on the scene. There are other inviting voices calling out: "Come unto me, believe in me, give your time and loyalty to me."

Having observed religion and tracked trends in Canada for the past 20 years, sociologist Reginald Bibby rightly concludes that "Pluralism at the group and individual levels has become part of the

Canadian psyche. Some time ago it left its cultural cradle. The pluralism infant has been growing up in the past three decades. It has been traveling across the country, visiting our moral, religious, family, educational, and political spheres."[13]

Missiologist Lesslie Newbigin clarifies what all this means. "In contrast to traditional societies, modern Western society leaves its members free, within very wide limits, to adopt and hold their own views about what is good and desirable, about what kind of life is to be admired, about what code of ethics should govern one's private life." One obvious repercussion of pluralism is that "rival truth-claims of the different religions are not felt to call for argument and resolution; they are simply part of the mosaic—or perhaps one should say a kaleidoscope—of different values that make up the whole pattern."[14]

It is obvious that a cultural code for Canadian pluralism has solidified. We have embraced the assumption that there are not only various ways to believe and behave, we have also concluded that these "many ways" are both valid and permissible. We have moved from simply accepting the inevitability of diversity to validating diversity.

We also need to acknowledge that the basic phenomenon of pluralism is not new. Canada was never a "one way" country. Cultural, linguistic, and religious diversity were imported from the beginning. "What is new is the intellectual response to this phenomenon; the suggestion that plurality of beliefs is not merely a matter of observable fact, but is theoretically justified—in intellectual and cultural life in general, and in particularly in relation to the religions. Claims by any one group or individual to have any exclusive hold on 'truth' are thus treated as the intellectual equivalent of fascism."[15]

Multi-mindedness—the modern Canadian way

In Canada's case, although there has always been ample room for ethnic diversity, historically there has been limited room for religious diversity. French-speaking Catholics and English-speaking Protestants may not have been able to communicate with each other, but they still spoke the same religious language. And as we have already noted, what resulted was a cultural consensus. The tenets of Christianity defined and established the one true way to conceive of or structure life. Even when people did not explicitly believe or obey the Christian way, there was a general cultural understanding that the Christian faith was "the right way." But in contemporary pluralistic society, instead of one way to believe and behave, there are many ways. Multi-mindedness is the modern Canadian way. Beyond being a multi-cultural society, Canada is a multi-moral, multi-faith, multi-family structure, multi-gender role, and multi-sexual orientation culture.

In the past three decades, pluralism has been given a cultural promotion. Rather than simply making cultural space for diversity, pluralism has been notarized at an intellectual level. It has gained the status of an ideology. Modern pluralism is a belief system. The pluralistic profession is that there are "many ways to believe and behave and these ways are equally valid." For reasons that elude a full explanation, what modern pluralists seem unable to accommodate in their ideology is making room for "the one way" that claims to be "the right way." Although the theory of ideological pluralism claims there are many ways to think, believe, and behave, the very idea that one particular way is the true way breaks the rules.

Case for cultural pluralism

In order to think clearly about pluralism, we must distinguish between "ideological pluralism" and "cultural pluralism." Ideological pluralism is really synonymous with relativism. In claiming that many ways of believing are not just "permissible" but also equally "valid," ideological pluralism reduces truth to a matter of personal opinion. As missiologist Lesslie Newbigin observes: "It has become commonplace to say that we live in a pluralist society—not merely a society which is in fact plural in the variety of cultures, religions, and lifestyles which it embraces, but pluralist in the sense that this plurality is celebrated as things to be approved and cherished."[16] Ideological pluralism denies the alternative of building one's belief system on a foundation of objective and knowable truth.

Even further, when pluralism parades in society as an ideology that does not make room for other ideologies that are based on the conclusion that objective truth exists, it becomes incompatible with biblical Christianity. Like relativism, ideological pluralism is an enemy of the faith. The absence of a truth base reduces life to subjective experience and personal opinion. As central as opinions and experiences are to life, they are not an adequate foundation for solid faith.

Cultural pluralism, however, is different from ideological pluralism. It stops short of becoming a belief system. Rather, cultural pluralism is a social response to and a way of dealing with our differences. Calling for attitudes that both accept and affirm differences, cultural pluralism supports its vision for society by creating social structures for cradling diversity. Cultural pluralism invites people in a single society, who believe different things, to live peaceably and productively alongside each other. While making room for a plurality of cultures, religions, and lifestyles it also leaves room for people who believe that truth exists as an external and knowable reality.

For God's people then, ideological pluralism, which is really synonymous with relativism, is an enemy of the faith. But cultural pluralism is another matter. Because it makes room for a diversity of beliefs and behaviors in a society, including the Christian faith, cultural pluralism can be a friend of the faith.

Friend of the faith

As a social structure for cradling diversity, cultural pluralism provides a place for the people of God to live alongside other people who have come to other conclusions about life. When cultural pluralism functions as it should, it makes room in society for church-attending Christians, as well as full-fledged secularists, semisecularists, agnostics, atheists, relativists, humanists, and hedonists. And because those of us who are visible Christians are now in the minority in society, it is clearly to our advantage to envision cultural pluralism as an ally. If the shared approach to society that cultural pluralism proposes doesn't work, Christians as a group will be pushed to the sidelines of society and be forced to watch the mainstream of cultural life pass us by.

One advantage for minority voices in a society that cradles diversity is that there is no officially approved pattern of beliefs or conduct. Consequently, cultural pluralism not only provides a legitimate place for Christians and others to co-mingle, it gives the various groups that make up the whole of society the prerogative to hold defined positions. While the social whole is undefined, the parts that make up the whole can clearly self-define if they choose to do so.

In contrast to being a closed system, cultural pluralism is an open system. And as an open system, Canadian society can be influenced. Unless people who live in open system societies take time to think and make deliberate belief choices, they will tend to conform to the prevailing consensus of the majority. In Canada's case, they will be pulled toward both secularism and relativism.

On a recent trip I had the delight of sitting next to a young Polish woman from Warsaw. In our conversation I asked her, "What are some of the biggest differences between communist Poland and life in your country today?" After reflecting for a moment, she said, "Today, we have freedom to say what we want to say. We can think our own thoughts. We can say the truth without fear. And of course, if we have the money, we can buy whatever we want without waiting in a long line."

As Christians living in an open social system, we not only have the freedom to voice our opinions without fear, we can express our convictions in the midst of other voices and invite people to consider Christ and his ways.

Perilous to the faith

Pluralism can be a friend of the faith, but in the present milieu, where a somewhat undeveloped cultural pluralism is blended with the tenets of ideological pluralism, there are dangers. As noted earlier, pluralism has already dealt a serious blow to truth. Half of those Canadians who regularly attend church have concluded that "what's right and wrong is a matter of personal opinion." Given all the possibilities offered by pluralism, "how can any of us have confidence in our own version of truth?"[17] A peril of living in a pluralistic culture is that it seeds uncertainty about any claims in life that appeal to truth.

Another potential impediment for the faith is that pluralism counters the tendency to hold strong convictions. When many ways of thinking and behaving are encouraged, then suggesting that any one way is better than all the other ways is discouraged. Accordingly, confidence in what one believes is easily undermined. Carving out deep convictions on various matters without being tempted to continually revise them requires a resolute spirit.

The outcome of pluralism also tends to foster excessive individualism and moral fragmentation. Excessive individualism asserts itself at the expense of community and collective concerns. Wherever it emerges, moral fragmentation inflicts wounds on its victims. Former assumptions about whatever was honorable and virtuous give way to unscrupulous conduct and unethical behavior. Instead of mutuality, vested self-interests control. Rather than keeping covenants in relationships, randomness rules.

Living in a pluralistic society can be hazardous to the church and the faith, but in my opinion, the advantages far outweigh the disadvantages.

But whether that judgment is valid or not, is not really the issue. That contemporary society is already pluralistic is an inescapable reality. Instead of denying that reality or attempting to turn back the clock, the better alternative is to make pluralism work.

In the meantime, as God's people, it will be important not to be casual about our beliefs and behavior. Consciously embracing the spirit Martin Luther demonstrated at Worms will be wise: "My conscience is captive to the Word of God; to go against conscience is neither right nor safe; here I stand, there is nothing else I can do; God help me; amen."[18]

• D. Religious pluralism—faith multiplied •

Today's world is like a giant kettledrum. When the drum is struck, the reverberations are felt around the world.

University of Toronto's Marshall McLuhan may have been the first to coin the term "global village," but as consumers of CNN's instant information, ours is the first generation to experience globalization. The global expansion of the world's religions is one of the reverberations we feel. And there are consequences for Canada. The globalization of religion creates another expression of pluralism. Our multi-faith society generates religious pluralism. Faith is multiplying inside our national borders.

Immigration policies that have imported the world and seeded the world's religions into Canadian soil have positively altered many people's perceptions. Surely the majority of Canadians would concur "that differences of sex, race, or religion, for example, are not inherently moral differences. Thus, they do not automatically imply differences in the human worth or moral standing of persons involved. A Hindu, for example, is not, as such, better or worse as a human being than a Christian or Muslim, nor is a woman better or worse than a man. It is therefore wrong to treat the one as if he [she] were somehow more deserving or more to be favored than the other."[19]

In his recent book *Crossing the Threshold of Hope*, His Holiness, Pope John Paul II, reminds us that people around the world and in all cultures "turn to various religions to solve mysteries of the human condition."[20] Informed Canadians are not surprised by the claim that almost all the great religions of the world are based on shared principles. The Bible enjoins us to "love thy neighbor as thyself"; the Koran reminds us that "human beings are worthy of esteem because they are human" and that the "kindness of God... has now bound our hearts together, so that through his goodness you may become brothers." And Buddha taught compassion and self-sacrifice alongside "right conduct" as one of the stages of the Eightfold Path.[21]

The basic Christian belief that God created the world opens the door to the presence of God and the activity of the spirit of God through the whole of creation. Cross-cultural experiences communicate the undeniable conclusion that people everywhere are spiritual beings. Pope John Paul II affirms his experience of shared prayer for world peace with those from other world religions and concludes, "Instead of marvelling at the fact that Providence allows such a great variety of religions, we should be amazed at the number of common elements found within them."[22] Canadians who are thoughtful about such matters also understand that "a list of virtues or duties drawn up by a Buddhist would not differ very greatly from one drawn up by a Christian, a Confucianist, a Muhammadan, or a Jew."[23]

Alister McGrath not only explains the geographical significance of religion, but also helps us comprehend why more and more people believe that all religions are equal. "Religion is often determined by the circumstances of one's birth. An Indian is likely

Fig. 2.2
"All world religions are equally valid"
Percent who "Agree strongly" or "Moderately agree"

By Region

National	B.C.	Alta.	Sask. Man.	Ont.	Que.	Atlantic
72	74	66	71	71	76	74

By Age

18–34	35–54	55+
73	77	66

By Gender

Female	Male
72	72

By Church Attendance

National	Weekly	Monthly	Occasional	Never
72	57	77	77	76

By Denomination

R.C.	Angl.	United	Luth. Presby.	Conserv.	World Rel.	No Rel.
78	74	74	73	45	75	78

Angus Reid Group: July '94. N = 1502

to be a Hindu; an Arab is likely to be a Moslem. On account of this observation, it is argued, all religions must be equal paths to the truth."[24] Those who study the trends of the times are not shocked by the reality that seven out of ten Canadians believe that all the world's religions are equally valid.

When we look at the data profiling various segments of Canadians, there are really only two groups of people that distinguish themselves on this issue. (*See Fig. 2.2*) Weekly church attenders and those who identify with the country's conservative evangelical churches are less enthusiastic about extending equality outside their religious boundaries. As with the issue of "right and wrong being a matter of personal opinion," perhaps the more startling finding is that approximately one-half of those who represent these two very religious audiences in Canada are ready to grant equality to multi-faith religion.

Affirming common commitments—discerning differences

A brief critique of religious pluralism in the nation is in order. First, theologians and scholars have long applauded the premise that "all truth is God's truth." If we believe that God created the world and everything in it, wherever we discover and discern what is real and what is true, we can only conclude that God is the source of that particular truth. Accordingly, we are set free to affirm truth wherever we find it. It doesn't matter if it is scientific truth, truth in Islam or Buddhism, or truth in the Christian faith, it is all accepted as a part of what God has released into creation. Following that line of logic, if we conceive of God as the source of all truth, then Christianity is not the only source of truth.

Living in the midst of religious pluralism invites a second critical distinction. It is the importance of distinguishing between people and their ideas. Only then can we have respect for people without necessarily affirming everything about the religion they believe and practice. Christians believe that every human being is created in the image of God. Accordingly, every person possesses inherent worth and is worthy of respect. Anything less pulls God's people away from the Great Commandment to "love our neighbors as ourselves." (Luke 10:25) Still, extending attitudes of regard to people who believe and follow other religions is not the same as affirming the faith they embrace. Wholesome multi-faith environments will bring people together who respect each other without the need to agree with each other.

The more radical demand to regard all the world's religions as the same or as equally valid is another matter. Showing respect to Muslims, Sikhs, Hindus, Buddhists, Jews and people of the Bahai faith is laudable. Making the theological declaration that all religions are the same is irrational.

Sincerely believing something does not create reality. "To say that whatever is sincerely believed and practiced is, by definition, true, would be the end of all critical discrimination, both intellectual and moral."[25] To allow "relevance" or "openness" to be given greater weight than truth is, quite simply, a mark of intellectual shallowness and moral irresponsibility. The first, and most fundamental, of all questions must be: Is it true? Is this worthy of belief and trust? A belief system, however consoling and reassuring, may prove to be false in itself, or rest upon utterly spurious foundations.[26]

Representing his worldwide communion and reflecting on other religions, Pope John Paul II asserts the following:

> The Catholic Church rejects nothing that is true and holy in these religions. The Church has a high regard for their conduct and way of life, for those precepts and doctrines which, although differing on many points from that which the Church believes and propounds, often reflect a ray of truth which enlightens all men. However, the Church proclaims, and is bound to proclaim that Christ is 'the way and the truth and the life' (John 14:6), in whom men must find the fullness of religious life and in whom God has reconciled everything to Himself." (*Nostra Aetate* 2)[27]

The cultural segmentation model introduced in chapter one illustrates how different Canadians view the world's faiths.

Reclaimers: Activated by the conviction that their way is the only true way to understand life, Christian reclaimers commit themselves to convert members of other world religions to their particular view of faith. They readily pray and give financial support to the efforts of missionaries sent to foreign lands.

Tribalizers: Living with a readiness to control, and if necessary, confront life around them, tribalizers are often blinded about what is sacred and important to others. They can be counted on to vote against turbans on the heads of RCMP officers, and to deny access to Canadian Legion halls when the rules say no headgear is allowed.

Accommodators: Motivated by compassion and concerned about not offending or judging anyone, accommodators roll out the welcome mat to people, especially if it is rumoured that they are subject to discrimination. Accommodators embrace the premise that "all religions are equally valid." They can be counted on to downplay what some contend are the "dangers of syncretism."

Cocooners: This group of Canadians are busy taking their children to dance lessons and hockey games. If they have no children, involvement in career development or in their latest personal interest occupies their time. Cocooners are indifferent to multi-faith issues unless an excessive number of visible minority people seem to be moving into their neighborhoods.

Collaborators: Striving to affirm their own convictions while accepting the convictions of others, collaborators seek to be bridge builders. Without reticence, they engage others about what they believe, but they do so with regard for what is important to others. While collaborators resist the idea that "all religions are equally valid," they are ready to make room in society for other religions and their practices.

◆ E. Christian pluralism—faith diversified ◆

The one other expression of pluralism in Canadian life that needs to be addressed is Christian pluralism. The idea behind Christian pluralism is to acknowledge the plurality of faith that is distinctly Christian and finds its diversity of expression in our different churches, denominations, and Christian traditions. The lines of distinctiveness and division that define Christian pluralism can be looked at in several ways.

Sociologists Glock and Stark suggest there are four great theological camps: the liberals, the moderates, the conservatives, and the fundamentalists.[28] In an often-cited essay entitled "Denominationalism as a Basis for Ecumenicity," Winthrop Hudson defined and defended denominationalism with the following affirmations: "No denomination claims to represent the whole church of Christ; none claims that all other churches are false churches; none claims that all members of society should be incorporated in its membership, none claims that society and the state should submit to its ecclesiastical regulation; but all recognize their shared responsibility for society."[29]

Richard Lovelace concludes, however, that denominational differences turn "one person's piety" into another person's "poison." Lovelace contends that different groups within the Christian church are at odds with one another because their models of the Christian life, its beginnings and its fullness, are so diverse. "One group of genuine believers can never remember a conscious conversion to faith in Christ; another insists that a datable experience of being 'born again' is essential; a third says that a second distinct experience of 'baptism of the Holy Spirit' is necessary for Christian maturity. When we 'test the spirits' in the lives of representatives among these groups, we often find an equal level of spiritual vitality—or deadness!—in each sector." Lovelace reasons that, although the Christian life is being offered in diverse packages, what is inside is the same—newness of life in Christ. "Nonetheless, the different groups enjoying this life are readily offended by another's packages."[30]

Novelist and sometimes theologian, Frederick Buechner manages to see humor in the midst of what he often thinks of as a religious mess.

> If you were to ask the average member of any congregation to explain those differences, you would be apt to be met with a long, unpregnant silence. By and large they all believe pretty much the same things and are confused about the same things and keep their fingers crossed during the same parts of the Nicene Creed.
>
> All the duplication of effort and waste of human resources. All the confusion about what the Church is, both within the ranks and without. All the counterproductive competition. All the unnecessarily empty pews and unnecessary expense...you don't know whether to burst into laughter or into tears.
>
> If all the competing factions of Christendom were to give as much of themselves to the high calling and holy hope that unites them as they do now to the relative inconsequentialities that divide them, the Church would look more like the Kingdom of God for a change and less like an ungodly mess."[31]

Common grace—competing doctrines

A more hopeful way to understand Christian pluralism is to see the people of God sharing their life of faith in various spiritual streams. Rather than slotting people into specific religious structures and organizations, this more hopeful way is to envision a diversity of Christian spirituality.

The following expressions of Christian spirituality will seldom exist as single isolated streams. Rather, they merge and converge. It is an oversimplification, but in all likelihood, each distinct denomination or Christian tradition will incorporate two or three streams in their emphasis. Individuals will then align themselves with churches that are compatible with their personal spiritual styles.

The various Christian expressions or traditions address the following needs:

The **Contemplative** tradition "addresses the longing for a deeper, more vital Christian experience" with an emphasis on the prayer-filled life.

The **Holiness** tradition "addresses the erosion of moral fiber in the contemporary church" with an emphasis on the virtuous life.

The **Social Justice** tradition "addresses the gospel imperative for equity and compassion among all peoples" with an emphasis on the compassionate life.

The **Evangelical** tradition "addresses the need for a center of certainty in Christian life and faith" with an emphasis on the word-centered life.

The **Charismatic** tradition "addresses the yearning for the immediacy of God's presence among God's people" with an emphasis on the Spirit-empowered life.

The **Charismatic-Power** orientation "addresses the desire to experience and express spiritual gifts" with an emphasis on the supernatural and the miraculous.

The **Sacramental** tradition "addresses the desire to access God's grace and affirm the sacredness of life" with an emphasis on ceremonial worship and receiving the sacraments.[32]

Affirming various styles of Christian spirituality invites churches to determine their particular doctrines and ways of worship. It also encourages individual Christians to experience God in their lives and express their faith in ways that are consistent with their perspectives and personalities.

Although Christians are the recipients of common grace from one God, they respond by embracing different and sometimes competing doctrines. Life in Christ is a shared experience, but the expression of that life is diverse. Ought we to expect anything else? "To some extent that's as it should be. We are finite beings, living in a complex, fallen world. We can't know every relevant fact, nor see the whole picture; our insights and conclusions will vary with our circumstances. Indeed, such diversity is actually a strength if it operates under a unity of purpose, for it improves our collective judgments and enables the Christian community to act with greater wisdom."[33]

Regardless of what we may think about religious streams and structures, theology and the distinctive doctrines that make up Christianity, there is one nonnegotiable to embrace. To believe in the God of Creation and the Christ of Redemption also means that we believe in the supernatural and the miraculous. Stephen L. Carter points out that to be genuinely Christian, after all, "is to believe in some aspect of the supernatural, whether the belief involves a certainty that God parted the Red Sea so that the Israelites could escape, a conviction that Jesus Christ is the Son of God and rules the universe as part of the Holy Trinity.... the belief in supernatural intervention in human affairs is a useful divider."[34]

◆ F. The case of gender equality ◆

In society at large and inside the nation's churches, diversity reigns. We are multi-minded. Our pluralism is more than theoretical. We are a culture that hands out permission slips to organizations and individuals that read, "pursue your preferences." We should not be surprised, then, that on the question of "gender equality" differences not only reign, sometimes they rage.

In Canada, women were not allowed to vote in federal elections until 1918. In provincial elections in Quebec, the freedom for women to vote was withheld until 1940. Aboriginal Canadians, both women and men, were not allowed to cast their ballots in federal elections until 1960.

During this time, roles for husbands and wives were clearly defined. The husband was the breadwinner. The wife worked at home and carried primary responsibility for raising the children. Father was the head of the home. Members of the "weaker sex" were restricted from entering higher levels of education until the '60s. In those days, when a woman had a profession, she was most likely either a nurse or a teacher. Even in the '70s, it was not unusual for women to be paid less for doing identical work to men. And today, the majority of women still work in support roles for men.

The feminist movement found its initial impetus outside the church. As occurs with the advent of most social causes, strident, angry, and sometimes harsh voices articulated the first-phase agenda. Thus, when the '60s emerged as the decade to champion change, the tone was not always courteous. In 1970, the Royal Commission on the Status of Women rather cautiously proclaimed, "The equality of opportunity for Canadian men and women is possible, desirable, and ethically necessary." Today, the National Action Committee on the Status of Women continues to contend that conditions of gender inequality remain and they lobby accordingly. At the same time, a conservative coalition calling themselves "REAL" women lobby for the retention of the traditional family and strive to keep mothers out of the workplace.

Once the issue of gender equality was solidly stated on the cultural agenda, some segments of the church began revisiting their theology and practices toward women in leadership and ministry. Advocates who champion the cause of gender equality inside the church frequently quote Galations 3:28 to support their case. "There is no longer Jew or Greek, there is no longer slave or free, there is no longer male and female; for all of you are one in Christ Jesus." Appealing to the biblical standard of being "one in Christ," they call for ethnic, socioeconomic, and gender equality. Thus:

- Ethnic equality is God's way—neither Jew nor Greek.
- Socioeconomic equality is God's way—neither slave nor free.
- Gender equality is God's way—neither male nor female.

At the same moment, somewhere else in God's family, other equally convinced followers of Jesus preach the theology of male "headship." The scriptures speak clearly for that perspective too. "For a man ought not to have his head veiled, since he is the image and reflection of God; but woman is the reflection of man. Indeed, man was not made from woman, but woman from man. Neither was man created for the sake of woman, but woman for the sake of man." (1 Corinthians 11:7–9)

Of note is the fact that the Anglican Church ordained their first woman bishop in Canada in 1994. In contrast, around the world and in Canada, Catholics hold to their traditional "male only priests"

Fig. 2.3
The Churches' Responses to Women in Leadership and Ministry

Church	Partial Ministry Function	Full Ministry Function
Catholics	Yes	No
Conserv. Protestant		
Alliance	Yes	No
Baptists	Yes	Yes & No
Pentecostal	Yes	No
Salvation Army	Yes	Yes & No
Mainline Protestant		
Anglican	Yes	Yes
Lutheran	Yes	Yes & No
Presbyterian	Yes	Yes
United	Yes	Yes

position. And if not by formal policy, the majority of evangelical churches in the nation also follow the practice of restricting the full function of women in ministry. *(See Fig. 2.3)*

Diversity reigns—truth and love resolves

What is the point of the above? This is how life works in Canada. We both encourage and permit diversity. Accordingly, every church has the responsibility and right to self-define. Particularly in today's multi-minded society, both organizationally and personally, it is crucial to be clear about who we are.

What can we expect in the future? On the matter of women in ministry, there will always be differences of opinion and conviction. It has ever been so and that reality will not change. What has changed, however, is the cultural mood. The pull toward genuine gender equality is clearly winning the day. Granted, the cultural mood can never be a justification for altering theology, but the negative consequences for churches that treat women as second-class citizens will be enormous in tomorrow's world.

In focus group research relating to effective churches,

several young mothers stated that they personally were prepared to attend churches where women were less than equal to men, but they refused to subject their daughters to messages of inferiority.[35] At the very least, churches that do not extend full access to women in ministry will be wise to assess the recent biblical scholarship on the matter.

Another motivation for revisiting the question of gender equality is that, as a social movement, both the tone and the content of the feminist agenda is evolving. Naomi Wolf represents a more recent and less extremist feminist voice. In her latest book, *Fire With Fire*, she argues for a new feminism, a feminism more driven by maturity and pragmatism than by the purity of ideology. Responding to both female and male critics, she says the following:

> We must return feminism to its best roots as an egalitarian, humanistic, tolerant, intellectually open, fair, civil rights movement, and reject any hint of any idea, no matter how "feminist" its costume, that involves notions of female superiority or male inferiority... Like any decent movement for social equality, feminism's main premise is the golden rule.[36]

This chapter started with references to the "truth man," Francis Schaeffer, and the "love man," Joseph Fletcher. Years ago those two messages seemed contradictory. But is that really the case?

The biblical way is to "speak the truth in love." Today, when I think about gender issues or other matters caught in the cradle of confusion, I wonder why didn't I make the "truth with love" linkage and work at the resolve between the two a lot earlier in life. The "truth with love" mandate liberates. Truth summons me to confirm my personal convictions on prevailing concerns, while love motivates me to give proper regard to the views of others. In the words of scripture,

> We must no longer be children, tossed to and fro and blown about by every wind of doctrine, by people's trickery, by their craftiness in deceitful scheming. But speaking the truth in love, we must grow up in every way into him who is the head, into Christ, from whom the whole body, joined and knit together by every ligament with which it is equipped, as each part is working properly, promotes the body's growth in building itself up in love. (Ephesians 4:14–16)

◆ Affirming Our Common Commitments ◆

Chapter Three

Introduction

Canadians are reasonably well-behaved people. We do not break the law most of the time. Most people are predisposed to lend a helping hand. At the very least, we leave modest tips at restaurants. It is only on rare occasions that we slam the door in the face of a stranger. Even when we feel like being first, we wait in line to get on the bus. If we have a job, we work productively, whether the boss is looking or not. When we play bridge, or poker, or monopoly with friends, we keep the rules. Even when we play solitaire, our conscience whispers, "Do what's right."

People around the world like Canadians. Our international reputation receives global applause. More cautious than aggressive, more cooperative than competitive, Canadians are likable and liked. Rumor has it that Americans who travel internationally sometimes pin the maple leaf on their lapels in the hope that they will be mistaken for Canadians.

A modern nation of 27 million people spread across a vast geographic terrain, Canadians have dealt with diversity from the very beginning. Being a "hyphenated Canadian" is not new. Anglophone Canadians and Francophone Canadians have lived out their cultural differences alongside each other. An early commitment to a mosaic concept of culture encouraged Ukrainian and German Canadians, Polish and Dutch Canadians, Italian and Greek

Canadians, and Mennonite and Jewish Canadians to keep their old ways alive. There was a sense of pride in being Canadian while retaining one's particular cultural heritage. Tragically, aboriginal peoples were not treated in the same manner.

Two realities from the past complicate our ability to deal with the disarray of diversity swirling around us in the present. Particularly in English Canada, the mosaic mentality that encouraged each Canadian to cherish his or her ethnic heritage, indirectly discouraged the cultivation of a strong Canadian culture. In French Canada, commitment to the preservation of a distinct society preempted the importance of nurturing a clear Canadian identity. Consequently, we may acknowledge the flag and sing *O Canada* together, but the absence of a strong consolidated cultural identity leaves us without defined reference points for comparing new issues with old assumptions.

Secondly, in the past, diversity was by its nature, less divisive. Certainly there was a wide array of languages, music, foods, festivals, and fashions. But at the same time, there was a common view of morals and ethics. A common religion provided the foundation upon which to build the nation. Catholics and Protestants may not have said kind things about each other in private, and they did not always speak the same language, but they **did** embrace similar beliefs. As a result, it was the Christian faith that shaped the historic assumptions of the nation.

◆ A. Yesterday's unstated strength ◆

After recently studying the nature of spirituality across Canada, Ron Graham, a political journalist and self-described skeptic arrived at the following conclusion:

> No student of Canadian politics and history can ignore the extraordinary impact God has had on those who have come here. Spirituality governed the aboriginal tribes of America before the Europeans. Bishops dominated French Canada from Laval to Leger. Religion ruled the issues and parties of English Canada... Denominations shaped our education system, our social services, many of our laws, even the ethics of our business elites. An obsession with sacred themes has characterized our culture. No less an authority than the Bible gave

> Canada its designation and motto, from the seventy-second psalm: that God 'will have dominion also from sea to sea, and from the river unto the ends of the earth.'"[1]

Prior to the 1960s, Canada had an unofficial core culture. Christendom gave Canada its cohesive cultural identity. The teachings of Jesus supported our plausibility structures, the assumptions of culture that we took for granted. They propagated the values we shared from the Protestant and Catholic pulpits of the land. Forgiveness, honesty, and generosity were uncontested virtues. We did not debate what behavior was sexually right and sexually wrong. The cultural consensus assumed that God's ways were right and good. Although we did not imprint "in God we trust" on our money, we reserved a place for the God of creation and the Christ of redemption in our souls.

University of Toronto historian Michael Bliss underscores the unstated strength of Canada's Christian heritage:

> Not too many years ago, I grew up in an Ontario community still profoundly influenced by its Christian heritage. The idea of divine commandments, many of them prohibitions, was the basis of a moral code that stressed our duties to God and one another, and the seed for self-denial, in matters both sexual and material. Doing one's duty was more important than self-fulfillment; ambition should be subordinated to the desire to serve. Life was to be lived by the precepts of the Ten Commandments, the Golden Rule, the Beatitudes. With faith, grace, and good works, corrupt humanity might find redemption and salvation.
>
> By the mid-20th century, organized religion had lost much of its public appeal and influence, and was dwindling to the margins of private belief and public aestheticism. In our time, practical unbelief has spread throughout society, and most of the values associated with the old Judeo-Christian moral code have become unstuck.
>
> What happens to a society when it loses faith in the central maxims of its cultural heritage? How do you rebuild ethics after the death of God? What do you do when you find yourself living in a society of appalling selfishness and communal

disintegration?[2]

A recent editorial in the *Globe and Mail* by Gordon Moir reminds us how central the faith was to our past:

> My father remembers a time not so long ago when people discussed the Sunday sermon over their Monday-morning java. Just try to find a fellow Christian, let alone a member of your parish or congregation, at your workplace now. Today, the Retail Council of Canada is a more powerful lobby than the Canadian Council of Churches.[3]

Symbols in society reveal current standards. In the context of the holiest week in Christianity's calendar, a seasonal billboard perched above the doors of a Toronto strip club read: "50 Luscious Babes to Tease and Please You. Open Good Friday."[4] As I have already asserted, the assumptions of secular pluralism define our unstated cultural beliefs in the present.

Although it is far too premature to mourn the "death of God," on behalf of the majority of modern Canadians, it is the time to lament the "loss of God." We are in the process of nurturing moral cultural poverty. Where do we look for the replenishing of our moral capital?

Noted Canadian, Michael Ignatieff observes, "Nobody knows what you integrate to any more. Before the First World War, you had the sense that here you had an Anglo-Saxon Protestant matrix and an imperial British culture—and everybody knew what hymn we were all singing. Now the question is, who's defining the context of integration at all, and what kind of Canada are you integrating yourself to?"[5]

◆ B. Yielding to the common good ◆

Canada's historic mosaic mentality is one social stimulus that produces pluralism in contemporary culture. That one can become a Canadian while retaining one's ethnic heritage mitigates against the establishment of a coherent culture. It contributes to a fragmented diversity that nurtures pluralism. In its present form, the basic notion of the pluralism that pervades society is relatively simple: "There are in society different people with different beliefs and different ways of life and they should as much as possible be free to live out their beliefs without being controlled by others."[6] Unchecked pluralism obviously leans heavily in the direction of individualism. Consequently, it is not an adequate creed for life in a society that is running low on moral capital.

A culture which simply lets "You do your thing" while "I do my thing" is set up for interpersonal tensions and social disorder. It is too independent and too self-oriented to foster wholesome community life. In order for communities to be healthy and for a country to function, its citizens must extend themselves beyond self-interest and be prepared to relinquish rights. To deal responsibly with our differences, there are times when treasured individual rights need to be surrendered to the best interests of the group.

Creating a society without an adequate group consensus is like running a public transportation system without a schedule or designated routes. The result is wildly unpredictable. Bus drivers are free to make up their routes at will. Depending on mood of the moment, they may or may not stop at designated pick up points. Likewise, culture cannot be built on excessive individualism. Individualism generates too much diversity, and the culture loses its strength and coherence.

Accordingly, there must be limits to cultural diversity. Just as we have the criminal code to protect the public from flagrant acts of violence or abuse, we must have social codes to keep from being tyrannized by unrestrained personal differences. This is not a new idea. We regularly relinquish rights in the normal routine of life. We listen when people speak to us. At the grocery store, we stand in line and wait our turn. As we drive our cars, we stop for red lights. We know that to live together, we must have regard for safety and the rights of others. In one sense, the equation is quite simple. Relinquishing individual rights is necessary in order to have a healthy collective life.

By stressing the importance of collective life, we do not relegate individual autonomy to unimportance. We do, however, balance the present unrelenting aspiration for personal choice and freedom with the needs of community life. In the end, individuals cannot have life all their own way. Existence in a healthy society is similar to life in a healthy family. There are inevitable limits placed on individual family members for the sake of the common good of the family. In the national realm, there has to be a "willingness to sacrifice private desires for public ends."[7] Each nation must solve in its own way what appears to be a contradiction: respect for free persons, and attainment of the common good.[8]

Catholic social teaching has used the term "common good" to point to the challenge of building the good society. The term takes on the concreteness specific to a historical context, but always, in this view, freedom is never an end in itself but rather the means to achieve the good society.[9] The Second Vatican Council (1962–65) defined the common good as "the sum of those conditions of social life which allow social groups and their individual members relatively thorough and ready access to their own fulfillment."[10] Therefore, the common good is all the arrangements and conditions that make it possible for the individual and for small social units to work together in an orderly fashion—the development of personality and the fostering of culture.[11]

The current community need to yield to the common good stands in contrast to increasing lawlessness in the land. All regions of the country are implicated. Reacting to cuts in service, villagers in Newfoundland seized a ferry. This past year, teachers in the Maritimes defied the law and went on strike. The Innu leaders at Davis Inlet physically refused to allow the provincial court into their community. For various reasons at different times, other aboriginal peoples have set up illegal road blocks and immobilized trains. In Montreal, business people threw furniture from the observers' balcony into the city council chambers when a decision went contrary to their interests. Day after day, truckers in Ontario inched their rigs along the country's busiest highways to get their way. Frustrated by unresolved grievances and reacting to an administrative decision to investigate the actions of two of their peers, the keepers of the law became laws unto themselves. A precinct of 50 Toronto police officers barricaded themselves into a downtown police station during a wildcat strike. Transgressing their own agreements, farmers in the prairies bootlegged grain across the border this past summer. When the courts ordered nurses in Alberta to stop their illegal strike and return to work, the nurses ignored the legal directive until they had negotiated a favorable new contract. In British Columbia, professor of philosophy Loren Wilkinson, from Regent College, was found guilty of disobeying a court injunction when he and others blockaded the logging road to Clayoquot Sound. Citing Socrates at the trial, Wilkinson reasoned, "There should be a complete identity between justice and the laws. When the laws do not serve justice, however, we have an obligation to disobey them—but always to do so in such a way that law and justice will be brought together.[12]

Advocates of various causes have long appealed to the tenets of "just war" theory. Although the rationale justifies breaking the law, in the prevailing mood that mindset also feeds self-driven lawlessness. The federal government's inability to either control or stop the smuggling and selling of American cigarettes in this country comes as no surprise. Even in the face of an enormous deficit, the prevalence of lawlessness forced them to sacrifice tax revenue instead of enforcing the law. Claims that the underground economy is flourishing fit the profile. In the face of these trends, all citizens would do well to remember that "Civilization is not a gift, it is an achievement—a fragile achievement that needs constantly to be shored up and defended from besiegers inside and out."[13]

◆ C. Discerning common commitments ◆

The parliament grounds in Ottawa are an impressive sight. They also shed light on some of the building blocks on which the nation was originally established. For example, due west of the library wing stands a statue of George Brown. A proponent of federalism and one of the Fathers of Confederation, Brown immigrated from Edinburgh via New York, and arrived in Toronto in 1843. To articulate his political views, he founded the *Toronto Globe*. In a similar spirit, he established the *Presbyterian Banner* as a vehicle to express his religious convictions. An advocate of representation by population, the inscription under George Brown's statue articulates a measure of his vision for the nation:[14]

"Government by the people
  free institutions
religious liberty and equality
  unity and progress of confederation."

In subsequent years, "the National Policy and railway construction, the Wheat Board and the CBC, participation in world wars or in U.N. peacekeeping operations, social security programs or the flag, have been defining characteristics of our identity."[15] Commemorating the nation's 100th birthday and hosting EXPO '67 linked us together in new ways. In 1972, we celebrated from coast to coast when our hockey players just barely beat the Russians. Whenever Canadians parade on the international stage, whether they are French, English, Black, Asian, or Indian, we all cheer—at least a little.

There have been three pieces of federal legislation that have been cultural watersheds in recent decades; the commitment to bilingualism in 1969, the Multicultural Act in 1971, and the Charter of Rights in 1982 altered the face of the nation. The following excerpts from the Charter help to define the character of the country:

> Whereas Canada is founded upon principles that recognize the supremacy of God and the rule of law:
>
> The Canadian Charter of Rights and Freedoms guarantees the rights and freedoms set out in it subject only to such reasonable limits prescribed by law as can be demonstrably justified in a free and democratic society.
>
> Everyone has the following fundamental freedoms:
>
> (a) freedom of conscience and religion;
> (b) freedom of thought, belief, opinion and expression, including freedom of the press and other media of communication;
> (c) freedom of peaceful assembly; and
> (d) freedom of association.
>
> This Charter shall be interpreted in a manner consistent with the preservation and enhancement of the multicultural heritage of Canadians."[16]

For whatever reasons, the nation's history, the influence of religion, subsequent legislation, and the Charter of Rights have not left us with a conclusive sense of what is a Canadian. Neither has the presence of the inherent drive for democracy, that fosters freedom and choices, been adequate to socially cement us together. Many voices expressing various views have addressed the longstanding debate about Canada's common commitments and national identity.

Former Prime Minister Pierre Elliott Trudeau has been one of the most eloquent: "Canada... is a human place, a sanctuary of sanity in an increasingly troubled world. We need not search further for our identity. These traits of tolerance and courtesy and respect for our environment and one another provide it. I suggest that a superior form of identity would be difficult to find."[17]

Referring specifically to English Canada, Historian Philip Resnick from the University of British Columbia agrees: "To emphasize tolerance as a cardinal principle of English Canada is a simple observation of fact, not a testament to moral superiority or hard prediction about the future."[18]

Noted Canadian Northrop Frye knew how consequential it has been for Canada to live next door to a global superpower. He said, "Historically, a Canadian is an American who rejects the Revolution."[19]

Pierre Berton picks up the same theme in his often humorous book, *Why We Act Like Canadians*. Envisioning a conversation with an American cousin, he proposes,

> We are cooler than you, as our people learned when your southerners invaded Upper Canada. Hot weather and passion, gunfights and race riots go together. Your mythic encounters seem to have taken place at high noon, the sun beating down on a dusty Arizona street. I find it difficult to contemplate a similar gunfight in Moose Jaw in the winter, the bitter rivals struggling vainly to shed two pairs of mitts and reach under several layers of parka for weapons so cold that the slightest touch of flesh on steel would take the skin off their thumbs."[20]

In a more serious tone Berton reasons, "Our identity has also been shaped by our negative reaction to your overpowering presence. We know who we are **not,** even if we aren't quite sure who we are. We are not American."[21]

University of Toronto political scientist Gad Horowitz's view on Canada's core culture is more cynical. "What has held our country together is not commitment to shared ideology but rather a tenuous willingness to coexist."[22]

Present Prime Minister Jean Chrétien has another perspective. "Canadians don't need their identity analyzed any more or any lessons in how to be Canadian because they already are living the experience." Speaking to Canada Day celebrants, he continued, "We all know the politicians, the pundits and the academics are busy trying to analyze what it means to be Canadian and what, if anything, unites us. Well, I can tell you the people I've met here on the Hill today, and 27 million other Canadians, are not asking themselves who they are. They are living the Canadian experience every day of their lives and they know this is the best country in the world."[23]

The Prime Minister's enthusiasm for the nation is commendable. However, the marginalization of organized religion, the failure of Meech Lake and the Charlottetown Accord, the present enigmatic configuration of Parliament, the pending referendum in Quebec, and our inability to deal productively with our increasing cultural diversity tell us problems remain.

From my own vantage point, we need to address several problems. First, it seems to me that tolerance is a deficient foundation upon which to build a society. Second, defining our identity on the basis of the fact that we are unlike another nation is inadequate. And third, it is an illusion to think that a coherent culture can be developed by simply championing pluralism and the diversity it spawns.

Neil Bissoondath, a journalist and a first generation Canadian, rightly contends, "Canada has long prided itself on being a tolerant society, but tolerance is clearly insufficient in the building of a cohesive society. A far greater goal to strive for would be an accepting society."[24]

Staking Canada's national identity on the claim of being "unamerican" is blatantly dissatisfying. The mere notion guarantees a negative national self-image. Countries that nurture confident citizens have discernible identities.

By its very nature, diversity cannot be the primary building block with which to construct a country. A nation must have glue to hold it together. Left to run its course, diversity fragments. Unchecked, diversity tears apart life. In the end, bowing at the "diversity is beautiful" shrine will shred the social fabric. A strong country cannot be built by simply extolling differences.

Talcott Parsons celebrated pluralism and "those aspects of secularization that freed social life from direct regulation by a religious code." But he also insisted that "societies—even highly modernized societies—need common values to legitimate the social order and to provide the motivational basis for social solidarity."[25]

Plato said, "Give me the songs of a nation, and it matters not who writes its laws." A nation's manners and morals are more important than the law. This is the business of culture.[26] In Canada's case, how can we pour more substance into our core culture? What are the marks of an "unamerican" identity? In our pursuit of "the business of culture," can we find new bonds for being unapologetically Canadian?

◆ D. Multicultural ambivalence ◆

In modern Canada, we have attempted to transmit common values and engender social order by affirming the tenets of multiculturalism. Typical of the Canadian style, however, we have diverse views on how we think multiculturalism should work. The federal government and nine of the provinces talk of multiculturalism and a mosaic; Quebec talks of interculturalism and a tree—a host country on which minority cultures are grafted.[27]

The Multicultural Act of 1971 officially designated Canada as a country that is multicultural in a bilingual framework.

> It is hereby declared to be the policy of the Government of Canada to recognize and promote the understanding that multiculturalism reflects the cultural and racial diversity of Canadian society and acknowledges the freedom of all members of Canadian society to preserve, enhance, and share their cultural heritage.
>
> —Canadian Multiculturalism Act

In a policy announcement to Parliament, the government declared,

> We believe that cultural pluralism is the very essence of Canadian identity. Every ethnic group has the right to reserve and develop its own culture and values within the Canadian context. To say that we have two official languages is not to say we have two official cultures, and no particular culture is more official than another. A policy of multiculturalism must be a policy for all Canadians.[28]

Analyzing the policy, University of McGill political scientist Charles Taylor suggests that multiculturalism means that, "Everyone should be recognized for his or her unique identity." He sees multiculturalism supporting "the politics of recognition." The politics of recognition, according to Taylor, fosters equal dignity "based on the idea that all humans are equally worthy of respect... What we are asked to recognize is the unique identity of this individual or group, their distinctness from everyone else. The idea is that it is precisely this distinctness that has been ignored, glossed over, assimilated to a dominant or majority identity. And this assimilation is the cardinal sin against the ideal of authenticity."[29]

In contrast to this lofty interpretation, University of Toronto political scientist Gad Horowitz suggests that multiculturalism in reality is "the masochistic celebration of Canadian nothingness."[30]

Policy prescription is quite different from cultural formation. Policies are posted as theory on paper. Culture is paraded in the positive and negative events of real life.

On November 11, 1993, five Sikh veterans who had participated in Remembrance Day ceremonies were refused admittance to the main hall of the Newton branch of the Royal Canadian Legion in the Vancouver suburb of Surrey. Branch bylaw prohibited the wearing of headgear, as a sign of respect for fallen comrades. Since the Sikhs would not remove their turbans, they were invited to "go into a separate room by themselves to drink coffee." The report acknowledged that at least one Legion member was angered by the treatment afforded the Sikhs. The television reports offered the ugly sight of angry members calling on the Sikhs to go back where they came from.[31]

On November 29, 1993, in the Montreal suburb of Longueuil, municipal court Judge Richard Alary expelled a Muslim woman for wearing a *hi jab*—a traditional head scarf—in his courtroom. In the view of the judge, court rules banning headgear took precedence over religious freedom as enshrined in the Canadian Charter of Rights and Freedoms. Although efforts were made to explain that the *hi jab*, like the Sikh turban, is an intimate part of religious identity, the explanation made no difference.[32]

Commenting on the incident, Jean Pare, editor of the influential magazine *L'actualité*, described the *hi jab* as "a rallying sign for Islamicists in their struggle against the 'Western devil.' In accepting this symbol, we are contributing to our own destruction, and that of our values of equality and tolerance, the very ones that Islamicists attack."[33]

Although formal policies are clear, national research data profiling 1502 Canadians reveals that multicultural ambivalence still lurks in society's public and private domains.

Multicultural ambivalence[34]	
A solid majority of Canadians are willing to describe discrimination against visible minorities as a problem in Canada. (72%)	A similar majority do not believe that the fabric of Canadian society is being threatened by the presence of visible minorities. (74%)
A strong majority of Canadians view Canada's multicultural composition as one of the best qualities of Canada. (77%)	A smaller majority would urge minorities to try to become more like most other Canadians. (57%)
Significant public concern exists that Canada's immigration gate is too wide open. (45%)	Very few Canadians believe that the country would be better off if recent immigrants returned to their country of origin. (13%)
On a "tolerance index" based on acceptance of diversity and views on immigration: 38% are highly tolerant 30% are moderately tolerant	On a "tolerance index" based on acceptance of diversity and views on immigration: 12% are highly intolerant 20% are moderately intolerant

The five cultural types defined in chapter one illustrate how Canadians can be expected to respond to the presence of multicultural diversity. **Tribalizers** are characteristically highly intolerant. Instead of making room in their world for men with turbans and women with *hi jabs*, they react judgmentally. Tribalizers cannot hear the argument that others in society should have the same religious or other freedoms they desire for themselves. **Reclaimers** also lean toward intolerance, but they are more moderate than tribalizers. **Accommodators** predictably embrace highly tolerant views of multicultural diversity.

Whether the focus is on religious symbols or other immigration issues, they champion full and equal rights for cultural minorities. Compared to accommodators, **collaborators** are concerned for tolerance too, but in a more moderate manner. They contend that we must make room for new expressions of diversity, but they are also ready to set limits on the forms of cultural diversity we collectively embrace. **Cocooners** weave their way through the issues of the age without strong feelings in either direction unless their immediate world is disrupted.

When identifying the five cultural types within specific situations, it is important to both avoid stereotyping and to distinguish between people's **attitudes** and their actual **practice**. For example, some people may well display attitudes that characterize them as reclaimers or tribalizers, but when particular people appear in their presence, they will be accepting and supportive. In contrast, accommodators are capable of talking the language of justice and equality, but in specific situations, they may be just as passive and indifferent as cocooners.

Within the current scope of government spending priorities, multiculturalism is a minor program. The current budget of about $27 million represents approximately one dollar a year for each person in Canada. In contrast to past years when multicultural monies were sometimes provided to build ethnic cultural centers and to support folk festivals, today the funds are channeled primarily into initiatives to reduce racial intolerance and discrimination.

A crucial part of creating a good society is making room for the people who want to live there. Wholesome societies include in their national identities the identities of those who make up the whole. At this stage in Canada's history, this means establishing cultural space for the diverse people who live within the borders of our shared land. Rather than thinking of the country as a multicultural mosaic, or as a very large and very old tree into which other trees must be grafted, is there value in envisioning modern Canada as a forest of many different kinds of trees?

The temperatures and terrain of the nation nurture different types of trees. There is ample room for birches and maples, for poplars, spruces, and giant Douglas firs. In some areas, the land graces its favor on trees to produce apples and cherries and peaches and pears. In other regions, the forest produces lumber to build homes, or timber for huge beams, or the sweet taste of maple syrup. Millions of trees with unique shapes and sizes display their array of colors and there is beauty in the land.

Although trees in the forest are different from each other, they all have similar needs and share common characteristics. To flourish, trees need a healthy ecology to support them. They all require soil for their roots to grow. Without enough light and moisture, trees remain stunted. When the winds howl or fires burn or storms wreak havoc on the land, the whole forest experiences the strain together. When acid rain falls, the whole forest is damaged.

A forest of trees that are all the same can still be pleasing to one's senses. But a forest of different kinds of trees is a statement of extravagant splendor. A tree standing alone has inherent beauty. A cluster of trees in the midst of other clusters of different types of trees is an impressive sight of creation and creativity.

Trees are not people and neither should the metaphor be overstated. But diverse people learning to live together in the same land is just as impressive as a diverse and mighty forest. Bissoondath is correct when he observes that, "A free society depends on a multiplicity of voices and visions, on the interplay of conflicting views. We would only diminish ourselves by diminishing that variety."[35]

◆ E. Celebrating collective commitments ◆

Offering a metaphor and making a case for the value of Canada's cultural diversity is relatively easy. Discerning what defines Canada's common commitments is much more difficult. As a nation, we readily celebrate our differences. We are less definitive, however, when it comes to identifying and affirming our shared commitments. Discerning a clearer definition of our nationhood will help guide both our collective and individual decision making.

The following affirmations and invitations are offered in the hope that they will contribute to the discussions around what constitutes the Canadian identity. Obviously these characteristics can be found elsewhere in the world. Accordingly, there is no basis to claim that Canadians are totally unique. When the individual dimensions are combined into a whole, however,

Canadians are distinctive. Consider the following affirmations that help describe the Canadian character.

Canadians are diverse people

The "hyphenated Canadian" has always been with us. The modern history of the nation began with French-Canadians and English-Canadians. Later, our embrace of the mosaic metaphor extended cultural status to Ukrainian-Canadians, Caribbean-Canadians, Chinese-Canadians, and a host of other national hybrids.

By way of comparison, the U.S. is now entering into a period of self-description that Canadians have experienced from the beginning. The surge in ethnic pride and the critical mass of people in the U.S. is just now creating a place for African-Americans, Asian-Americans, and Hispanic-Americans. Canada's historical experience may be inescapable in the modern world where the movement of people is inevitable.

The marginalization of the Christian faith in Canada's cultural life has made room for moral multi-mindedness and lifestyle alternatives. The Charter of Rights and Freedoms and the formal policy of multiculturalism has protected minority groups and ordained ethnic diversity in new ways.

The Canadian soil and soul is genuinely and increasingly pluralistic and diverse. However, a coherent culture cannot be developed by simply championing pluralism and the diversity it spawns. Learning to live more constructively with our differences will serve us all.

Canadians are compassionate people

Medicare, over its first 30 years of existence, has become an integral component of the Canadian psyche. Research has long identified social services such as 'universal healthcare' as the most important factor, of many benefits received, in defining "what it means to be Canadian."[36] The readiness of the population to support a tax base to fund the high costs of medicare is an indication of both Canadians' self-interest and compassion.

Although there has been resistance to present levels of immigration, Canadian people are quite ready to make room for new Canadians. When television images tell the story of horrors in Rwanda, millions of Canadians empathetically write cheques in response to the needs of others. In fact, 61% of Canadians say, "I would really like to help people who need it, but I just don't know what I can do to help." Surprisingly 33% of Canadians go as far as to say, "I would be prepared to pay higher taxes so the Canadian government could do more for poor people in developing countries."[37]

Canadians are peaceful people

One of the historical marks of Canadians is their reputation for being peacemakers. In contrast to the American way, Canada's severance from Britain was both piecemeal and peaceable. Although Canadian soldiers served honorably in two world wars, our modern reputation is founded on the role of our soldiers as United Nations' peacekeepers.

Admittedly, the Canadian Airborne Regiment has stained the Canadian reputation for peacekeeping with Somali blood. The overt racism and despicable behavior of members of the Regiment offended Canadians deeply. In one measure, it was the collective conscience of Canadians and their concern for peaceful civility that forced the disbanding of the Airborne Regiment in military disgrace.

One of the distinctly un-American characteristics of Canadian life is our attitude to guns and violence. "In 1990, handguns killed only 22 people in Great Britain, 68 in Canada, and 87 in Japan; in the U.S., the total was 10,567."[38] When it comes to violence, Canadians are not like Americans. And if that is what Canadians mean when they say "we are not American," then so be it. However, to suggest that the primary mark of the Canadian identity is that we are "un-American" is neither complimentary nor true.

Canadians are spiritual people

Documentation has already established that Canadians are less and less enamored with organized religion. At the same time, Remi de Roo, the Roman Catholic bishop from Victoria, contends that, "People are as spiritually inclined as ever, in the sense that they still dream, they still have visions and aspirations for a better world, they still look for some kind of paradise."[39]

Reflecting the spiritual interest of young adults sometimes called "Generation X," Canadian Douglas Coupland writes, "I must remind myself we are living creatures—we have religious impulses—we must—and yet into what cracks do these impulses flow in a world without religion? It is something I think about every day. Sometimes I think it is the only thing I should be thinking about."[40]

In the 1960s, the potent influence of science tended to reduce life to what could be empirically proven in a laboratory. The realm of the rational ruled the day. If reality could not be measured, it was considered suspect. However, the human spirit could not be contained. In the years that followed, the yearnings of the heart overpowered the logic of the mind. The hunger for experience pushed life beyond the rational. The desire for transcendence broke through the boundaries of the natural in pursuit of the supernatural. For many Canadians, the search for the spiritual also extended beyond the traditional forms of faith nurtured by organized religion.

Canadians may appear spiritually disinterested. But churches, other religious groups, and those who invite experiences with the supernatural will find an openness to phenomena that is personal and spiritually intriguing.

To affirm our common life is not to say that Canada is a nation of cookie-cutter people. The differences among us are real. And yet, "For all our disputes about language and ethnicity and regional rights, our differences shrink beside our similarities, and the things that unite us dwarf those that divide us."[41] The point is that we may have more in common than we think.

In the future, there are other critical initiatives for Canadians to pursue. The nation's citizens can distinguish themselves even further as a distinct people as they link what they **are**, to what they **can be**.

Canadians can be principled people

Even though we currently live with a certain amount of cultural ambiguity and moral complexity, specific codes of conduct still remain. Political abuse of power and privilege to gain financial advantage, extramarital sex, lying, cheating, and stealing are all forms of behavior that violate the moral consensus, and our moral conscience.

Thirty years of public advocacy on justice issues uniquely qualifies The Citizens of Public Justice to articulate a strategy for dealing with differences and developing public policy. Spokesperson Gerald Vandezande, an innovative collaborator, spells out a criterion for pursuing a just and principled society:

Human dignity: the right of all persons and their communities to be treated with justice, love, compassion, and respect, and their responsibility to treat others likewise.

Mutual responsibility: the duty of all persons to contribute to the well-being of the community as they are able, and the duty of each community to contribute to the well-being both of its members, regardless of their ability, and of those in the larger society.

Economic equity: the right of all persons and communities to adequate access to the resources necessary for a full life, including access to worthwhile work, fair employment conditions and income-security provisions, and our communal responsibility to use such resources responsibly.

Social justice: the right of all persons and communities to full participation in the life and decision making of Canada, and to adequate access to the resources necessary for a full life, including access to adequate education, health care, housing, and child care, and our communal responsibility to use such resources responsibly.

Environmental integrity: the duty of all persons, communities, and institutions to live in harmony with, and to practice responsible stewardship of the earth and the environment.

Fiscal fairness: the right of all persons, communities, and institutions to fair fiscal treatment and the responsibility of all to contribute fairly for the well-being of all.[42]

Taken as a whole, the above criterion is worthy of careful evaluation and strategic implementation, but it will not preclude social battles in the future. After the tensions surrounding abortion, mutliculturalism, aboriginal land claims, fair and just taxation, and the place of religion in the public forum get resolved, other matters will inflict more strain and stress. Still, to allow our culture to fragment into disarray would be inexcusable.

Principled people lift the level of life above polite behavior and good manners. They engage in social interaction that demands openness to the claims of others, combined with a willing restraint of one's own claims in the service of our common aspirations.[43]

Canadians can be collaborators

Differences between people in society do not need to result in adversarial social interaction, endurance tests of tolerance, or painful poundings. Living with a commitment to collaboration can instill attitudes of mutuality that set the ground rules for living together in constructive ways.

The commitment to collaborate with others quiets adversarial attitudes. Addressing personal problems or social tensions with an understanding that there is more than one valid way to view the world lessens the likelihood of damaging confrontation. The spirit of collaboration addresses the underlying tension that often exists between the vested interests of individuals. People who live with clear convictions but who also have regard for the views of others are more inclined to negotiate than they are to come out of their corner with the intention of knocking out their opponent.

Collaboration lifts life above the tone of both tolerance and intolerance. If one has to choose between the two, tolerance is much preferred to intolerance. But tolerance also falls short of being the ultimate virtue with which to foster healthy social life. The temperament of tolerance says, "I will endure you. I will acknowledge your existence and put up with your difference." Collaborative temperaments say, "I will not only acknowledge you, I will live with a commitment to understand you and to cooperate with you."

Cultural collaborators are also aware of the probable imbalance between individual preferences and community needs. Commenting on the spirit of the age, sociologist Robert Bellah appeals for people to be "less trapped in the clichés of rugged individualism" and "more open to an invigorating, fulfilling sense of social responsibility."[44] Collaborators intentionally seek the balance between personal entitlements and corresponding social rcsponsibilities.

In *Restoring the Good Society*, author Don Eberly writes:

> The good society is a society with shared values and personal and social order. It consists of positive ideals, strong communities, civility, and manners. It can neither be doled out as just another entitlement, nor pieced together through programs, nor

stimulated into existence by tax cuts. Instead it must be achieved through the cooperative efforts of individuals from all sectors and society.[45]

Canadians can be cultural contributors

Augustine believed that, "Where there are good Christians, there are good citizens."[46] It seems, though, that many visible Christians "in our culture may think long and hard about what it means to be a good parent, but they won't often ponder what it means to be a good citizen or to have a just society."[47]

There is a Christian and common-sense virtue in thinking and talking about the cost of citizenship. For all people in a country's population, responsible citizenship involves more than just keeping the law and paying taxes. Keeping the law and staying out of jail is morally neutral behavior. In a country like Canada, with its extensive social programs, paying taxes is more an obligation of duty than it is an extraordinary cultural contribution.

Cultural contributors ask, "What can I do?" rather than "What should the government do?" They are ready to reach into their own pockets to respond to other people's needs without requiring tax receipts. Cultural contributors are more motivated to create or look for work than to automatically line up for unemployment insurance. At the same time, they know that not everyone who wants to work is able to find employment. Accordingly, cultural contributors pay their unemployment insurance premiums without complaining. While they resist the notion that "the world owes me a living," they are ready to support those who need assistance.

Cultural contributors also ask, "What can I give?" rather than "What can I get?" They give a portion of their time to something they value without being paid. Cultural contributors canvass the community to collect for their favorite charity; they take people with disabilities on shopping trips; they look after their neighbors' homes when they go away; they buy extra groceries for food banks, and roll up their sleeves at blood donor clinics.

As more citizens intentionally live as cultural contributors, not only do they, as individuals, escape the tyranny of selfism, but the collective life of society moves toward its potential.

Canadians can be grateful people

In recent years, Canada has been cited internationally as one of the best countries in the world in terms of education, personal freedom, and standard of living. Deeply etched in my memory is a conversation with a farmer from Western Canada. There was no hint of "Canadian complaining" in his view of life. The man had come from a stable Canadian home, had completed his education, and was running a successful farming operation. He was particularly grateful that he was able to provide spiritual support and economic security for his own family. The final comment of his story was profound. With a face weathered from years of working outside, he smiled and declared, "I won the biggest lottery in the world. I was born in Canada."

Life divorced from thankfulness is maimed; it merely limps along. John Henry Jowett lived in another century and culture, but his message is wise counsel in this age too:

> Life without thankfulness is devoid of love and passion
> Hope without thankfulness is lacking the fine perception
> Faith without thankfulness lacks strength and fortitude.[48]

There is no need to lament the state of the nation as Canadians celebrate their common commitments and take their social responsibilities seriously. As people from sea to sea affirm what they are, and pursue what they can be, we find substantial reason to be unapologetically Canadian.

◆ Dealing with Levels of Life ◆

Chapter Four

Introduction

I am a "born in Canada" white male. I had no choice. My parents brought me into the world that way. I like red meat and drink too much coffee. Some members of my family and other friends and colleagues counsel me to change my ways. Sometimes they lecture me. I also love desserts. Having been raised with the aroma of fresh baked cinnamon rolls and luscious apple pies, I keep blaming my mother for my lust for sweets. And again, people who care for me keep saying, "Don't you know, too much sugar is bad for you. Have you had your cholesterol checked lately? Isn't there a history of heart disease in your family?" I just keep eating my steaks, medium rare, draining coffee pots, and savoring decadent desserts.

I enjoy people and value relationships. My personal schedule, travel patterns, and monthly long distance telephone bills confirm that I place a high priority on making memories with friends. Quite regularly, couples and singles, males and females sit around our dinner table and sleep in our extra bedroom. Over the years, we have savored hundreds of remarkable conversations, engaged in scores of emotionally charged debates, and repeatedly regaled with laughter. If only the walls could talk.

I've been living with the same marvelous woman for over 30 years. We got married just as we exited the teenage years. As we keep figuring out how to grow up together, we also keep celebrating our love for each other. Without Beth in the picture, I flirt with dysfunction. Our relationship has long since convinced me that sex is one of God's best ideas. Can there be a better way to experience belonging to each other? Such pleasure. Such intimacy. Such profound joy in mutual surrender. Only God could be that creative.

As I reflect on my circle of relationships, I do not have any close friends who are homosexuals. I do, however, interact occasionally with several acquaintances who are active gays. We have had discussions with each other about our sexual lifestyle decisions and feelings. In the department of disappointments, one of the very few mentors in my life was eventually revealed as a long-term closet homosexual. Frankly, homosexuality is a turn-off for me. Although there have been occasions when I think individuals would have welcomed a same-sex encounter, I've never been sexually attracted to another man. In the sexual realm, that's who I am.

Sexuality is like a lot of other things in life. People are offered alternatives and then they make decisions. God's ways are believed and pursued by many. Other people can choose to ignore or reject God's design for life. Accordingly, as I understand how God created the world and how a democratic society functions, if adults choose to embrace same-sex partners, they have the freedom and prerogative to do so.

The aim of this chapter is to use the issue of homosexuality as an illustration of how we can deal with diversity at different levels of life. Because the questions surrounding homosexuality generate such strong emotion and debate among many Canadians, it is important to address the issues directly. The first part of the chapter offers an overview from various voices on the subject. Jesus' commitment both to conviction and to compassion frames the biblical focus. The interplay between the personal, organizational, societal, and global dimensions of our lives forms the substance of the chapter and concludes the discussion.

◆ A. Shredding of society ◆

One only has to read the newspaper to conclude that a current concern troubling many Canadians is how to respond to the pervasive presence of homosexuals. The small but vocal contingent of Canadians championing the homosexual cause is disrupting the status quo. They are pressing the majority of heterosexual Canadians to rethink and reorder their past assumptions about sexuality. To no one's surprise, organizations and individuals are reacting differently. Canadians in the cultural categories we previously described are predictable in their responses.

Reclaimers tend to react with emotion and an honest desire to protect the traditional heterosexual family. Their judgments and sense of rightness are enthusiastic and genuine. With clear consciences, they are comfortable castigating homosexuals.

Tribalizers line up on both sides of the issue. As people who segment and polarize themselves, they become either "pro-gay" or "anti-gay." Embracing one of the two extremes, they are quite ready to confront each other and, if necessary, segregate themselves from the mainstream.

Accommodators predictably include and embrace homosexuals and their drive for full-scale equality. They believe that a legitimate segment of society is being treated unjustly. In order to restore justice, they are ready to act. Sometimes, without careful reflection, they readily judge those who judge homosexuality to be morally wrong. They take pride in not being homophobic.

Cocooners simply disengage themselves from the debate. Unless a member of the family comes out of the closet, they don't really care what happens to gays and lesbians. They keep working, watching television, cutting the grass in the spring and summer, and shoveling snow in the winter. They keep spending time with their families and doing whatever "cocooners" do to maintain the status-quo of their self-framed lives.

Collaborators add their particular twist to the demands of homosexual activists. Their sensitivity and concern about human rights prompt them to make room in the culture for those with same-sex aspirations. However, collaborators are clear about who they are and they do not necessarily believe they should include homosexuals inside their particular organizations, nor do they necessarily feel any need to advance the cause of homosexuality.

Carving up culture

The media-fed homosexual agendas have gained so much momentum that it has been impossible for churches, governments, and other organizations to remain neutral. In an open letter to the constituency of the Evangelical Fellowship of Canada, Executive Director, Brian Stiller, writes with conviction on the subject of homosexuality:

> There's no doubt in my mind that we're standing at a dividing moment in history. The family is part of the glue that God, through history, has used to hold societies together. As I watch it being consistently undermined, I wonder just how far our society is going to go!

Stiller asks,

> On what grounds should the benefits afforded to marriage and family be extended to same-sex relationships?
>
> Of all the issues in which the EFC has become involved on behalf of Canadian evangelicals like you, this is one of the most serious. And we must make sure that we remain squarely in the middle of this crucial debate... I've tried to write as compassionately and compellingly as I can. I want to emphasize that... unless we act now, we may lose the opportunity to defend the biblical view of the family."[1]

When the Ontario government introduced legislation that would have given same-sex couples workplace rights and legal access to adoption privileges, Catholic Archbishop Aloysius Ambrozic spoke out strongly too. In a pastoral letter that was to be read from church pulpits, the archbishop of Toronto asserted that "any attempt to promote a homosexual lifestyle as the equivalent of legal marriage must be vigorously opposed." In a letter to the priests in his diocese, Ambrozic stated, "It is time for us to place our concerns before the people and ask them to let their voices be heard."[2]

The United Church of Canada, on the other hand, is at the forefront with those championing equality for homosexuals. One of the church's social initiatives calls for "changes to federal income tax regulations so it can extend survivor benefits to same-sex partners of church employees." Already offering health benefits to their employees who live with same-sex partners, Canada's largest Protestant denomination laments that "Income Tax Act regulations permit only spouses of the opposite sex to be eligible for spousal pension benefits." To no one's surprise, the United Church's position is "lauded by homosexuals as a positive step forward, but the church's action is also condemned by church conservatives as a further attack on the traditional family."[3]

The Anglican church's historic position to deny homosexuals right of access to formal position and public blessing is being subjected to inside pressure. As Michael McAteer points out in his column in the *Toronto Star*, bishops and priests are increasingly divided over the issue:

> A high-ranking Anglican cleric says it's time his church approved some form of service or rite that would bless the union of committed same-sex couples. The Very Rev. Duncan Abraham, Dean of St. James Cathedral in Toronto, said in an interview that the blessing of same-sex unions could ease the pain of homosexuals who feel excluded from the church. 'It seems to me the only solution is to acknowledge some form of commitment and then get on with our work.'[4]

The current unresolved debate on homosexuality invites extremists on both sides of the issue to parade their views. "A new report by feminist researcher Shere Hite scorns the traditional family as outdated, authoritarian, and the cradle of many of society's injustices." According to Hite, "The western nuclear family, with its hierarchical, male-dominated structure is not worth saving."[5]

Looking at life from another extreme, Rev. Joseph Chambers, a fundamentalist minister from Charlotte, N.C., alleges that *Sesame Street* muppets Bert and Ernie are gay. In his radio show, Chambers declared, "They're two grown men sharing a house—and a bedroom! They share clothes. They eat and cook together. They vacation together and they have effeminate characteristics. In one show, Bert teaches Ernie how to sew. In another, they tend plants together. If this isn't meant to represent a homosexual union, I can't imagine what it's supposed to represent." Representatives from *Sesame Street*'s producers, Children's Television Workshop, were not impressed. In an exasperated tone they chided, "Bert and Ernie have no sexual orientation. They're cloth puppets, for Pete's sakes."[6]

National Film Board decision-makers could not resist allocating some of their tax-based resources to feed the controversy. Concerned about protecting the interests of "gays and lesbians as they battle prejudice, overcome challenges, and live and love with dignity and courage," the board continues to market ten videos entitled *The Gay and Lesbian Collection*. Extolling the "rich tapestry of lifelong friendship," the series can be purchased for $224.95 with a complete satisfaction guarantee.[7]

When homosexuality is the subject in today's society, divisive diversity is the norm.

◆ B. De-escalating the debate ◆

During his public ministry, Jesus had to deal with the pressures and complexities that swirled around him. For example, when Jesus was teaching in the temple, he was not only interrupted, but was also confronted with a profound dilemma. The event is recorded in John 8:1–12.

> Jesus went to the Mount of Olives. Early in the morning he came again to the temple. All the people came to him and he sat down and began to teach them. The scribes and the Pharisees brought a woman who had been caught in adultery; and making her stand before all of them, they said to him, "Teacher, this woman was caught in the very act of committing adultery. Now in the law Moses commanded us to stone such women. Now what do you say?" They said this to test him, so that they might have some charge to bring against him. Jesus bent down and wrote with his finger on the ground. When they kept on questioning him, he straightened up and said to them, "Let anyone among you who is without sin be the first to throw a stone at her." And once again he bent down and wrote on the ground. When they heard it, they went away, one by one, beginning with the elders; and Jesus was left alone with the woman standing before him. Jesus straightened up and said to her, "Woman, where are they? Has no one condemned you?" She said, "No one, sir." And Jesus said, "Neither do I condemn you." Go your way, and from now on do not sin again." Again

> Jesus spoke to them, saying, "I am the light of the world. Whoever follows me will never walk in darkness but will have the light of life.

This particular passage is subject to scholarly debate. Absent from the earliest manuscripts, the question is often raised about whether the incident was included in John's original writing. The concern is valid. However, there can be no serious debate about whether or not the account is historically feasible and consistent with how Jesus responded to people. The description of the encounter fits the context of the times and is compatible with Jesus' attitudes and actions throughout his ministry. The encounter is not only full of suspense and surprise, it affirms the strength and profound insight of Jesus under pressure. For us, Jesus' handling of this socially complex and morally delicate situation can be a model for dealing with parallel situations in our own day.

Jesus—still a prototype

Linking the New Testament incident to our own social dilemmas, the first observation to note is that **Jesus responds with a strong sense of personal identity**.

People may not agree that Jesus actually was who he said he was, but there is no ambivalence in his **self**-perception. He confidently asserts that, "I and the father are one." Jesus repeatedly makes "I am" declarations. "I am the bread of life. I am the door. I am the way, the truth and the life." And in the context of the woman humiliated by her accusers for her adultery, Jesus declares, "I am the light of the world." (John 8:12) Jesus is not stifled by an inferiority complex. Waffling is never Jesus' way. His strong sense of identity releases him to live with decisiveness. He can project an assurance that communicates "I know what is right in this situation."

In the midst of our cultural multi-mindedness, people who are clear about who they are have an advantage. Their strength of identity stabilizes them. Being relaxed about who they are frees them to be relaxed with other people who are different from themselves. Assurance about who they are brings the freedom to accept others as they are.

While protecting the dignity of the woman who is about to be attacked, **Jesus de-escalates the emotionally charged situation**.

The accusing crowd had a malicious agenda. An earnest desire to obey the sacred law was not the motivation for their actions. Their real target was Jesus. The situation was a setup. The woman was just a pawn, an opportune means to serve an abusive end. Seeking to entrap Jesus, the pious religious establishment was out to discredit him as a reputable teacher. If they could entice Jesus to contradict Moses, then they could build their case against him. (Leviticus 20:10)

Confronted with their devious agenda and hostility, Jesus takes charge. Bowing down to write in the sand, he takes time to plot his rebuttal. Instead of offering a legal answer to the legalists, Jesus turns the attack into a spiritual dilemma for the accusers themselves. With theatrical flair, Jesus stands to his feet and counters, "If you are without sin—start throwing rocks." The mob knows they have met their match and within moments they start to disperse.

Jesus' strategy is brilliant. Rather than throwing tear gas into the crowd and inciting more anger, Jesus forces the people to deal with their own hypocrisy. He diffuses the anger and de-escalates the situation by turning the attackers' attention from the woman's sin to their own sin.

Deflecting the condemnation targeted at the woman, **Jesus protects the vulnerable person in the situation**.

Instead of the mob throwing rocks at the victim and then congratulating themselves for their self-righteousness, they are sobered by an inescapable sense of their personal sin. In the turmoil, Jesus is the peacemaker. Rather than ask his disciples to physically stand with him to intimidate the crowd, or dial 911 for police backup, Jesus disarms the thugs. Without even raising his voice, he disperses the ugly crowd.

In this predicament, Jesus is consistent. He is predictably redemptive. He lives out the meaning of the cross before he surrenders himself to die on the cross. Jesus' life is given to the same purpose as his death. He is compelled to translate the brokenness of people's lives into new patterns. Anything else is a sham for Jesus. And in this situation, both the disgraced crowd and the humiliated woman are allowed to escape their ruin and begin again.

If there is a pattern in his attitude and behavior, it is that **Jesus embraces both conviction and compassion**.

Jesus' first instinct is to be compassionate. His heart reaches out to the woman. She is the one facing the death threats. The crowd wants Jesus to come over to their side. They want his endorsement so they can apply the letter of the law. But Jesus says "no" to legalism. His compassion compels him to stand with the woman. He is more concerned about giving the woman a fresh start than he is about staining his own reputation by associating with her. In Jesus' mind, no one in the temple is innocent. Everyone in the scenario is in need of grace and mercy.

Jesus is ready to deal with the tensions in this situation. Compassion pulls him in one direction while his sense of conviction pulls him in the other direction. His conviction about what is right and what is wrong is clear. Jesus knows that sin is wrong, legalism is destructive, and immorality is evil. But Jesus is not afraid of sin. He is neither reticent about calling sin by name nor is he intimidated by the force of sin. He knows that sin can be dealt with. Consequently, Jesus keeps his balance. He also knows it is not the time to preach a sermon on the fact that "all have sinned and come short of the glory of God." Jesus did not ask the crowd to go and find the man who partnered in the adultery. Rather, he gives himself to the circumstances of the moment. But between the lines of this event we hear the refrain of the whole of Jesus' ministry and mission: "Give up on sin. Stop destroying yourself and others."

The combination of conviction and compassion is the key to unlocking Jesus' attitudes and actions.

Compassion compels Jesus: "Woman, where are they? Has no one condemned you?" She said, "No one, sir." And Jesus said, "Neither do I condemn you."

Conviction obligates Jesus: In a direct and specific way, Jesus says to the woman, "Go your way, and from now on do not sin again."

Linked together, conviction and compassion feed the spirit of collaboration. Affirming one's convictions results in clear self-definition. Calling for compassion instills empathy for other people's convictions. Conviction nurtures self-affirmation. Compassion nurtures regard for others. Conviction is a virtue that enhances one's

Fig. 4.1

Cultural Segmentation Comparison on Conviction and Compassion

	Compassion: Low	Compassion: High
Conviction: High	Tribalizers Reclaimers	Jesus Collaborators
Conviction: Low	Cocooners	Accommodators

- **Tribalizers** are high on conviction and low on compassion.
- **Reclaimers** are also high on conviction but low on compassion.
- **Cocooners** are low on both conviction and compassion.
- **Accommodators** are low on conviction but high on compassion.
- **Collaborators** are high on both conviction and compassion.

personal beliefs. Compassion is a virtue that engenders respect for the beliefs of others.

Jesus' embrace of both conviction and compassion is an invitation to compare the extent to which reclaimers, tribalizers, cocooners, accommodators and collaborators embody these two virtues. (*See Fig. 4.1*)

Dealing with a crisis is one issue. Positioning yourself for the morning after and the rest of life is another matter. In the instance of the trauma between the crowd and the woman, **Jesus offers fresh beginnings**.

The good news of the gospel is that in spite of the times when we mess up, we should "get on with life." The cross is not about making people pay for their sins or their misjudgments, their laziness or selfishness, their victimization or foolish choices, or their blatant self-righteousness. The death of Christ is about restoration. It is about beginning again and getting on with life.

The cross is God's powerful move in history to make peace with an alienated creation. In some profound and ultimately unexplainable fashion, the cross is morally charged with goodness. It is the ultimate answer to evil. It is an expression of God's grace and mercy. In the divine strategy that transcends human logic, the cross is an instrument of justice. In God's design, Jesus' surrender to death and triumph in resurrection is an invitation to deal with the past and start again.

If Jesus' response to the malicious crowd and the vulnerable woman is a prototype for dealing with modern moral dilemmas, such as adultery and homosexuality, what specifically have we learned? How can Jesus' attitude and behavior inform our responses today? How can a mix of conviction and compassion in the events of life guide our behavior?

Four levels in life

Life is multi-dimensional. If we choose to do so, we can interact with the issues of life at different levels. Imagining our interaction with the various levels of life as taking place inside a four-story building is one way to think about how we relate to the rest of the world and function in Canada's democratic society.

In this four-story structure, the main floor is where we experience interpersonal relationships. For the majority of people, main floor living is where most of life happens. It involves friends and neighbors, colleagues at work, family members, and other people who call us by name.

The second floor represents life inside organizations. For Christians in today's world, the second floor includes the church.

Fig. 4.2 **Four-story strategy for living**	
Level	**Relationships**
Main Floor	Interpersonal— Relating with acceptance
Second Floor	Organizational— Involvement with compatibility
Third Floor	Societal— Lobbying with intent
Fourth Floor	Global— Contributing with compassion

The third floor is where interaction with society occurs. We might join a lobby group to influence government legislation, petition a city council on behalf of local community concerns, join a parent association, or intervene before the Supreme Court.

The fourth floor has a lot of vacant space. This is where activity that has a global focus takes place. (*See Fig. 4.2*)

◆ C. Interpersonal—relating with acceptance ◆

Most of us function best on the main floor; maybe because that's where we spend most of our time. Unless we live in unusual circumstances, we cannot escape regular contact with people. Some of that contact will be with people who are different from ourselves.

From our childhood, we remember teachers who were warm and supportive as well as others who couldn't remember our names. As we began to grow and mature, we may have noticed that, in our neighborhoods, some people were uneducated and a few had advanced degrees. In our churches, there were white collar workers and blue collar laborers. On special days of prayer, we ended up in the same building with Christians from other denominations. As Protestants we remember meeting Catholics and realizing they were a lot like us. As Catholics we remember thinking that maybe Protestants were a part of God's family too. Along the way, in one situation or another, most of us met couples living common-law and others who were single parents. We were exposed to people who were abstainers and we knew others who had reputations as alcoholics. We met people with different skin colors from our own and even talked occasionally with a person who had spent time in jail. There was no escaping the obvious conclusion that people were different from each other. For most of us, accepting those differences was just part of growing up.

What is more recent in the "differences department" is encountering people who publicly advocate for same-sex equality.

Homosexuality has never been a "secret" in the sense that people were ignorant of its presence. In the 1940s, the Kinsey report seeded the assumption that approximately 10% of the population was homosexual. News reports occasionally referred to raids on bath houses. In other instances, we heard about police putting hidden cameras in public washrooms, and about charges that were laid as a result. But until the past decade gays and lesbians pretty much stayed in the closet, for obvious reasons.

Recently, however, gay activists have received an enormous amount of media coverage—and this despite the fact that evidence exists which suggests that this group is much smaller than previously proposed.

For example, a three-country study conducted in 1988, which involved 6,000 people between the ages of 15 and 50, found that while no more that 1% of the respondents said they had been exclusively homosexual in the past five years, the number reporting same-sex fantasies during their lifetimes was substantially higher. The study found that roughly eight to 12% of the men and women (from the United States, Britain, and France) who responded, had experienced homosexual attractions but did not act on them.[8]

In agreement with virtually every similar survey taken over the past five years, roughly 1% of men and one-third of 1% of women reported having only same-sex relations over the past five years. When bisexually was included, the numbers went to about 7% for men and 2.5% for women.

During this moment in time, the media are parading the homosexual cause. Telephone companies portray same sex couples in their marketing. American Express is spending their advertising dollars to sell travelers cheques to female and male couples who vacation together. The homosexual community may be receiving a lot of attention, but it is a small market niche. In the summer of 1994, a comprehensive study on the Canadian family was conducted which involved 2050 families. Even though the front cover story of *Maclean's* magazine reported that one of the new family trends in society is same-sex couples, a total of .08% fell into that category.[9] The perception may be otherwise, but the relatively small size of the homosexual community in today's society means that the advertising investment will generate a meager return.

Examining general population patterns and observing social trends concerning homosexuality is interesting. But for most Canadians, the issue doesn't really hit home, so to speak, until a family member "comes out." At that point, the issue generates emotional trauma.

I recently listened to long-standing friends describe the consequences of their son's homosexuality. Their son Steven married in his early 20s and was soon the father of a son. Then, one day, Steven announced that he was moving in with Mark. Steven's wife suddenly became a lone parent. My friends were devastated and felt humiliated. They were also committed to staying connected with their son. Even so, several years after the announcement they still lament, "We love Steve, but we still can't understand what happened." Edging toward retirement, my friends are the ones who emotionally and financially support Steven's former wife and para-parent their grandson.

Codes for next door neighbors

When the apartment down the hall becomes vacant, or the house next door goes up for sale, it's natural to wonder who your new neighbor will be.

My first hope is that, beyond being civil, my new neighbors will be stimulating people who are open to enjoying a relationship. But I'll also be honest with you. Rather than Steven and Steven, or Jennifer and Jennifer, I'd prefer that Jennifer and Steven buy the house next door. My stated preference for heterosexual neighbors, however, is made with a strong qualifier. The qualifier is that, if Steven and Steven **do** move in next door, I will treat them the same way I would have treated Steven and Jennifer had **they** moved in. I will welcome them. I will seek to get to know them as persons. And, if there is openness to the relationship, I will eventually ask them how they like their steaks barbecued.

The code for interpersonal relationships is not all that complicated. Whether we are Christians or people who believe otherwise, when we share life in a neighborhood or workplace, we recognize the rights of others. We relate to them with acceptance. Whether we agree with what people think or believe is not the issue. The rights we extend to others are the same rights we expect to have for ourselves. Accordingly, when other people act within the boundaries of the criminal and social codes of the times, if we are fully human, we will respond to them with civility and courtesy.

Most of us have more casual acquaintances than we have significant relationships. Not every person, whether he or she is a colleague at work or a neighbor, represents a potential friendship. However, whether the person is an acquaintance or a valued friend, everyone deserves to be accepted for who they are. Particularly if we are Christian, the people in our lives should get signals from us that we believe they are created in the image of God and that they are therefore profoundly valuable.

In the event that the house next door is put up for sale and Steven and Steven become my neighbors, I would hope that our relationship would become significant enough to allow us to talk about stuff that matters in life. I expect that would only happen after they had a meal or two on our deck and my wife and I had also experienced their hospitality. Eventually, I would like to be able to hand them the following editorial by Kelvin Browne, which appeared in the *Toronto Star*, and then for all of us to openly discuss the issues involved.

> If having gay pride means accepting your own sexuality, good. It is a step toward the self-acceptance that every mature person needs to function reasonably. On the other hand, if gay pride implies that your sexuality defines your life, that is adolescent. Too much pride in being gay, or seeing sexuality as the major defining factor in life, is a formidable restriction to realizing your potential as a human being... Therefore, if you are gay, put being gay further down the list of the things that make you

the person you are. Get on with your life and achieving the things you would do if you weren't gay."[10]

◆ D. Organizational—involvement with compatibility ◆

Second-story living also involves interpersonal relationships but they are embodied within organizations. For visible Christians, organizational living includes participation in the church. It can involve experiencing worship, committee meetings, social events, work parties, service projects, and outreach events. Also for Christians, the broad organizational division is between Catholics and Protestants. For Protestants, there are almost as many options available to accommodate personal preferences as there are models of cars on the market. But even though there are a myriad alternatives to choose from, like other organizations in society, inside our churches "like people group together. Unlike ones do not."[11]

Formally, a denomination is defined as "a voluntary association of like-hearted and like-minded individuals, who are united on the basis of common beliefs for the purpose of accomplishing tangible and defined objectives."[12] Informally, whether the religious alliance is Protestant, Catholic, Jewish, or with one of the other world religions, faith communities are places where people gather to express their faith. As organizations, religious groups provide opportunities for people to worship, serve, participate, belong, and to affirm each other's shared beliefs.

Choosing where to belong

Denominations and religious traditions are a lot like people. They have distinct personalities. Their worship styles, doctrinal distinctives, and ministry methods define their identities. The range of organizational diversity allows individuals to stay involved in the church of their birth, or to switch to the church of their choice. There are both advantages and disadvantages to participating in a church where there is a mesh between the organization's identity and one's personal spiritual preferences.

On the positive side, people feel safe when they are in the presence of others who share their views, who believe in God in similar ways. In compatibility groupings, communication is free and easy. Having the same slant on life generates shared laughter, stimulates prayer for common concerns, and generally removes resistance so that people can readily act together. When similarity is removed, levels of "discomfort set in, barriers are raised, and interaction is hampered."[13] Increased diversity leads to less natural interaction. Excessive diversity can either reduce interaction to zero or increase conflict to levels where people simply cannot function together.

On the negative side, people can be stifled by too much sameness. Psychologist Gordon Allport observes that small affiliated circles of people "fashion tiny islands of security."[14] They tend to become more exclusive and less affirming of what the whole body of Christ includes. They are also vulnerable to their narrow convictions that "are a downward spiral fed by... homogeneity of membership and outlook and unspoken, tight consensus."[15] The organizational tension is to find the balance between affirming enough sameness to generate a common vision while encouraging enough diversity to discourage stifling small-mindedness.

The individual challenge is to find a church that is compatible with one's beliefs and spiritual convictions. Some people are content living on smaller islands. They value highly the security of clarity. They welcome rules and regulations. They usually treasure, preeminently, the promise of personal salvation. In exchange, they are happy to offer their personal commitment in support of the aims and objectives of the church where they have a strong sense of belonging. Canada's evangelical churches are often the recipients of the vibrancy that is fostered when people live with these high-level faith commitments.

Other people desire to live on larger islands that are surrounded by large bodies of water and perhaps other islands. These people are more ready to live with ambiguity. They place a high value on the role of their personal convictions and are consequently more open to venturing into uncharted waters. Especially in recent years, the United Church of Canada has been ready to explore the concerns of its collective conscience. An example of concern for marginalized peoples is the church's sensitivity to aboriginal injustices. In 1986, before it was fashionable for churches to publicly acknowledge the plight of Canada's First Nation peoples, the United Church formally confessed and proclaimed:

> Long before my people journeyed to this land your people were here, and you received from your elders an understanding of creation, and of the Mystery that surrounds us all that was deep, and rich and to be treasured.
>
> We did not hear you when you shared your vision. In our zeal to tell you of the good news of Jesus Christ we were blind to the value of your spirituality.
>
> We confused Western ways and culture with the depth and breadth and length and height of the gospel of Christ.
>
> We imposed our civilization as a condition for accepting the gospel.
>
> We tried to make you like us and in so doing we helped to destroy the vision that made you what you were. As a result you and we are poorer and the image of the Creator in us is twisted, blurred, and we are not what we are meant by the Great Spirit to be.
>
> We who represent the United Church of Canada ask you to forgive us and to walk together in the spirit of Christ so that our people may be blessed and God's creation healed.[16]

Some of God's committed people respond to the above statement with both enthusiastic approval and genuine contrition. They are drawn to associate with like-minded people in their churches. Others in God's extended family are also concerned about past inequities inflicted on aboriginal peoples, but they are more concerned about preserving the purity of the gospel. They are also attracted to being in a church with others who share their views. The same polarities and similarities prevail on the issues relating to homosexuality. Organizational biases abound and individuals are faced with finding compatible places to belong.

Not surprisingly, the official Catholic perspective champions the conservative side of the homosexual debate. Drawing sharp moral lines, Pope John Paul II reasons that traditional family structure is not just a Christian ideal, but the "natural right" of all religions and cultures. His statement, which was reported in the *Globe and Mail*, expanded on a papal encyclical which asserted that morality is not a matter of opinion and that confusion about "moral certainties" threatens the human race. "The marriage, which is a stable union between a man and a woman...is not only a Christian value, but is an original value," said the Pope in his weekly address in St. Peter's Square. "To lose this truth is not just a problem for only the [Christian] faithful, but a danger for all humanity." The Pope called the traditional family a "natural right that unites all people and all cultures."[17]

The Metropolitan Community Church in Toronto looks through another spiritual window. Although it looks like an average, middle-class Canadian church, on the Sunday closest to Valentine's Day, a ceremony takes place unlike any other, anywhere else. Couples are asked to come forward to be blessed. And they do. Almost 200 gay and lesbian couples, arms clasped about each other, go to the altar to receive a special benediction.

"There isn't much support for heterosexual couples in this society," said Brent Hawkes, the pastor of Metropolitan Community Church, in a recent story which appeared in the *Toronto Star*. "But gays have almost **no** support systems. We want to visibly show support. To acknowledge to people that we know that staying together is difficult, but that it is God's will that their relationships grow.[18]

Like some other denominations, the Presbyterian Church in Canada recently made a policy statement. Although the tone is empathetic the position is thoroughly orthodox.

"We tried to make it both principled and pastoral, courageous and compassionate," says church doctrine committee convenor Clyde Ervine. In a tone more pastoral than legislative, the statement affirms that the proper place for sexual activity is a monogamous marriage between a man and a woman. "We see in scripture a thorough-going commitment to the union of male and female in marriage, a pattern for both unitive and procreative sexual relationships," explains Ervine. "Negatively, we see scripture speaking against sexual relationships that deviate from that."[19]

Several questions invade this discussion. What is the correlation between the organizational and the personal? If the church a person attends views homosexuality as a sin, should that affect how one relates to Steven and Steven or Jennifer and Jennifer if they live next door? In other words, does the organizational impinge on the personal? What about the reverse scenario? If a person believes that homosexuality is a sin but the church one attends decides to bless same-sex marriages, is one obliged to express dissent or even leave and attend another church that holds a different view?

The question of the organizational encroaching on the personal is the easiest to address. Just because one attends a church that deems homosexuality to be a sin is no reason to treat gays and lesbians in a demeaning or negative fashion. What churches and their members believe is one matter. How people are treated, regardless of what they believe, is another. Holding different beliefs from another person is not a license to judge or mistreat them. Surely it is consistent with Christian consideration for the choices other people make that we could even join a church-sponsored public lobby against homosexuals and still develop a healthy relationship with homosexuals who live next door. Holding different convictions could well create complications in the relationship, but having interpersonal differences is no reason to negate a valued relationship.

The issue of belonging to a faith community that embraces positions that are in opposition to one's personal beliefs is a different, complex matter. One point to acknowledge, however, is that it is highly unlikely that any fully alive person would ever agree with everything an organized church affirms. Belonging and participating in churches is more about compatibility than it is about total agreement with doctrines and decisions.

In the event of disagreement between the organization and the person, two other factors become evident. Obviously, all doctrines are not equal. Debate about the uniqueness of Christ is a weighty matter. Conversely, differences of opinion about how frequently the sacrament of the Lord's Supper should be served do not merit consideration as a possible basis for switching churches. Also, some people's temperaments require more organizational compatibility than others. Some people are relaxed with dissonance. Others are unable to live at peace with themselves unless they are in agreement with others who surround them.

Churches are living organisms. With help from God, they are made by human hands. And with continued help from God, they evolve in human hands. Participation in particular churches and decisions to continue participating in those same churches is a human decision.

• E. Societal—lobbying with intent •

Third-story living is expressed inside and between the structures in society. Within democracy, the exchange occurs wherever organizations work together in coalitions and where lobby groups seek to wield their influence as government policies are drafted and voted into binding legislation. Individuals may also take the initiative to influence public life. Activities might include attempts to keep public housing out of neighborhoods, lobbying the federal justice minister on abortion, or intervening before the Supreme Court to counter workplace rights for homosexuals. In society, the debates take place inside political caucuses, between polarized religious groups, and sometimes between political leaders and religious spokespeople. Successful leaders have to be adept at dealing with the diversity inside their ranks as well as in the society around them.

Soon after Jean Chrétien became the leader of the Liberal party, he told about 1,500 delegates at the party's policy convention that he respects pro-life campaigners. But he was adamant in his refusal to allow them to force their views on the party's agenda. "In a pluralistic society like ours, none of us can impose his own morality on others," Chrétien said to loud sustained applause.

Speaking with an intensity nurtured by his own experience as a Roman Catholic and as the 18th child in a large French-Canadian family, Chrétien told the anti-abortion campaigners: "I respect you and I will never shut you down..." But if the issue were to come back to the House of Commons, he said he would "give MPs the freedom to vote according to their consciences." Chrétien also told Liberals they should look deep inside themselves and consider not only their own positions but those of others in the debate.[20]

As Prime Minister, Mr. Chrétien faces the reality of division within his caucus on the homosexual issue. Bill Graham, a Liberal MP, is one of those leaning on the government to recognize same-sex couples and change immigration, pension, and tax laws to eradicate discrimination against gays and lesbians. Liberals Tom Wappel and Roseanne Skoke are at the other end of the spectrum on the debate; both adamantly oppose recognizing homosexual couples.[21] In an attempt to avert an internal split and dodge emotional public controversy, Chrétien employed the tactics of avoidance and called for caucus solidarity. Sources said that the Prime Minister told his MPs that such dissension is only divisive to the party.[22]

Religious leaders have often been active in the political forum. Since the 13th century, following the example of Pope Innocent III, various church leaders have used their office to intervene in politics. In fact, many Christians argue that they have a moral responsibility to speak up when political decisions could negatively impinge on their belief system.[23]

Participating in the public arena

Missiologist Lesslie Newbigin writes passionately about God's people participating in the public arena:

> There is no room for a piety that seeks personal holiness by opting out of the struggle for a measure of justice and freedom in public life. This faith enables us to be politically realistic without cynicism, to be sensitive to the supreme rule of love without sentimentality. It enables us humbly to acknowledge that even the best social order is—in God's sight—an organization of sinful men and women and therefore always prone to corruption; and yet not to use this knowledge as an excuse for political quietism, but rather as an inspiration to work tirelessly for the best possible among the actually available political alternatives.[24]

In the summer of 1994, the issue of equality for same-sex couples was on the legislative agenda in the Province of Ontario. Following intense lobbying and emotional debate from both sides, the legislation was defeated in an open vote, 68 to 59. A poll conducted following the defeat of the legislation found that half of the people questioned want the province to reintroduce same-sex spousal rights legislation at some time. The poll also suggests that most Ontarians would prefer such legislation be limited to economic rights and not family rights such as adoption. For example, 53% of respondents favored gay and lesbian couples having the same pensions, survivor and employee benefits as heterosexual couples, while 44% were opposed.[25]

Within the same time frame, Jim Egan and Jack Nesbit from Vancouver Island took their case for spousal benefits to the Supreme Court of Canada. Having lived together for nearly 40 years, and pleading that "there's very little difference between us and any married couple," the two men asked the courts to rule in their favor.[26] In the barrage of media coverage surrounding the legal initiative, Jim was interviewed on CTV's *Canada AM*. Referring to a legal intervention from a multi-faith coalition countering his claim, Mr. Egan contended that "Religious coalitions have no right to attempt to influence the courts."[27] The interviewer did not ask the obvious question. "If religious groups do not have the right to represent their positions before the courts, why would any other group have the right of access either?" In Canadian democracy, all segments of society can have their say if they have the will and resources to do so.

Even without resources or extraordinary motivation, we can all come to our own conclusions about these matters. To press the issue, if you were sitting as a member of a provincial legislature and same-sex legislation was being debated before the Assembly, would you vote in favor or would you be opposed?

And how would I cast my vote? With one hand, I am opposed, but with the other, I vote in favor.

Because God's original intent was to affirm heterosexual families as the ideal for creation, I believe advocating that same standard for the whole society is the better long-term goal. Consequently, I am opposed to allowing same-sex couples to legally adopt children. Although the Christian response to circumstances in life that are less than the ideal must always be redemptive, that is not a valid rationale for abandoning God's stated preference for heterosexual family life. A truly pluralistic society makes room for many voices and seeks the common good. I choose to stand with other voices that collectively support the historic and biblical ideal of heterosexual families.

The commitment to protect people's human rights, however, demands that I vote in favour of workplace rights and pension benefits for everyone in society. In my view, granting the dignity of dental benefits for the Jims and Jacks of this world is the right and humane thing to do. Those who argue that extending workplace benefits threatens the traditional family are simply alarmist. To withhold common cultural privileges lacks compassion.

Jesus protected the vulnerable woman in her predicament. My vote is to protect children from the social and psychological vulnerabilities they would face in today's society. The current norms are in place for sound social and biblical reasons. The argument that two women or two men can provide a healthy and nurturing environment for children is not the issue. Obviously, a caring couple, regardless of whether they are of the opposite sex or of the same sex, has the capacity to do so. My concern is that we not set up children for unnecessary negative stigma when they are parented by same-sex couples. In a hierarchy of values, protecting powerless children is the value to advance.

In reaction to this viewpoint, others will contend that we need to sensitize society to emerging realities and make room for new norms. They will turn the lens back to times when slavery was condoned by both the state and the church. They will point out that, until recently, people who were divorced suffered from similar strains of social and religious stigma. Some will support their claims with careful interpretations of biblical texts. The viewpoints are all valid. For Christians who desire to be true to themselves, however, seeking to preserve what they believe is God's stated standard takes precedent.

Some people in God's family are judgmental and even harsh toward homosexuals. Others committed to the same faith are ready to grant full family privileges to same-sex couples. Whatever our feelings and convictions about homosexual rights and family structures, we will be wise to turn to the New Testament. In the gospel of John, Jesus offers counsel to his disciples (16:13). In Jesus' eyes, they still have much to learn about his ways. He also assures his followers that the spirit who will be given to them will lead them into all truth.

◆ F. Global—contributing with compassion ◆

The view from the highest floor of life allows us to look out the farthest. People who spend at least part of their lives on the fourth floor carry two passports. They have a national and international perspective. Without disregarding local concerns, they value their global citizenship.

Canada is not the only nation mired in public debate on the issues relating to homosexuality. The cultural power of the religious right in the United States is pervasive and sometimes disruptive. European and Scandinavian countries are at various stages of legislative liberation regarding same-sex matters.

In Bermuda, as late as 1994, homosexuality remained in the criminal code. In response to a private member's bill to decriminalize homosexual acts, a march and demonstration was orchestrated by a Christian coalition. Consistent with Bermudian culture, the protest paraded in an orderly manner. Several members of the Human Rights Alliance, which disagreed with the protestors' position, watched quietly from the sidelines. When asked to comment on the rally, a member of the Alliance said, "While we do not agree with the marchers' position, we respect their right to march."[28]

Countries in Africa and Asia are both geographically and culturally distant from Canada. The norms of the sex-slave trade in Thailand push us outside our social boundaries. In Kenya and Tanzania, the practice of Masai elders planting their spears outside a tent to signal ownership of another man's wife for the night stretches our imaginations. Of all the film clips I have watched portraying the problems of the Third World, none has troubled me more than the one which showed the plight of Lucy Wamboi from Uganda.

Lucy innocently contracted the AIDS virus from her husband. When asked how she first reacted after finding out she had the dreaded disease, she gasped, "I couldn't believe it was me... especially me... why me?" Pictured with her baby son in her arms who was also born with the virus, Lucy is asked, "What is your greatest fear about your disease?" With a pain any mother anywhere in the world could experience, she sobs, "My son, my only son. He's innocent."

In the modern world where we know so much about each other, do we simply muse and groan at such indecencies? When the horrors of apartheid in South Africa finally moved the international community to exert pressure, positive change began. Without a worldwide media platform for Bishop Desmond Tutu, restrictive trade sanctions and other international pressures, instead of being

Prime Minister, Nelson Mandela would likely still be in jail.

Because life inside Canada and around the world involves far more concerns than just those associated with homosexuality, there is merit in expanding this discussion to other issues and perspectives. Especially when globalization is so rapidly becoming an everyday experience—and one which also accelerates our diversification—it is critical to look out at global life from the fourth floor window.

Citizenship beyond national borders

We must ask whether or not God's people should be giving a higher priority to fourth floor living? When do we act? When are we silent?

During the Iraq-Kuwait conflict over borders and oil, the United Nations was ready to mobilize Canada and other countries with their armaments. Using military might for humanitarian reasons, and in the floodlights of CNN, the U.S. navy and air force stormed the shores of Somalia. Pressed by a flood of refugees and in defense of democracy, the Pentagon ordered an invasion of Haiti. When is global intervention justified? When is international passivity morally irresponsible?

The hell-on-earth horrors of Rwanda remain in our minds. Before the world cared very much, the cover of *Time* magazine proclaimed a missionary's warning: "There are no devils left in hell. They are all in Rwanda."[29] The real holocaust was still to come. Two months later, in an article published in the *Globe and Mail*, journalist Andre Picard charged, "the world stands accused."

> You can stand in the middle of the place they call Camp Cholera, choking on the air, bending under the heat, nauseated by the sight of Rwandans vomiting and defecating their way to cholera-induced death, and still hear the fires crackling. We have all heard that hell was hot, dark and foul-smelling, but no one ever said it would be so eerily quiet... But what gnaws at you long after you walk away from the mass graves and the ever-growing piles of bodies, is the silence—not only the quiet resignation with which the Rwandans die (heeding requests to lie in straight lines to facilitate the work of the body collectors), but the silence of the international community.[30]

When do we stay at home and when do we get involved outside our national borders? At what point does the protection of human rights overrule national sovereignty? What are the conditions when silence from the international community should be judged immoral and unjust? When does a commitment to global justice on behalf of the world's women and children justify confronting cultural practices in other countries?

And how should we respond to economic exploitation? In 1992, Michael Jordan earned $20 million to promote Nike shoes. Jordan's endorsements were more than the entire annual payroll of the Indonesian factories that make them.[31] Admittedly, these issues are not simple. Who would argue with the conclusion that employment for meager wages is better than no employment at all?

Lesslie Newbigin's response turns us in the right direction.

> The church today cannot without guilt absolve itself from the responsibility, where it sees the possibility, of seeking to shape the public life of nations and the global ordering of industry and commerce in the light of the Christian faith. Even where the church is a tiny minority with no political power, it has the duty to address the governing authority of the civil community with the word of God.[32]

Responsible Christian living involves deliberate activity on all four floors of life; interpersonal, organizational, societal, and global.

Some days we get special gifts from God. One particular spring morning I was scheduled to speak to public school guidance counselors about research relating to teenagers. The morning light was bright but soft. The birds in the backyard were creating their usual clamor. The massive 40-year-old cherry tree that shades the deck behind our house was blanketed with pink blossoms. While sipping a second cup of coffee, the gift arrived.

As I gazed out the window, a shower of tens of thousands of cherry blossoms suddenly began falling from the tree. Like tiny feathers, in wave after wave, they fell softly and silently to the ground. As I absorbed the beauty of that moment, a lusty red male cardinal landed on the grass. It was like we were watching a special moment in creation together. The cardinal didn't stay long but he did take time to perch on a yellow forsythia bush at the back of the yard. I was overwhelmed by the splendor of it all.

Within two hours, I was in another section of the city waiting to be introduced to the guidance counselors. People were called together, I was graciously profiled and introduced. But before I moved toward the microphone, a representative from the teachers' union was invited to make a statement.

At the time, everyone employed in the public sector was dealing with government demands to renegotiate their social contract. In the face of forced financial cutbacks, the atmosphere was charged with dissent. The union representative informed the educators about the negotiations. His tone was controlled but tough. His final comment before he excused himself was that he would represent the teachers' interests so that they would get what they deserved. He walked away from the podium. Then it was my turn.

For a moment, I stood motionless behind the microphone. As the room full of educators shifted their attention from their paycheques to the reason for their vocations, my mind replayed the drama that had taken place earlier that morning in my backyard. I began the presentation with descriptions of the cherry tree, the shower of blossoms, the cardinal, and the beauty and privileges of living in a country called Canada.

Then we journeyed from the back yard to the Third World. We acknowledged that even though education is under provincial jurisdiction, the federal government is administering an 84 million dollar "stay in school" initiative in an attempt to reduce the number of high school dropouts. To contrast this situation, I told them about one of World Vision Canada's school projects in Guatemala. Three years ago, the project began with grade one. In sequential years, grade two and grade three were added. When I visited the school, the question was whether or not there would be enough money to hire another teacher so that grade four could be offered. Because the state school is 15 miles away from the village and there is no public transportation, those young children will complete their education before they turn ten years of age.

In an attempt to bring perspective to the very real pain inflicted by the social contract, I talked with the educators about other portraits of everyday poverty that exist around the world. My last overture was to ask the question, "Can we live rich without making the rest of the world poor?" For a few moments, people in the room sat in silence.

It seems that when left to run its natural course, life shrinks. The close-at-hand demands preempt bigger picture needs. In a recent national poll, Canadians were asked, "if you had $100 you could give to charities helping the poor, how much would you want spent to help the poor in Canada, and how much would you want spent to help the poor overseas?"[33] The respondents answered decisively. A total of $75 would be spent in Canada and the balance of $25 would be allocated to overseas need.

Fourth-floor living pulls our attention beyond the borders of our own society to the desperation of life across the globe. Illiteracy, malnutrition, preventable diseases and other forms of human misery are a plight on God's hope for creation. As believers in the Creator of the whole world, God's people cannot ignore the needs of children in Uganda who are AIDS orphans. If our vista extends to the rest of the world, educating Masai elders about the dangers of their sexual lifestyles becomes imperative. If we take our global citizenship seriously, we cannot rest or remain silent when international debt, unfair trade policies, unchecked violence, and other injustices cripple the world's poor.

Living as a global citizen involves more than a commitment to charity. It is not just a matter of responding generously to Third-World need or working systematically to help people help themselves. The relationship with people across other cultures involves learning from those who live in other countries.

Long before Israel's Yitshak Rabin and the PLO's Yasser Arafat signed their peace accord, Father Elias Chacour modeled how to live out a commitment to reconciliation.

Historically, one response of the international community to the atrocities committed against the Jewish people during the Second World War was to decree into existence the State of Israel. At that time, Bishop Chacour's family were Palestinian land owners. They lived with the dignity that employment and self-sufficiency brings. However, soon after the 1949 international declaration, the Chacours lost their land and became refugees. Elias suddenly became a boy without a country or a passport. The story of the beauty of this godly man and the injustices with which he has lived is told in the book *Blood Brothers*.[34]

Overcoming circumstances that have driven lesser men to suicide or violence, Father Chacour gave his energy to God and to a vision of a better future. As a Palestinian Christian priest committed to finding ways to de-escalate the tensions, Father Chacour started an integrated school in Ibillin, Galilee. In 1982, a mix of 82 Muslim and Christian students and staff began living and learning together. Ten years later, 1250 students shared life in a government-recognized community college. Today, a staff of 125 Christian, Muslim, and Jewish teachers collaborate together as a community of radically different people bonded to a common cause.

During his visit to Canada in 1990, I had the privilege of sharing part of two memorable days in the presence of Father Chacour. At the time, with a poised spirit and steady voice, he advocated a two-state Israel. His vision was to make room for both the Palestinian and the Israeli peoples. But he always qualified his proposal with the statement, "Restoring past injustices cannot come at the cost of future injustices."

Touched by Jesus in his inner spirit, Father Chacour's words ring with the conviction and compassion of Jesus' spirit. "I do not condemn you, but let's stop sinning and destroying each other." Other words of Jesus ring right for the rest of us. The summons is to "go and do likewise."

No escape from diversity

There is no escape from diversity in today's world. The interdependent and connected nature of countries and continents invites all people everywhere to spend more time on the fourth floor. Those of us who place our faith in the Creator and Redeemer of the whole world are mandated to live out our global citizenship. As we extend our reach beyond our national borders, we will quickly understand that those who live in the developing world confront survival issues more than they do sexuality issues. We will also realize that the presence of tribal mentalities, cultural and religious intolerance and the frequency of wars are often rooted in the inability to resolve differences. As we find ways to live more amicably with the differences we face interpersonally, organizationally and in Canadian society at large, we will be more able to respond creatively to the complexities of global diversity too.

◆ Resolving the Troubling Tensions ◆

Chapter Five

Introduction

Effective organizations are like rivers. They are in perpetual motion. They possess an unrelenting drive to push ahead even when what looms around the corner is unknown. Whether it is a church, a business, or a government department, in healthy organizations purposeful activity flows like water down a swift-moving stream.

Like organizations, rivers are different from each other. They have distinctive names and unique characteristics. Some are small; others are massive. Some are narrow and run deep; others are wide and shallow. Some rivers have reputations for rapids and whitewater. By contrast, others just keep placidly rollin' along.

Rivers have one striking similarity. Whether they twist around the Rocky Mountains, wind across the Prairies, or meander their way through the Maritimes, they all have banks. Rivers may be slow-moving streams or torrents of water surging forward, but it is the banks that give rivers their definition. Remove the banks and rivers are no longer rivers. They become lakes or swamps or they spread out so far that they dissipate and eventually vanish.

Banks for rivers are the same as boundaries for organizations. They keep an organization's activity on course. They allow organizations to self-define. Practically, organizational boundaries serve a double purpose. They let people in and keep people out. Boundaries establish who belongs. They determine who is inside and who is outside. Organizations that do not have a clear understanding of their boundaries will also be confused about their purpose and identity. They will be like rivers without banks.

For individuals, participating in an organization is similar to launching a canoe into a river. The river is already flowing in a predetermined direction. The channels are clearly carved. Sometimes the banks are set in concrete. And although many people have spent their lives attempting to remake organizations in their personal images, rivers are bigger than canoes. Is it any wonder that so many entrepreneurial people have launched so many organizations?

In a world charged with diversity, organizations and their leaders face two temptations. The lure of inclusiveness is enticing. But the attraction of exclusiveness is also compelling. One extreme motivates lowering the banks and removing the boundaries. The other excess prods the building of high banks and the creation of clear boundaries. Reclaimers and tribalizers specialize at building banks. Accommodators are the ones who keep scaling down the banks and expanding the boundaries. In the eyes of reclaimers, tribalizers, and accommodators, those who strive to live as collaborators often look like they can't make up their minds. Cocooners just keep rollin' along.

The purpose of this chapter is to look at attitudes that polarize people from each other. The intent is to reveal why some people build high banks while others are prompted to lower theirs. Accepting the reality that differences often create tensions, the approach will be to acknowledge the inevitable instinct to value our personal points of view, but also to be sure that we value the perspectives of others. The tension is to find the balance whereby we neither overvalue ourselves nor devalue others. The hope is that, as we better understand why polarities remain among us, we will be less divided by the diversity that exists between us.

Perplexity of complexity

Leading organizations and living thoughtfully in today's world is often confusing. While some issues are straightforward, others are more perplexing and injected with tension. Considering some of the matters currently being debated, the desire to straddle the fence often seems overwhelming.

For example, it is feasible to create a scenario to support abortion under extraordinary circumstances, but that is much different than supporting abortion under all circumstances. Affirming the value of life while philosophically opposing euthanasia seem to go hand-in-hand. However, computing the implications of medical technology and being categorical about when "life is really life" and when "death is really death" is far more complex.

Most people have no difficulty advocating compassion for single parents while at the same time affirming the ideal of a heterosexual, married-for-life model of marriage. Few would argue that expressing empathy for teenage mothers is the same as condoning permissive sex. Yet the same people will vigorously debate whether or not condoms should be easily accessible to teenagers.

The maze of modern life produces a flood of examples. It is easy to oppose censorship at the local library while favoring some form of censorship when it comes to the unrestricted public consumption of pornography. Championing the cause of gender equity for women in the workplace while still affirming the advantages for young children of the traditional single-income family, with a stay-at-home parent, is more difficult.

As we have already shown, the argument which would support human rights and workplace privileges for homosexuals while withholding permission for homosexuals to function in society as full-fledged families is complex. And clearly, the mental and emotional reach on these matters is greater and causes more stress for some people than it does for others.

The complexity of life produces perplexity. Tensions inevitably result whenever people with opposing points of view want their point of view to be accepted by others. My personal assumption is that society belongs to all its members. Consequently, one premise that plays throughout this book is that no group has the sole proprietorship of Canadian society. Whatever our family histories, skin color, socio-economic status, or religious convictions every group in society must stop short of believing it has the divine right to rule over others.

Many of God's people will give their mental assent to this idea but also be left with emotional ambivalence. After all, aren't Christians taught to believe that their way is both the right and the best way? And what about the scriptures? Doesn his people to go into all the world and make disc and right way? (Matthew 28:19–20)

Whether we like it or not, living in our multi- like putting together an extremely difficult jigsaw thinking about the types of puzzles where the ima almost all alike; puzzles in which large bodies of w[...] blur into different shades of blue sky. Or perhaps they show a basket of baseballs, a box of chocolates, or a collection of Christmas tree ornaments all the same shape and color and size.

Yet there is no defensible reason for Christian lament. In the midst of the quandaries and complexities of modern life, God's people still have a profound advantage. The Christian edge is that, as we search for the pieces that join together, we have a view of the top of the puzzle box. People who have inside information from the Creator and Redeemer of the world also know what life is supposed to look like. As a cautionary note, however, Christians do well to remember that other people are working on other puzzles that make sense to them too.

◆ A. Urgency of self-defining ◆

People who accept the idea of a "multi-puzzle world" naturally conclude that there is more than one way to put the pieces of life together. Especially in the midst of increasing diversity, they see the urgency of making sense out of their own existence. They also understand that others who are different from themselves face the same need to figure out what makes sense to them.

For Christians, Jesus is not only the source of salvation, but also a model for how to live. His human example knows no equal. Philosopher Immanuel Kant was correct when he said, "Out of the crooked timber of humanity, no straight thing was ever made."[1] In Jesus' case, however, there is no crookedness in his character or twistedness in his spirit. If it is possible to establish measurable criteria for a flawless human life, Jesus is the standard.

We have already noted, in the previous chapter, that Jesus functioned with a clear sense of his personal identity. One reason Jesus was so able to respond capably to the different people and circumstances that swirled around him was that he knew who he

Likewise, in order for those of us who are followers of Jesus to respond coherently to the current issues of life that swirl around us, we will need a clear sense of our identities too.

Reference points for decision-making

Self-defining is similar to saying, "These are my ingredients. This is who I am and this is what I am."

Christians are often called "believers." They accept common beliefs with other Christians while also embracing beliefs that are distinctive to their particular faith communities. What people believe and what they choose to disbelieve determines the content of their belief systems.

Writing in 1960, Rokeach defines a belief system as "all the beliefs, sets, expectancies, or hypotheses, conscious and unconscious, that a person at a given time accepts as true of the world he lives in." In contrast, one's disbelief system, "is composed of a series of subsystems rather than merely a single one, and contains all the disbeliefs, sets, expectancies, conscious and unconscious, which, to one degree or another, a person at a given time rejects as false."[2] As belief systems are consciously affirmed by both accepting some ideas and rejecting others, a basis for building one's self-definition emerges.

The process of self-definition begins at birth and continues until death. The influences and experiences of healthy family life, or the absence of a supportive family, have a profound effect on self-development. But whatever one's age, having a clear sense of self provides a foundation for stability.

A coherent view of self empowers people. Self-defined people have a solid basis for establishing morals and values. They function with a framework that gives them the freedom to fit in or stand apart. They are comfortable inside their boundaries and not afraid to be venturesome. Self-defined people are grounded people. They have reference points for decision-making and are able to draw selectively from a wide behavioral repertoire. Self-defined people are also likely to live with healthy self-images. Having deliberately thought about who they are, they can be more accepting and confident about the attitudes they hold and behaviors they express.[3]

The intent of the above is not to suggest that we can resolve all of life's maladies on the merits of self-definition. It is, rather, to contend that unless we are clear about our ingredients, modern life will be utterly confusing. A wise person is the one who has ceased "to be whirled around" by external determination. Wisdom arises when you take possession of your life and your strings cease to be pulled by someone or something other.[4]

One caution and one warning at this point is crucial. Self-definition is not just a matter of right beliefs and solid theology. Impeccable theory without corresponding behavior is a sham. People who excel at thinking lofty thoughts and articulating splendid words without translating the essence of their theory into practice, are self-deluded. This is not meant to imply that it is possible to convert perfectly one's intentions into reality—no one can. It is simply a call to acknowledge that one's real self-definition is expressed both in behavior and in words. Personally and organizationally, we will have integrity as we both **define** our beliefs and **do** our beliefs.

The warning is simply this: in Canada's future, the right to retain organizational self-definition will be critical. A recent scenario in Ontario illustrates the concern.

Joanna Manning has just won a two-year fight to teach religion again in a Metro Toronto separate high school. On the surface, it's a simple case of a teacher who fought to regain her job. But as an outspoken critic of the Roman Catholic Church, two years earlier Ms. Manning was barred from teaching religion to Roman Catholic students. Pitting teachers against the separate school system and the church hierarchy, the incident stirred up a cauldron of tension and hostility.[5]

Deciding not to appeal the decision that reinstated Manning as a religion teacher, the chair of Canada's largest publicly funded school board still reasoned, "The Catholic faith must be strong and maintained by the teachers—if it's not, then what are we doing? Why are we here?"[6]

When organizations lose their right of self-definition, they face the possibility of being diluted by excessive diversity. When that happens, "there are not enough common beliefs and goals upon which to base the group's existence, motivation and direction. In short, the 'glue' is missing and the energy expended simply to hold the fragments of the group in close proximity to one another robs the group of any power to act."[7] Although it may sound harsh to some, "We must exclude someone from our gathering, or we shall be left with nothing."[8] Otherwise, organizations can end up without glue, banks or boundaries.

◆ B. Matters of life and death ◆

As organizations and individuals seek to self-define in today's world, they face both complexity and controversy around life and death issues. In new ways and with increasing passion, abortion and euthanasia are being debated on the streets and in the courts.

The Royal Commission on Reproductive Technology concluded its four-year, $28.2 million study with the publication of a 1,250-page report. The two volumes containing the report, entitled "Proceed with Care," include 293 recommendations. The Commission calls for a ban on research into controversial techniques such as genetic alteration and the use of embryos in cloning and animal-human hybrids. Other recommendations call for the ban of surrogate motherhood, prenatal diagnosis to determine the sex of a fetus, sex-selection techniques, and the sale of human eggs, sperm, embryos, fetuses, or fetal tissue.[9]

The number and complex nature of the recommendations remind us that although abortion captures the most attention, there are other profound matters relating to how and when life begins.

Just as we must face new issues concerning birth, we must also address contentious questions surrounding death. When 42-year-old Sue Rodriguez, who suffered from Lou Gehrig's disease, sought the court's permission to end her life, the thorny issues linked with euthanasia made a sudden entry into the public forum.

And while religious leaders, ethicists, and the courts continued to wrestle with the implications of doctor-assisted suicides, the next piece in the life and death puzzle arrived. Robert Latimer, a loving father from Saskatchewan, was convicted of second degree murder and sentenced to a minimum of ten years in jail for the mercy killing of Tracy, his 12-year-old severely disabled daughter. Within days, *Maclean's* magazine put Tracy's picture on the cover alongside the probing question, "What would you do?"[10]

The abortion debate is not new. Pro-life and pro-c
cates have paraded their points of view for decades. "P.
extol the sacredness of life, plead for the rights of unbor.
and often quote scripture. Sometimes they point their fin
their opponents and charge "murder."

"Pro-choicers" advocate the right of women to have co..trol over their own bodies. They contend that "if the fetus is life, it is not human" any more than an acorn is an oak tree. If they are Christian pro-choicers, they may argue that it was when God breathed the breath of life into Adam that he became a living person. Accordingly, the sign of breath is the sign of life.[11]

In Canada, Dr. Henry Morgentaler has been the long-time leader of the pro-choice cause. His supporters acclaim him as a champion of women's rights. He has also had to appear in court repeatedly.

In 1988, the Supreme Court of Canada threw out the criminal law on abortion. Three years later, the Senate defeated a bill that would have recriminalized the procedure. Last year, the Supreme Court clarified the matter further by condemning Nova Scotia's attempt to prevent legal abortions by banning abortion clinics. Yet, in defiance of the court, Prince Edward Island pays only for abortions if they are judged medically necessary and performed in a hospital. Hospitals perform them only if it's a medical emergency.[12]

In the United States, several abortion-performing doctors have been shot and killed by anti-abortion activists. In Canada, doctors who are known to perform abortions have had protestors picket their homes. A doctor in Vancouver was shot in his home in what is suspected to be an abortion motivated act of violence.

The euthanasia debate persists

On the issue of euthanasia, the Supreme Court of Canada split 5–4 against, on the question of whether or not Sue Rodriguez should be allowed medical help to take her own life.[13]

In a national poll conducted by Angus Reid-Southam News shortly after Sue Rodriguez died, three out of four Canadians supported legislation that would allow doctors to terminate a dying patient's life. Of those surveyed, 74% favored doctor-assisted suicide for terminally ill patients who want it.[14]

In the midst of the controversy, the *Toronto Star* published a carefully reasoned piece by Brian Stiller, the religious leader representing the Evangelical Fellowship of Canada::

> The waves of sympathy and respect for Sue Rodriguez are camouflaging the real issue at stake in this debate: should a person be allowed to help another kill themselves?
>
> We respect the courage and dignity Ms. Rodriguez displayed in advocating her point of view. Her claim for autonomy resonates with the commonly held assumption that our bodies are our own and we should be able to do with them as we want. Lending increased acceptance to this assumption was the tragedy of her affliction and the way in which she won the hearts of many Canadians.
>
> At the heart of this debate, however, is an understanding of what we have commonly understood to be the meaning of murder. While "murder" is a word most wish to avoid, we really are talking about taking a person's life.
>
> In our history, the protection of life has been considered central to our societal values. We have laws to protect life and laws that punish those who injure or end life. To change that and now say, "We'll allow you, on the basis of someone's request, to end a life," is a departure from what we as a society have held.[15]

Preston Manning, a conservative Christian himself and leader of the Reform Party, responded in a manner consistent with his commitment to popularist politics. The results of a televised town hall meeting persuaded Mr. Manning and four other Calgary Reform MPs to vote in favor of physician-assisted suicide, although they personally oppose it. Acknowledging "strong constituent support for physician-assisted suicide under specific conditions," the Reform party leader said, "If a government bill was presented to Parliament tomorrow permitting physician-assisted suicide under those conditions, the participating MPs would vote for it in accordance with the expression of those constituents."[16]

At the other end of the spectrum, columnist Frank Jones, writing for the *Toronto Star*, took a stand against the majority in the polls and exclaimed:

> Proper palliative care largely removes the fear that makes peo-

> ple seek suicide; but doctor-assisted suicide removes the pressure for decent palliative care...
>
> Forget about safeguards; if Canada became the first country in the world to legalize euthanasia, a new breed of Jack Kevorkian-style death doctors would be operating out of motels along the border, disposing of the depressed and the lonely as well as the terminally ill.[17]

In the case of Robert Latimer and his second degree murder conviction, the judge ruled that the father and farmer from Saskatchewan would be allowed to be with his family while he waits for his appeal.

Journalists and others were quick to point out that whether fathers kill their disabled daughters out of love or frustration or hate, there is an immense difference between individuals themselves requesting the end of their lives and those who have their lives taken from them. Writing in the *Globe and Mail*, columnist Andrew Coyne warned about the slippery slope and observed that "It is revealing how instantly the link was made in the public mind with Sue Rodriguez and the issue of assisted suicide... But the beatification of Mr. Latimer, like that of Ms. Rodriguez, suggests what really is at stake in each case. It never was about rights or dignity. It was and is about death."[18]

The questions are unyielding. Is abortion an act of murder? Do women and their sexual partners have the right to rule over their own bodies? Should we open the door to euthanasia? Is there room for leniency in the case of mercy killings? What do you think? What would you do? What do I think? What would I do?

◆ C. Intolerance and Tolerance ◆

Tolerance has long been applauded as a Canadian virtue. In these pluralistic times, tolerance is the cultural golden rule. Ironically, there is also escalating intolerance toward those who are presumed to be intolerant.

Tolerance is a value that fits naturally with the world we live in. "Having pretty much decided that truth is not attainable," writes S. D. Gaede, "we have made tolerance of a plurality of truths a virtue. Having no truths worth defending, we have made nondefensiveness a mark of distinction."[19]

Tolerance is not just a matter of current cultural etiquette. It also emerges as the ultimate answer for dealing with diversity. "Live and let live" is the code. Consequently, it is no surprise when those who are not tolerant of other people's views offend the status quo and get judged.

Certain people have less difficulty tolerating groups and individuals who have different, even opposing, belief systems, while others very quickly feel compelled to go on the offensive against those who are "different."[20] Accommodators naturally gravitate toward tolerance. Tribalizers and reclaimers are inevitably pulled toward intolerance. Collaborators get caught in the tension of both attempting to be tolerant and setting limits. Cocooners opt out of the debate. Religious belief, particularly conservative religious belief, is also frequently linked with intolerance.

Tolerance examined

G. K. Chesterton is quoted as saying, "Tolerance is the virtue of the man without convictions." What is Chesterton proposing? Is he suggesting that when tolerance is postured as a virtue it is difficult to differentiate between real goodness and moral weakness? Or is he blatantly presuming that people without convictions are spineless and feeble? Chesterton's Christianity is stated too clearly to conclude that he is recommending that God's people sell out to duplicity. We can be sure that Chesterton is not suggesting that "tolerance for one another's heresies is a virtue."[21]

An analysis of tolerance can lead to no other conclusion than that tolerance itself tends to trivialize other people's views. Instead of genuinely engaging people, attitudes of tolerance tokenize people. Rather than taking people seriously, tolerance treats people superficially. Instead of conveying "Who you are and what you believe is to be valued," tolerance says, "I will endure you." In essence, "I will tolerate you" is just another way of saying, "I will put up with you." And in doing so, the inferred message is, "I do not take you seriously." In the guise of tolerance, people are treated more like things than as persons to be valued and respected.

Tolerance also takes the urgency out of life. As a mindset for living, tolerance undercuts motivation and turns passion into passivity. When tolerance rules, anything and everything becomes a matter of other people's state of affairs. Tolerance can serve as an escape hatch which replaces responsible caring. Using the issue of single parenthood as an example, tolerance simply accepts the reality that lone parents are more common now. "So what? People create their circumstances, let them live with the consequences of their decisions."

Extolling tolerance as a principle for living can simply be a rationale for disengaging from other people's needs. At least for serious Christians, tolerance is an inadequate response to genuine need. Listen to a real live single mother: "It's too simple to say that single parenting is more common now, when we are more tolerant of various family configurations. Tolerance is no help when I'm pushed beyond the end of my energy and patience and find myself alone.[22]"

Religious tolerance is not always a sign of goodwill either. Often, it can be a sign of ignorance about the claims of a given religion, a simple failure of someone to take the time to sit down and listen to what a religion says about itself. Religious tolerance can be nothing more than careless religious indifference, which is an offense to all religions.[23] Simply wrapping one's arms around other people and their beliefs may be motivated by good intentions but that doesn't mean it is marked by thoughtfulness or integrity.

Referring back to Reinhold Niebuhr, religious studies professor Douglas Hall of McGill University makes the important point that in pluralistic cultures, Christians are called to get beyond tolerance. While they, along with others, are required by law to tolerate other people, they are also required by the Christian faith "to recognize that tolerance is not enough." Tolerance too easily reflects a decision to simply look past people, allowing them to have their beliefs. "It **may** be good enough, legally and politically, for the pluralistic society; but it is not good enough... for the one who did **not** say 'Tolerate your neighbour,' but 'Love your neighbour.'"[24]

Still, we must be careful not to become too idealistic. In many situations, tolerance is definitely preferable to intolerance. Bigotry, judgment, and prejudice are ugly in the presence of courteous endurance that is nurtured by tolerance. But neither should tolerance be elevated to the status of an unexamined virtue. Especially for God's people, there are higher ways and more noble callings.

When left unchecked and allowed to run their course, both tolerance and intolerance fall short when it comes to the issues of abortion, euthanasia, and mercy killings. Tolerance trivializes and produces passivity. Intolerance generates harsh judgment. Still, a comparison of what influences people to be tolerant and intolerant in their views on these life and death matters helps us to understand why they believe and behave the way they do.

Issue	Mainly Tolerant	Mainly Intolerant
Abortion	Ambiguity about when life begins A mother's choice No compromise on right to choose Government-supported medical service	Life begins at conception Life of unborn protected No compromise on sanctity of life Lobby to deny access and medical support
Euthanasia	Viewed as an act of compassion Doctor-assisted suicide is permissible	Viewed as a criminal act Participants treated as criminals
Mercy Killing	Leniency No compromise on right to choose Limited consequences	No leniency No compromise on sanctity of life Treat as murder

◆ D. Exclusive and Inclusive ◆

Another polarization exists between those pulled toward being "inclusive" and those who tend to be "exclusive." When faced with the complexity of modern-day diversity, some people resolve the tensions by widening their boundaries. They become more and more inclusive. Other people say "no" to inclusiveness and keep their boundaries firmly in place. They design their worlds to exclude people who disagree with them. Religious traditions and denominations have followed the same patterns for centuries.

Until quite recently, the Roman Catholic Church not only held strongly to the Christian exclusivist claim on truth, but went even further and maintained that it alone represented the true form of Christianity. Following the Reformation, Protestants often lived with the same point of view.

For Catholics, changes both in the official position and in attitude appeared during the Second Vatican Council, held in Rome from 1962 to 1965. Some dramatic shifts took place. While Roman Catholics still saw their form of communion as the best manifestation of the church of Jesus Christ, it was no longer considered the sole or the complete manifestation of the whole church. The other Christian churches were accorded a new respect, a respect extended to other forms of religious faith as well, especially to Judaism. That respect went further than general esteem; these religions were seen as possible ways to the salvation which was, according to previous preaching, only to be had through Catholicism.[25]

Marks of exclusivists

First and foremost, "exclusivists" are "truth people." Consequently, they are also clearly self-defined people. Exclusivists can be so absolutist about their beliefs, they conclude that any and all beliefs different from their own are false. Deeply desiring clarity, exclusivists live with an attitude that says, "I am right. And if we don't agree, then you are wrong." They very seldom ask the question, "What might be true about other people's views?" In the heat of an argument, rigid exclusivists deliver, as their final blow, the exclamation, "There's your way and there's God's way—I'm going God's way!" In that vitriolic mode, exclusivists excel as tribalizers.

Exclusivists also live with a closed belief system. They usually belong to churches that have definitive statements of doctrine, specific lifestyle codes for membership, and high commitment expectations for participation. Their predetermined acceptance of systemized theology provides ready answers to life's spiritual dilemmas. There is limited motivation for exclusivists to open up discussion on issues that historical decrees have already settled. Newcomers either convert to the prevailing commitments, or they soon discover they do not belong.

Closed-system exclusivists "see the world as a dangerous place, full of chaos and unpredictability."[26] The closed group is a place both to belong and to feel secure. Closed groups can also be places that foster fear. Individuals can feel threatened by the presence of groups in which they do not have a sense of belonging; if they cannot identify, they must oppose; if a group is not "acceptable," it is "alien."[27] People who feel particularly vulnerable, can also be the people who are predisposed towards joining a group that provides the safety of a closed belief system.[28]

Exclusivists are in-group/out-group people. They tend to project stereotyped negative imagery and even hostile attitudes toward out-groups. In contrast, stereotyped positive imagery and submissive attitudes are embraced with regard to in-groups. In-groups usually invite a hierarchical and authoritarian view of group interaction.[29] Accordingly, members are either clearly inside or outside the stated organizational boundaries. There is little middle ground for any dissent. One either supports the group agenda or is pushed out by the group.

Exclusivists also tend to be "evaluators." They pass statements made by other people through the filters of their own belief grids. They have difficulty appreciating points of view outside their own frame of reference. Understanding other people from their point of view is not easy. It involves risk and takes considerable courage. After all, exclusivists are undoubtedly right when they reason, "If we really understand another person in a way that enters into his [her] private world to see how life appears to him [her], without any attempt to make evaluative judgments, then we run the risk of being changed ourselves."[30]

Marks of inclusivists

In contrast to "exclusivists" who are categorical about truth, "inclusivists" are content to confess that they "look through a glass darkly." Christianity might well be affirmed as the fullest revelation of the Creator to humanity, but it is accepted that "we can only know in part" what God is all about. Glimpses of truth are the most inclusivists hope to discern. They seldom ask the question, "What's wrong with people's ideas?" Instead, divergent thinking is the norm and conflicting conclusions are deemed inevitable. Placing limits on what can be known about God's truth can also set up inclusivists to be absolutist. Unlike exclusivists who are convinced they can know all they need to know about God's will and ways, inclusivists can be just as dogmatic that it is impossible to really know very much about God's revelation.

Accordingly, inclusivists live easily with open belief systems. Holding beliefs in common is not a critical criterion for evaluating others. People are positively valued, often, despite their beliefs.[31] Inclusivists are relatively relaxed with ambiguities. They are also comfortable with contradictions. They are often content to leave the pieces of the puzzles of life disconnected.

Inclusive-type churches embrace people without requiring high levels of conformity. However, compared to exclusive-type churches, inclusive churches do not generally receive as high commitment levels from their people. Because of their open belief systems, inclusive churches broaden their boundaries. In the current milieu, they may open their doors to the benefits they see represented in New Age and Native Spirituality.

Rather than being "evaluators," inclusivists are "acceptors." They typically embrace the assumption that all belief perspectives are valid and, therefore, ought to be included or at least affirmed. For the inclusivist, "to be exclusive about truth (to assert that one can distinguish between truth and error) is bad, while to be inclusive of all truth claims is good."[32] High acceptance levels increase the likelihood that inclusivists are relatively open to change. Because change is "often linked with flexibility, independence, nonconformity, and open-mindedness" inclusivists are inclined to vote for new ways to think and behave. Because living with openness to what is new fits the mood of the age, the inclination also makes inclusivists vulnerable to being embraced by the spirit of the age. Enthusiastic inclusivists are susceptible to compromise.

In contrast with inclusivists, exclusivists are inclined to vote against change. Accordingly, they are often characterized as people who are rigid, close-minded, compulsive and intolerant of ambiguity.[33] In a more positive light, exclusivists are also "evaluators" and "protectors." Ready to resist the mood of the moment, they are less apt to be dislodged from some of the virtues of the past. Their reticence to embrace the latest trend not only slows down the pace of change, it can also preserve what is right and good.

Exclusivists and inclusivists also tend to read the Bible through dissimilar lenses. They are attracted to different texts. They both interpret what they read through the filters of their preset beliefs. The following statements from scripture illustrate the types of biblical passages exclusivists and inclusivists cite to articulate their differing perspectives on who belongs inside God's family.

Exclusive	Inclusive
John 14:6 Jesus said to him, "I am the way, and the truth, and the life. No one comes to the Father except through me."	Acts 10:34–35 Then Peter began to speak to them: "I truly understand that God shows no partiality, but in every nation anyone who fears him and does what is right is acceptable to him."
Revelation 3:15–16 "I know your works; you are neither cold nor hot. I wish that you were either cold or hot. So, because you are lukewarm, and neither cold nor hot, I am about to spit you out of my mouth."	John 10:16 I have other sheep that do not belong to this fold. I must bring them also, and they will listen to my voice. So there will be one flock, one shepherd.
John 3:5–7 Jesus answered, "Very truly, I tell you, no one can enter the kingdom of God without being born of water and Spirit...Do not be astonished that I said to you, 'You must be born from above.'"	Matthew 13:47 "Again, the kingdom of heaven is like a net that was thrown into the sea and caught fish of every kind."
Matthew 12:30 "Whoever is not with me is against me, and whoever does not gather with me scatters."	Luke 9:49–50 "Master, we saw someone casting out demons in your name, and we tried to stop him, because he does not follow with us." But Jesus said to him, "Do not stop him; for whoever is not against you is for you."

In his book *Culture Wars*, James Davison Hunter refers to a deep division which runs across America between traditionalist and progressive alliances. Each side holds a view of the world that is diametrically opposed to the other; each harbors a deep hostility against the other. Hunter says that each side of the cultural divide judges the other to be ideological extremists, illegitimate "by virtue of the substance of its message."[34] Inclusivists and exclusivists have the same potential as the traditional and progressive alliances to polarize and turn against each other. In regard to the segmentation of "types" referred to throughout this book, in similar and destructive ways, accommodators can be pitted against reclaimers and tribalizers.

Can we acknowledge our differences and still ask, how can we treat each other with more regard? Even with hotly contentious issues such as abortion, euthanasia, and mercy killing before us, can we treat others as we treat ourselves?

Most people are more lenient with themselves than with others. One consistent pattern I have observed is that many of us judge ourselves at the level of our intentions. We know what we **meant** to do and so we give ourselves the benefit of the doubt. Even when our behavior misses the mark, we let ourselves off the hook because we intended to do better.

When it comes to others, we reverse the standard of judgment. Instead of looking at what people intend to do, we more often judge them on the behavior they display. Instead of assessing internal motivations, we judge external actions.

This double standard calls for higher levels of performance from other people than it requires of ourselves. Our virtue is found in good intentions, but others are measured by their actual achievements. As Edmund Burke said of the French revolutionaries, "in the manifest failure of their abilities, they take credit for their intentions."[35] The grace factor would rise and less polarization would result if we more often judged other people as we judge ourselves.

◆ E. Counter and Complement ◆

Appreciating the perspectives and motives of others while also valuing our personal points of view is a demanding way to live. And try as we might, sometimes the tensions are unresolvable. Commitment to a moral principle can make it impossible to find a middle ground. In some situations, the attempt to find a balance whereby we neither overvalue ourselves nor devalue others is no justification for spiritual or personal compromise.

The Bible regularly tells us to exercise judgment about questions of truth and value: "Woe to those who call evil good and good evil" (Isaiah 5:20, NIV); "Test the spirits to see whether they are from God" (1 John 4:1). In the same passage in which Paul the apostle calls God's people to cultivate kindness, patience, and generosity, he insists that we also take a strong stand against such "works of the flesh" as sexual immorality, impurity, and drunkenness (Galatians 5:16–23). Whether we like it or not, faithful Christians cannot avoid "judging" certain attitudes and behaviors.

At the same time, many texts warn against judgment. Jesus tells his followers, "Do not judge, so that you may not be judged." Jesus' own example invites us to accept people—including prostitutes and people who drink too much, among other "undesirables"— just the way they are.[36]

Despite what the Bible teaches and how Jesus lived, many Christians are still reticent to either judge others, or be judged by others. Christopher Lasch explains that often there is a "refusal to draw a distinction between right and wrong, lest we 'impose' our morality on others and thus invite others to 'impose' their morality on us; our reluctance to judge or be judged."[37]

Recently, a friend and I met for lunch. Over the years of our relationship, I've valued Raymond's friendship and also developed a high regard for his judgment. During the time we had together, Raymond told me about another lunch encounter he had with his long-standing friend Dan. Over that meal, Dan confessed to Raymond that he had been losing his temper more than usual, and on two recent occasions he had physically hit his wife. Raymond told me that he carefully laid down his fork and knife and looked Dan straight in the eyes and said, "If I were sitting across the table from Karen at this moment, I would advise her to leave you immediately." With the emotion of the previous encounter rekindled in his inner spirit, Raymond continued, "I know Dan's confession was undoubtedly a call for help and he went on to convince me how sorry he was, but the whole mess is just too wrong to accept."

Raymond also said to Dan, "Listen, I care deeply for you as a friend, but I've always believed that anyone who abuses his wife is a loser, and right now, I can't change that just because a good friend of mine is the one hitting his wife." Raymond continued, "Dan, promise me it won't happen again. Let's get some help for you. I know a good therapist who can help you. And I don't care if it is three o'clock in the morning; if you get in trouble, call me. Don't hit Karen, call me."

Raymond reflected, "It was a sobering moment for Dan, but this abuse stuff has to stop. I told Dan that if I hear from Karen that it is continuing, I'll do whatever I can to get her out of that abusive relationship."

Even though every person in society must stop short of believing he or she has the divine right to rule over others, we must establish limits. Some behaviors are blatantly wrong and must be stopped. Abdicating to law enforcement agencies and relying on the criminal code to maintain social order is not good enough. Relationships entail obligations. Raymond was right to be confrontational and forceful with Dan.

The issue is, when do we go with the social flow and complement the culture, and when do we dig in our heels and say "enough is enough"? When do we counter the prevailing norms in our presence?

Catholic theologian David Tracy, from the University of Chicago, rightly contends that, "Despite their own sin and ignorance, the religions, at their best, always bear extraordinary powers of resistance. When not domesticated as sacred canopies for the status quo nor wasted by their own self-contradictory grasps at power, the religions live by resisting."[38]

Stephen Carter, in his book *The Culture of Disbelief*, articulates a similar message: "A religion is, at its heart, a way of denying the authority of the rest of the world; it is a way of saying to fellow human beings and to the state those fellow humans have erected, 'No, I will not accede to your will.'"[39]

Tracy and Carter should not be interpreted as saying that religious people have the right or obligation to operate as a law unto themselves. At the same time, Tracy and Carter underscore the importance of refusing to be domesticated by the culture. Rather than being controlled by the culture, religious folk should "be prepared to resist the culture." Instead of quietly bowing to the ways of the world, we are called to hear the voice of God and keep true to the faith. God's committed people must expect, at times, to be called to stand tall and counter what the world says and does. In order for the reign of God to be experienced in the present tense, the people of God must bring the presence of God into the moral disorder of the modern world.

Surely the first invitation to God's people at any time in history is to bless what God blesses. It is to celebrate what God celebrates and to affirm what God affirms. Only in this way can we play a role in bringing the reign of God into the here and now.

As Christians, we believe that God created the world as a place for relationships. God had love affairs in mind when the world was set in motion. Husbands were to love wives and wives were to love husbands. Children were to love and be loved. People were to care for each other as well as for the environment. Justice was to rule within all of creation. Employers and employees were to be honest and fair. Widows were to receive extraordinary protection. Special consideration was to be extended to the poor. God affirmed the preeminent value of human life from the very beginning.

Accordingly, in these days, our aim should be the same. We too should lay hands of blessing on what God blesses.

But we should also resist what God resists. Lying and stealing and envy have never met with God's approval. Murder has been wrong in God's eyes from day one. Breaking marriage covenants or taking another person's wife or husband has never received God's blessing. The Old Testament consistently portrays faithful Israelites as speaking out and acting against any attempt to ignore or push God to the sidelines. They resisted whatever demoted God into insignificance.

God also resists being ignored and counters what is evil. Instead of abdicating and leaving creation to run its dreadful course, God intervenes. Refusing to be ignored and disregarded, God persists and reappears again and again. Through people and events, and eventually in Jesus Christ himself, God keeps interjecting, "Remember me and my good ways."

The story of redemption is not finished yet. As in times past, God's people of the moment are invited to play a role in redeeming what God hopes to redeem. In today's world, that will include getting in the way of evil. Even when it is unpopular to do so, being a contemporary ally with God demands making moral judgments. As well as pursuing what is right, it demands resisting what is wrong.

If we follow God's lead, our resistance to what is wrong will be cast in the mode of "redemptive resistance." "Getting in the way of evil" will involve providing compassionate alternatives for young mothers who might otherwise choose abortion. It will mean providing personal and social support for families burdened with disabled children. It is unlikely that anyone who advocates increasing taxes so that palliative care can be more widely available will receive much applause or support. Yet the strategy of redemptive resistance is to "overcome evil with good," and that will mean doing what is necessary to allow the sick and the dying to live with dignity until their life on this earth ends.

I personally believe that it is appropriate to make a moral judgment on the issues of the value of life and the cultural codes regarding death. In the midst of all the ambiguities and all the complexities, some issues merit a conservative position. Affirming the value of life in general and more specifically saying "no" to doctor-assisted suicides and mercy killing is a case in point. Rather than offer an elaborate defense to support the position, I would encourage you to listen to excerpts from a letter written by 11-year-old Teague Johnson of North Vancouver. Suffering from severe cerebral palsy, Teague used a spelling board to write his feelings and thoughts:

> The Latimer case in Saskatchewan has caused me a great deal of unhappiness and worry over the past few weeks. I feel very strongly that all children are valuable and deserve to live full and complete lives. No one should make the decision for another person about whether their life is worth living or not...
>
> I had to fight to live when I was very sick. The doctors said I wouldn't live long... I have pain, but I do not need to be "put out of my misery." My body is not my enemy... Life is a precious gift. It belongs to the person to whom it is given. Not to her parents, nor to the state...
>
> My life is going to be astounding.[40]

The end of the human story has yet to be written. The hope that God interjects into the story is that life is redeemable. The essence

. is to restore and renew. The privilege of God's people is to .cipate in the story.

◆ F. Conviction and Compassion ◆

There are ditches on both sides of the road. In today's world, one can easily be pushed off into either one of them. Tolerance and intolerance can be difficult to hold in balance. The extremes of inclusivity and exclusivity are also good to avoid. Then there is the tension between fitting in and complementing what is going on in the world, and carefully countering some of the more damaging trends.

This chapter began by talking about banks and boundaries and underscoring the urgency to self-define personally and organizationally. Steering around the obstacles and staying on the road is not a simple matter. However, there are two guard rails which buffer and protect. On one edge of the road there is compassion; on the other there is conviction.

Religion without conviction is spineless and weak, powerless and indecisive. Without conviction, faith lacks passion. It is like weak tea. Furthermore, passiveness prevails.

By comparison, religion with conviction brings clarity and design. Questions have answers and doubts can be resolved. People with convictions know who they are and what they believe. Conviction checks the excesses of trivializing tolerance, unexamined inclusiveness, and the readiness to simply accept whatever the world proposes. Conviction stirs confidence in God and often produces a vibrant faith that can inspire others to believe too. Religion with conviction rings with an inviting certainty in a world that is so uncertain and often afraid. Conviction keeps God's people on the road and out of the ditch.

At the same time, religion without compassion is harsh and judgmental, arrogant and rude. Without compassion, faith lacks empathy. It blocks out the possibility of seeing God's love and concern. People who have not tasted God's compassion don't know much about the heart of God. They can blindly believe that intolerance is a virtue and that their ways are the only ways to serve God faithfully.

Religion with compassion puts a human face on God. Forgiveness becomes attractive. Beginning again is somehow believable. Compassion invites belief without the requirement to get it all right. Compassion keeps God's people on the road and out of the ditch.

Left to stand alone, conviction and compassion can become religious villains. When held together, however, they form a formidable alliance. They protect the people of God from destructive excesses. The following alignment demonstrates how the two virtues positively reinforce each other when they are linked together.

CONVICTION	COMPASSION
Truth People	**Love People**
Theologically correct Defenders of the faith Focus on certainty Inclined to closed systems Bible is the word of God	Theologically empathetic Reminders of grace Focus on complexity Inclined to open systems Bible contains the word of God
Great Commission People	**Great Command People**
Authority to make disciples Priority on words Evangelism as proclamation Head over heart	Mandate to love Priority on deeds Evangelism as presence Heart over head
Inclinations	**Inclinations**
Know what they believe Confident and certain Clarity is a virtue Rigid and dogmatic Intense about beliefs	More open to others' beliefs Self-assured and content Ambiguity is necessary Flexible and accepting More casual about beliefs

During the past decade, no other issue has generated more emotional debate and social polarization than abortion. However, in some centers, there's a gentle wind of change blowing that has caught pro-life and pro-choice activists by surprise. Conviction is being blended with compassion and compassion is being mixed with conviction.

Called the Common Ground Network for Life and Choice, the

idea is to try to find creative, constructive, and peaceful ways of dealing with differences as fundamental as those inspired by the abortion issue. The aim is for opposing sides to develop an understanding of each other's position by sitting down and talking—person to person—instead of shouting, harassing, protesting, or going to court. They do so without trying to convert or dissuade the other of their belief, with a spirit that encourages learning from the other. They try to reach an understanding, not necessarily an agreement—and certainly not a compromise.[41] The Psalmist spoke of such occurrences:

> Steadfast love and faithfulness will meet;
> Righteousness and peace will kiss each other. (Psalm 85:10)

◆ Conclusion ◆

During a recent dinner party with a few friends, the conversation circled around to the issues addressed in this chapter. The discussion was often spirited and sometimes sobering. At one point in the conversation, one person introduced her contribution with the comment, "I remember when Canada was a good country." She then went on to talk about the virtues of the "good old days." I later linked the "good-old-days" dinner-party comments with the following historical account which I found written on a placemat at the Globe restaurant in the small southern Ontario community of Rosemont.

> In the early days, Rosemont boasted four hotels, one of which was the Globe. One night, a fire broke out in the hostelry built where the Anglican church now stands. The wife of the owner of the Globe rose from her bed. Grabbing her husband's shotgun, she ran outside in her nightgown and mounted guard over the well—which happened to be located on her husband's property and which was also the main source of water for the village. She stood there daring anyone to fetch water to aid her chief rival for business until the burning building was past saving. The pump she guarded so valiantly is still to be seen outside—a tribute to the competitive instincts of our forebearers![42]

Canada's past does have many virtues to put on parade. However, our history books are also filled with tensions and troubles.

Often, we quiet the memories that stimulate pain and stress and humiliation. The more crucial question for us today is what mindset do we bring to the issues of the day? Is it best to be small-minded, empty-minded, close-minded, or open-minded?

Small-minded people reduce life to their own size. Their small-mindedness is an attitude that travels everywhere with them. They may play a good game of Trivial Pursuit, but they are remembered as petty people who major in the small stuff in life.

Empty-minded people have not taken time to think very much. They are like people who take trips with empty suitcases. They come face to face with the issues of the day without any real conviction about what they believe. Even when they do take time to reflect, they tend to "question everything" and are "agnostic on all things." Empty-minded people are content to remain in a perpetual state of "adolescent questioning and skepticism."[43] Whenever something new arrives on the horizon of their lives, they begin at zero.

Close-minded people travel through life with their suitcases fully packed; almost everything is neatly folded. Some have locked their suitcases and don't even realize they have lost the keys. When they talk with others, close-minded people seem unaware that to "listen with one's mind already made up is an empty gesture."[44]

Open-minded people carry some rather heavy suitcases, but they always leave room to put in more stuff. Although their cases have strong latches that get used frequently, they do not worry about losing the keys because their suitcases do not have locks. Open-minded people believe "the mind is like a parachute, it works better when it is open."

Healthy Christians are not afraid to open themselves to other people's ideas or to submit their own convictions to scrutiny. It is lack of faith that brings the fear of being adversely affected by the wisdom of other people's ideas. Truth can stand scrutiny. Neither do stable Christians let themselves be swept off their feet by forceful arguments, so that they "continually vacillate like a broken weather-vane."[45] As John Cobb has written, "If we trust Jesus Christ as our Lord and Savior, we have no reason to fear that truth from any source will undercut our faith. Indeed, we have every reason to believe that all truth, wisdom, and reality cohere in him."[46]

◆ Pursuing Principled Pluralism ◆

Chapter Six

Introduction

There are rituals in modern life for more occasions than just going to church. We frequently expect unstated ceremonial standards to set our behavioral rules and regulations. Whenever *O Canada* is sung, audiences automatically rise to their feet. At orchestral performances, whispering is disrespectful and coughing is uncouth. Clapping between movements is a sign of musical ignorance. Protocol at funerals demands hushed tones; laughter is unacceptable. Even at baseball games, unofficial rules state, "Do not leave your seat until the third batter is out and the players on the field are headed for the dugout." Our rituals and codes of conduct help keep our behavior inside the limits of approved social etiquette.

At this stage in Canada's history, our cultural etiquette for living in a pluralistic society is not as clearly defined as our other rituals. We are making progress, but problems remain. Many facets of our emerging "cultural pluralism" have taken up residence in our shared perceptions. We continue to be proactive when it comes to establishing social structures for cradling our diversity. The courts in the land regularly hand down judgments that press us to find new ways to live together. However, there are numerous times when we don't know when to stand or sit, when to offer applause or express disapproval, and when to whisper in hushed tones or speak out passionately.

The intent of this chapter is to define more clearly the nuances of our emerging cultural etiquette. The aim is to offer a framework for pursuing principled pluralism that will enhance our ability to deal with diversity. The hope is to articulate a cultural creed that invites all members of society to live with strong convictions without trampling on each other. The case study focuses on evangelism etiquette in these pluralistic times.

We must address and resolve two contrary points of view in order to practice principled pluralism in the church and in society. In the church, too many of God's people hang on to majoritarian attitudes. They have been used to life on their terms and they think life should continue to march to their beat. In the culture at large, many people have downsized pluralism to their particular perspective too. They want an open society in which "all views are equally valid," but with one exception. They are unwilling to accept the view of those in society who believe that truth really does exist and that there is one right way to believe and behave.

The problem on the church side of the equation is even more complicated than in the culture. Diversity inside the church divides the church against itself. There are visible Christians who hold high views of truth and believe that even on complex issues God's ways are definitive and absolute. These people of God are often exclusive and judgmental. There are other church-attending Christians whose views on truth and God's ways are less decisive and dogmatic. These people of God tend to be more inclusive and permissive.

To complicate the church scene even more, there are committed Christians in both categories who hang on to assumptions that worked when the majority of Canadians attended church. They remember when the church had cultural power and social status. They remember when politicians drafted legislation that addressed a social policy or moral issue. In former days, it was simply assumed that church leaders could make an appointment with the cabinet minister in charge to express their point of view. They understood that their perspectives would be taken seriously. It was unthinkable that public officials would simply disregard the Christian position. After all, more than simply being influential, the Christian voice was considered both right and best. Today's majoritarian Christians still live with that same mindset. Unfortunately, their attitudes and actions are sometimes detrimental. They often seek to exert their influence in ways that are both disruptive to others in society and frustrating to their own psychological well-being.

On the society side of the equation, in its present stage of immaturity, cultural pluralism only tolerates other ideological pluralists. Only those who voice the conviction that "all views are equal" receive the cultural seal of approval. When the majority in society conceives of life in this way, those in minority groups tend to feel like outsiders. Consequently, Christians who think that truth exists and that there is only one way to believe often feel unwelcome in their own culture. They sometimes feel psychologically intimidated about acknowledging their views in the public forum. Singing an explicitly Christian carol at a public school Christmas concert breaks the pluralists' rules and regulations. At ceremonial celebrations, any word of quiet witness or expression of prayer breaches protocol. Even in interpersonal relationships, it is often assumed that communication about personal beliefs is off limits. Christian evangelists feel about as welcome in the modern world as skunks at a garden party.

But why should Christians who deeply value their faith feel so marginalized? Just because they are members of a minority group in today's society, do they need to feel so unwelcome? Surely, there is a healthier way to live together.

In order for "principled pluralism" to make an entrance, people in our churches and in the culture at large will need to shift their assumptions. Otherwise, we will not be able to live peaceably and productively with our increasing diversity. People with various views of God's truth and others in the culture must be prepared to live by the same rules. All segments of society must give up the presumption that they have the right to reduce society's norms to their biases. Without sacrificing their own principles, they must make room for each other. While retaining the prerogative to be true to themselves, individuals and organizations must give to others the same freedoms they desire for themselves.

One basic premise of principled pluralism is that people in the church and in society should neither be judgmental of others nor permissive themselves. Resisting permissiveness encourages us to establish personal convictions and thereby be true to **ourselves**.

Relinquishing the right to judge others who are different from ourselves gives other people room to be true to **themselves**. Specifically, ideological pluralists need to stop judging Christians who believe truth can support one-way thinking. And Christians need to stop judging pluralists who believe many views are equally valid. If they choose to do so, both committed Christians and ideological pluralists can retain their particular views of each other, but they must give each other unjudged cultural space. In other words, principled pluralism will advance when people grant others the same privileges they desire for themselves.

The cultural groupings illustrate how people in society and in the church nurture different attitudes toward diversity. Tribalizers and reclaimers tend to resist diversity and are often judgmental. Accommodators welcome the arrival of diversity and are more permissive. When cocooners notice that people around them believe and behave differently, they may wonder what is happening, but mostly they will remain uninvolved. Collaborators analyze what is changing. As they establish their own opinions they also look for ways to relate constructively to others around them. (*See Fig. 6.1*)

◆ A. Getting ready for God's next move ◆

There is an instance in the New Testament when the church was edging from one stage to another that reveals both how God works and how we can move toward a more desirable future. The history-making incident is recorded in the New Testament, Acts 10:1–48.

In its infancy, the church is limited to a Jewish sect. The vision of the leaders for the future of the church is blocked by their cultural containment.

The main characters in the drama are Peter and Cornelius. In the Acts account, Peter is no ordinary member of the flock. He has credentials. Just a few months earlier, Peter was a member of Jesus' inner circle and now he is the revered leader of a surging new spiritual movement. Peter has tasted the limelight and what it is to have access to God's power. He has enormous organizational clout.

Cornelius is the other main participant in the drama, but he is not a Jew. He is a Gentile, a Roman centurion. Cornelius is not just any ordinary soldier. He is an army man with enough rank to be in

Fig. 6.1
Degree of acceptance of diversity

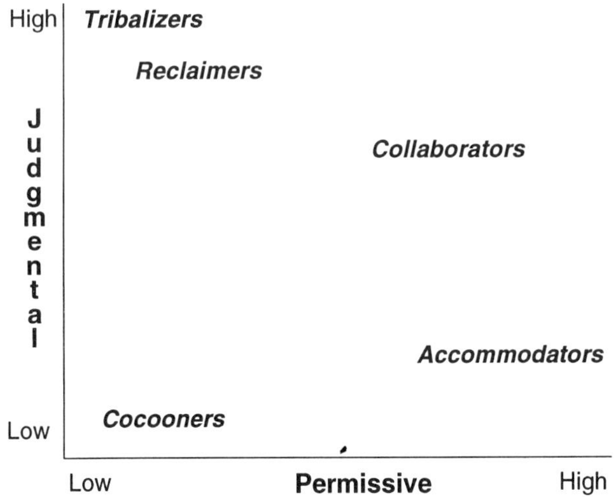

Tribalizers: convinced, entrenched and closed
Reclaimers: traditional, concerned, and fearful of compromise
Cocooners: passive and indifferent
Accommodators: innovative, inclusive and experimental
Collaborators: progressive, experimental but with set limits

charge of a Roman regiment noted for its bravery. His privileges include servants and a place large enough to house his family. Cornelius is a devout and godly man. He consistently prays to the same God the Jews believe in and has a reputation for being generous. Although Cornelius has a heart for God, he doesn't have the proper ethnic credentials to qualify for membership in the new spiritual movement.

At the time of the event, Peter is in Joppa looking for a little time off and taking advantage of the hospitality of a businessman convert, Simon the tanner. Cornelius is 30 miles north in Caesarea, at home with his family and servants. God is present both in Joppa and in Caesarea.

Cornelius is on stage for the opening scene. At three o'clock in the afternoon, Cornelius is interrupted by a vision; an angel comes and gives him detailed directions. He is to send representatives to

Simon the tanner's house in Joppa. They are to find Peter. (3–8) Cornelius obeys immediately.

The following day, Peter is up on Simon's roof looking out at the sea, enjoying the sun and preparing to pray. Before long, he nods off and falls into a deep sleep. God turns on a video tape in Peter's mind. For Peter, the vision is more like a nightmare. Just before he fell asleep, Peter had requested that some food be brought to him. Now, in his trance, Peter receives a vivid portrait of a white sheet holding all the kinds of animals, reptiles, and birds that Jews do not eat. God says, "Peter, get up and kill and eat." Peter said, "I can't, they are unclean." God responds, "They are clean now. I've taken them off the forbidden list." The same script is replayed three times; Peter's convictions run deep and he stays within his ritual boundaries. (11–16) Then he wakes up and realizes that he has suddenly lost his appetite.

As Peter puzzles over what has just happened, Cornelius' emissaries knock on the door. Peter knows enough about how God works that he readily welcomes these people he has never met before. That night they talk about their visions and first thing in the morning they leave for Caesarea.

The 30-mile walk along the sea gives Peter a chance to think and pray. He can't escape the connection between Cornelius, a Gentile, and the forbidden animals in the sheet. The question keeps gnawing at his mind: "Are Gentiles off the forbidden list too?"

Cornelius is expecting Peter and his men and has already called together his relatives and close friends. (25) As Peter looks across the room at Cornelius, he knows what the message has to be. But just to be sure, he asks Cornelius to repeat his vision one more time. Peter listens, and then begins by acknowledging the old ways, "It was unlawful for Jews to associate with Gentiles." But, Peter continues, "God has shown me a new way. (28) I now understand that God treats all people the same. Whatever our nationalities, when we believe in God and do what is right, God accepts us." (34–35)

Once Peter realizes what is happening, he can't stop. He shifts from prophet to evangelist and says, "You know the message God gave to the people of Israel. Jesus of Nazareth, he is Lord of all... and everyone who believes in him receives forgiveness of sins through his name." (36–43) True to God's ways, the surprises don't stop. While Peter is still speaking, the Holy Spirit makes an entrance, and what used to be a small, culturally controlled sect takes the first steps toward becoming the church of Jesus Christ.

Principled and pluralistic

Today, Christians who continue to live with majoritarian mentalities toward the culture are similar to Peter and his view of the church before he encountered Cornelius. They desire to control the rules and regulations governing society. Although they live with clear commitments that protect them from being permissive, they resist diversity at a cost to others who are different from themselves. Followers of Jesus who are absolutist about truth and who judge other Christians from their exclusive point of view do the same thing. The problem also exists for Christians who live with more open belief systems, but who judge other Christians whose faith is contained in closed belief systems. Peter had a confined view of Cornelius. Christians who insist on judging each other also have confined views of each other. Just as Peter was unprepared to let people who were different from himself have a place, the same is true of Christians who insist on judging one another.

Ideological pluralists who are generally accepting but who, at the same time, are intolerant toward committed Christians whose truth compels them to conclude that there is one true way to believe, make the same mistake. They live like Peter before he encountered Cornelius. Ideological pluralists who only affirm other ideological pluralists reduce the world to the size of their own view. Instead of being inclusive of the views of others, they are exclusive. Rather than making room for people who are different from themselves, they fashion all of life in their own image. The paradox is that in denying cultural space to people who are different from themselves, these pluralists deny the very premise they parade.

After the Cornelius event, people who were different from Peter had a place. Diverse voices were considered equal. God's family of faith grew larger. Peter and Cornelius walked together on level ground. It will be a sign of progress when followers of Jesus from different denominations and Christian traditions welcome each other's presence in God's family. When visible Christians and ideological pluralists live with understanding and other, it will be a sign that the present immature st pluralism is well on the way to becoming principle

A genuinely pluralistic society is a post-Cornel culture that is both "principled" and "pluralistic" in be true to themselves, but also makes room for dive we are visible Christians actively involved in churches, or whether we design our lives without God and a concern for truth, we will all gain as we intentionally make room for each other. Only then will our cultural pluralism be truly principled and pluralistic.

◆ B. Give permission—take permission ◆

There is nothing new about the church needing to make sense out of who God is and what Christ has done within the context of a multi-minded and pluralistic society. The Christian proclamation has always taken place in a pluralistic world, in competition with rival religious and intellectual convictions.[1] There are many parallels between New Testament times and today. However, there is also an essential difference. In the early period of New Testament history, followers of Jesus were a small minority in the culture. It was only in succeeding centuries that Christians moved from being a minority group to a dominant voice in society. Then, in AD 313, the emperor Constantine decreed the Roman Empire to be Christian. The age of Christendom was born.

Recent history has seen the reverse of this process take place within Canada. Our nation was founded on the assumptions of Christendom. From the beginning, the Christian way was woven into the Canadian way. The Catholic **and** Protestant presence gave Canada the full expression of historic Christendom. Now, instead of moving from minority status to the majority voice in society, visible Christians have experienced the opposite. Rather than gaining cultural power, they have lost both cultural power and social status. It is only natural for the people of God who have been a part of the shift to feel a deep sense of loss, even to the point of lobbying intensely for life as it used to be. Particularly for those who have known the former ways, majoritarian thinking may be understandable, but it is no longer helpful. Trading in majoritarian thinking for an egalitarian mindset will be a move in the right

...tion. Relating to others in society with a vision of equality will be the attitude required to design a desirable future.

Working within a framework of principled pluralism, the first move toward people who are different from ourselves is to **give permission**. Whether we are visible Christians, people who hold privatized beliefs, members of other world faiths, or confirmed agnostics or atheists, we need to give each other the prerogative to be what we choose to be. In a two-way-street manner, we must grant each other the personal and social space we all need to be true to ourselves.

Giving permission to each other allows everyone to self-define. It involves relating to people in a manner that releases them to be who they are at the point in time when we encounter them. It is meeting and enjoying people in the neighborhood, at work, at church, or wherever with an attitude that conveys, "I give you permission to believe and behave as you choose."

In our associations with others, giving permission is not **approval** of what they believe or do. Approval extends beyond giving permission. It is more like an endorsement. Approval notarizes people. Granting approval is like bestowing a blessing. Giving permission stops short of endorsing or blessing others.

Giving permission to people is also different from **agreeing** with how people believe and behave. Agreeing with people means that we share the same opinions or profess the same beliefs. Agreement says, "I am ready to sign your statement of belief." Giving permission says, "I acknowledge your statement of belief."

Neither is giving permission **compromise**. Compromise involves making concessions at the cost of personal integrity. Compromise requires that people surrender their principles to the ways of others. In contrast, giving permission simply secures cultural space for other people and says, "There is a place for you in the world we share."

When we give permission to people to be who they are and what they are, we extend ourselves to them and say, "I **accept you**." Acceptance is neither judgmental nor permissive. Acceptance simply says, "Just as I have the prerogative and privilege to self-define, I understand that you have the prerogative and human privilege to do the same. I assume that is how God set up the world and I accept you and your choices."

Acceptance is not the same as approval. It is also different than agreement. Neither is it compromise. Acceptance involves treating the people in our lives like loving parents treat their children. It would be difficult to find a parent anywhere in the world who would say they have always agreed with or approved of everything their children have said or done. But those same parents would undoubtedly also point out, "My disagreement and disapproval does not negate my acceptance of my children."

Mature Christians have always distinguished between accepting people and agreeing with their ideas. It has never been necessary to withhold acceptance from people just because they are not everything we think they ought to be. The idea that the role of Christians is to judge those who do not comply with God's ways may be well-intentioned, but it is wrong.

At its most profound level, "giving permission" **treats people like God treats people**. God created the world, but, in the beginning and forevermore, God decided not to control how people live in the world. Instead of treating people like pawns on a chess board, the laws of creation dictate that people have options. Rather than forcing and coercing people, God gives choices. "Come unto me," Jesus invites. But if we choose to go elsewhere with our will and wishes, that is our prerogative. Certainly God loves and lobbies and entreats, but human choice rules human destiny. And along the way, without approving or agreeing, God accepts.

The second critical step to make in the pursuit of principled pluralism is to **take permission**. That is, claim your prerogative to be what you choose to be. Instead of embracing and being embraced by a spirit of permissiveness, affirm what it means to be true to yourself.

Taking permission invites clear **self-definition**. The appeal is to carve out cultural space for who one is and what one believes. For active Christians, the aim is to respond to God's will and ways, all the while affirming, "I know who I am. I know what I believe. And I aspire to certain forms of behavior."

Taking permission also encourages people to **take a stand**. God's people are not passive and innocuous. They live with ideals and convictions. Christians can take a stand because they have some set standards. Although they know there is more than one way to view the world, they are confident and content with their way of putting life together. Church-attending Christians are often encouraged to make a case for what they believe. Particularly in our multi-minded and multiple-choice world, they are aware that "If you don't stand for something, you could fall for anything."

Taking permission promotes speaking with a **clear voice** amidst the chorus of voices which make up society. Without being simplistic and naive, God's people search for God's truth. They raise their voices above the static of the age and speak out with conviction. Exposed to as many voices as anyone else in society, concerned Christians risk committing themselves to what they believe is true and right. Although they may represent a minority voice in the culture, they possess a clear voice.

Giving and **taking permission** protects the people of God, and others in society, from one-way-street living. They cannot escape the reminder that the world is bigger than one's personal world. Other people's worlds count too. As a visiting professor, Frederick Buechner noted that Harvard Divinity School was proud of its pluralism—feminists, humanists, theists, liberation theologians all pursuing truth together. But in his class, the dark side was also exposed. "At least for a moment we all saw, I think, that the danger of pluralism is that it becomes factionalism, and that if factions grind their separate axes too vociferously, something mutual, precious, and human is in danger of being drowned out and lost."[2]

Committed to preserving an interdependent world, principled pluralism abides by a nonnegotiable; it makes room for various voices. But making room must not mean living in isolation from each other. People with differences who have no contact with each other are like patients under quarantine in a hospital. They are protected, but it is hardly healthy living. Paul Marshall rightly reasons that, "A good form of pluralism is one in which we live together in peace and mutual respect, while acknowledging that our differences are real and important."[3]

The dynamics of life dictate that people who **give permission** also **get permission**. Mutuality is necessary to make life work in a society where diversity reigns. Those who give permission to others end up getting permission for themselves. In this sense, life is reciprocal. Otherwise, life ends up being a tug of war between opposing differences.

Many chaplains in our hospitals, universities, and prisons are learning to express their ministries with mutuality. They are making principled pluralism work by both giving and getting permission.

In the past, the pattern of praying among chaplains inevitably took a Christian form. In keeping with Canada's religious history, prayers were first expressed in the "name of the Father, Son, and Holy Spirit," along with frequent references to "Jesus." However, when Jewish, Islamic, or Buddhist chaplains joined the circle, they were uncomfortable with the exclusive nature of the Christian prayers. Out of respect for their differences, what often ensued was an inclusive style of praying. But the prayers became more of an exercise in not offending someone else's religious tradition than they were free expressions of communication with God. Dissatisfaction with this style of innocuous praying prompted the next stage to emerge. The chaplains encouraged each other to pray in ways that were consistent with their own beliefs. In giving permission, they also got permission to pray without reservation. Because of their understanding of each other, rather than praying offensively, they gave each other the freedom to pray with integrity.

These chaplains demonstrate a critical balance. They are neither judgmental toward others nor permissive with themselves. They understand and accept people from different faiths, but they are unwilling to surrender their own faith commitments. In accordance with principled pluralism, they secure their own space as they give space to each other.

◆ C. Discern the good ◆

We live in a world where honesty is front page news. Recently, the *Toronto Star* featured the story of 11-year-old Adam, who turned in a wallet he found containing $1,400. The owner repaid the act of honesty with a measly $10 reward. When the story became public, "hundreds of people wanted to reward the boy." Adam received numerous gifts and benefits for his deed of honesty; so many, in fact, that Adam's grade six teacher was quoted as saying, "honesty really does pay."[4] The cheapskate loser of the wallet ought to be chastised, and Adam deserves the accolades he received. But whatever happened to simply expecting honesty as a way of life? Doesn't honesty deserve applause as a virtuous ethic whether it pays or not?

"Political correctness" seems to be on almost everyone's agenda these days. The movement has functioned as society's conscience, ensuring that society includes various marginalized groups. It has raised our awareness of the ways we describe people. Political correctness in communication has been more than just a language game. Its presence has served to reduce racist comments and has removed demeaning descriptions of many marginalized people from our vocabularies.

But political correctness has also tended to curtail free-flowing discussion. Current pressure to be "politically correct" tends to preempt open discussion which might contain or imply anything negative about feminism, gay rights, aboriginal peoples, other minorities, or other world religions. The informal social policy pronounced by political correctness seems to elevate social sensitivity above truthfulness. A more discerning approach would propose that all views should be subject to scrutiny, including the "politically correct" agenda.

In his book *Mosaic Madness*, Reginald Bibby correctly points out that "Pluralism legitimizes the expression of viewpoints. But, if anything, it makes the evaluation of viewpoints not less important but all the more important. Precisely because we encourage choices, we need to champion the critical concept of discernment. People need to learn how to choose."[5] The present is no time to downplay discernment. If ever there was a need for ethical, moral, spiritual and intellectual discrimination on all matters, these are the times.

Discernment quickly reveals that all values are not equally valid. Contending that dishonesty is as virtuous as honesty is absurd. Students who doctor their transcripts to get into medical school do not deserve confidence when a patient needs an operation. Put honesty next to deceit, and honesty will win out every time. Generosity makes greed look bad. Compared to self-giving, selfishness is offensive. To contend that greed is good, or that the purpose of life is to exalt self at the expense of others is ludicrous. A rapist appears morally repulsive when compared to a faithful lover. The very idea that breaking marriage vows is more virtuous than keeping a covenant with one's husband or wife is preposterous. Even in a pluralistic society that intentionally makes room for diverse ideas and views, the mere suggestion that all values are equally valid is mindless relativism. It is irrational and an affront to principled pluralism.

I am not suggesting that ethical and moral decision making is always obvious or categorically black and white. The issues surrounding reproductive technologies, abortion, and immigration policies are not straightforward. Legislating just punishment for euthanasia and mercy killing is profoundly complex. However, I do believe that we must continue to seek the truth. Our hope for the future will be found in refusing to surrender the struggle to discern the right from the wrong, and the good from the best.

I recently listened to John Perkins. A black social activist from Mississippi, he has experienced overt racism and has survived physical violence at the hands of white men. He has been asked publicly, "What has kept you from hating white people?" Dr. Perkins' answer is simple: "Love is more powerful than hate."

All values are not equally valid. As we understand and implement God's ways and preferences the whole world will benefit, not just Canadian society.

Downside of pluralism

Pluralism opens the door to the belief that criticism is off limits. Particularly when we emphasize accepting people and giving them permission to be what they choose to be, both discernment and criticism may seem unacceptable. Writing about civility in an uncivil world, Richard Mouw observes, "Being civil doesn't mean that we cannot criticize what goes on around us. Civility doesn't require us to approve of what other people believe and do. It is one thing to insist that other people have the right to express their basic convictions; it is another thing to say that they are right in doing so."[6]

In the mood of the moment, critiquing other religions is not just discouraged, it is sometimes considered disrespectful. Yet, when I recently read a feature article documenting how Islamic courts in Somalia continue to hand down harsh punishment for crimes in the name of God, I wanted to weep. Public stonings and the cutting off of hands and feet may be prescribed by the Koran, but please don't ask me to believe that the God who died on the cross at Calvary is the same God behind the justice being meted out in Somalia.[7] Of course, as Christians, we have to accept the reality of our own harsh history. And public stonings were prescribed in the Old Testament. Today, however, the teachings of the New Testament and the life of Jesus set the standard for Christians when it comes to how to respond to the evils in the modern world.

Pluralism without discernment can lead to a convictionless culture. When various ways of believing and behaving are simply accepted and left unexamined, life tumbles to its lowest common denominator. Instead of striving for conviction, we surrender to consensus. Discriminating right from wrong is no longer part of the process of making daily decisions. What is good, better, and best receives limited scrutiny. We lose our motivation to establish standards, exercise value judgments, or take stands on controversial issues. The consequences for society are truly frightening to contemplate.

Discernment itself can be pursued in at least two different ways. One is to ascertain what is good and right, and then pursue that course. The other is to look for the lies in life, to resist embracing and being embraced by what is dark and destructive. The more people and organizations strive to practice critical discernment, the greater the prospect will be that a strong principled pluralism will emerge in the culture.

◆ D. True to self—regard for others ◆

The willingness to give and take permission is an important attitude to embrace. A mindset which encourages discernment and discrimination is also something to be cultivated, especially in the maze of modern life. But as virtuous as these things may be, life can still remain passive and private unless we express our convictions in appropriate behavior. The substance of principled pluralism only develops as we translate solid theory into pertinent practice.

True to self

Last year, a Christmas advertisement was pushed through our front-door mail slot. The invitation was printed in bold letters:

"Join your neighbors for... BREAKFAST WITH SANTA." The event featured a saxophone quartet and gifts from Santa. It was billed as an opportunity to greet and meet your neighbors.

Reading the attractive invitation, I wondered to myself, "Who is sponsoring this event?" Eventually, I figured out that it was organized by a church in the neighborhood. Realizing it was a local church initiative, I examined the advertisement more carefully. There was nothing, not one word, that was distinctly Christian or religious. "Breakfast with Santa" could have just as easily been sponsored by the local community league.

The organizers of the event undoubtedly had outreach in mind. Christmas is a time for getting together and it makes sense to offer something special to the community. But it doesn't make sense for churches to extend invitations to events that have no distinctly Christian components. When churches cloak their identity in the shroud of relevance and function without clear spiritual objectives, they belie their purpose. Instead of being true to themselves, they betray themselves. Rather than sounding a clear voice in a multi-voiced world, they speak with a muted and confused voice.

Whether we function as organizations or as individuals, being true to ourselves in a pluralistic society requires that we behave like a prospector looking for gold. It means we must venture out into the cultural landscape and stake a claim.

The process is quite involved and can take a significant period of time. Surveying the topography, taking soil samples, analyzing alternative locations, and projecting the probability of finding gold is a complicated matter. The ability to distinguish real gold from fool's gold only comes with experience. Sorting the real from the illusionary and the genuine from the fraudulent can only be done confidently after careful assessments are made. But after the analysis is complete, the time comes to take the risk and stake the claim. Fully cognizant that other people are staking out other claims, the people of God choose to risk their claims on God's claims. And it is only after the claim has been staked that one can begin mining for the gold.

In the next period of cultural history in Canada, those organizations and individuals who are ready to stake their claims are the ones who will also experience positive futures. Those who are content to lapse into ambiguity and vagueness will continue to exist, but they will wane into insignificance. People and organizations that choose to speak clearly and stay focused on who they are will solicit followers of like-minded individuals. Those who carve out a clear self-definition but who also relate with positive regard to others who are different from themselves will have the opportunity to flourish.

Regard for others

The point has already been made that a genuinely pluralistic society invites people to be true to themselves while making room for diversity. Accordingly, an egalitarian mindset, the belief that we should relate to others in society with a concern for equality, will be indispensable if we are to design a hopeful future.

Grand Chief of Canada's First Nations, Ovide Mercredi, observes that, "Some Canadians believe that equality means everyone must be the same and that differences in lifestyle, culture, language and religion should be ignored if we are to share a democratic society. This is not an approach that First Nations peoples share because it means assimilation. Democracy must include respect for differences and the promotion of diversity if it is to reflect the realities of Canadian history."[8] I agree, but also contend that it will take more than just acceptance or tolerance of differences to create a positive future. Unless we can **appreciate** each other's differences, working toward mutual respect will be exceedingly difficult.

Expressed as an attitude, acceptance recognizes people and establishes the legitimacy of their existence. Appreciation is an attitude that reaches out to people. The implicit message is, "I not only recognize you, I affirm your uniqueness." Appreciation extends beyond acknowledgment and searches for inherent value in people. Appreciation is ready to give people the benefit of the doubt but stops short of bestowing approval or of saying, "I agree with you." Neither do we give people the "Good Housekeeping Seal of Approval" just because we appreciate them. Still, appreciation opens the door and makes it possible to respect other people.

We can cite many examples. Just because one prefers classical music doesn't mean one cannot appreciate the energy and creativity expressed in other styles of music. When one understands the intent of every serious artist to create good art, it should be possible to stand in front of a "bad" piece of art and still appreciate what the artist desired to portray on the canvas. Thoughtful Christians who engage in conversation with thoughtful agnostics or reflective atheists find it natural to appreciate those people even though they disagree over crucial concerns.

In the midst of a public forum debate about the prominent place of Christmas and Easter on the Canadian calendar, Jewish journalist Lorrie Goldstein spoke out in defense of understanding and appreciation for Christian content in Canadian culture.

> Wherever did we get the dumb idea that respecting the religious beliefs of roughly 2% of the population composed of other faiths should shut down the expression of the Christian faith...
>
> I would argue, that when our politicians play down the idea that Canada is a Christian country—as they always do—and when our schools take the Christ out of Christmas—they are ignoring the religious beliefs of almost 80% of the Canadian public for the sake of about 20%, most of whom are non-believers...
>
> The better route would be to guarantee the religious freedom of minorities, which Canada already does better than most any other country on Earth, while acknowledging the obvious truth that Canada is a Christian country.[9]

At the World Vision Reception Center for refugees, where people arrive from troubled countries around the world, an "Interfaith Worship Directory" prominently lists alternatives for worship. In this government-funded facility, the intent is to acknowledge and appreciate the place of religion in all cultures. Accordingly, options for local worship at Catholic, mainline and evangelical Protestant churches, Muslim, Hindu, Sikh and other world religion places of worship are identified and encouraged. Principled pluralism readily asserts that "my views count" but just as readily affirms that "other people's views count too." When we adopt principled pluralism, we are neither judgmental toward others nor permissive with ourselves.

◆ E. Influence without apology or attack ◆

At some point in my own journey, I remember realizing that, regardless of all our differences, everyone believes **something** about life. It was a revelation at the time; I suddenly realized that "if you breathe, you also believe—something."

Of course, that does not mean everyone has a formal belief system that they have consciously constructed. However, it does mean that, at some functional level, people everywhere have morals and ethics that frame their decisions. They have values and beliefs that inform their behaviors.

Our cultural etiquette is woefully inadequate when it comes to how we interact with each other about our beliefs. Tensions exist between "committed Christians" and pluralists who do not make room for each other. The majority have intuitively concluded that beliefs are private matters which should be quietly contained within our inner selves. There is a smaller group of Canadians who think that beliefs should not only be openly examined, they should be shared. These people have concluded that convincing others to believe as they believe is a big part of the purpose of life.

These two groups also hold definite views of each other. The "keep-your-beliefs-private" people disdain those who zealously seek to convert others. And the "my-beliefs-are-worthy-of-becoming-your-beliefs" people suspect those who keep their beliefs to themselves to be either "uncommitted" or "spiritually lost." Scholar Martin Marty describes our predicament: "In a world where the religiously committed are not very civil and the religiously civil do not often seem very committed, we look for a new style of consciousness that combines civility and commitment."[10]

In a national survey, Canadians were asked whether or not they agree with the statement, "I feel it is important to encourage non-Christians to become Christians," two out of three said "no." Although there are significant regional differences—B.C. showing the lowest percentage and Saskatchewan and Manitoba the highest—one out of three respondents agree with the statement. Weekly church attenders and those who identity as conservative/evangelicals are the most enthusiastic about converting people to Christianity. (*See Fig. 6.2*) Of particular interest, for each Canadian who strongly agrees that "it is important to encourage non-Christians to

Fig. 6.2

"I feel it is important to encourage non-Christians to become Christians"

Percent who "Agree strongly" or "Moderately agree"

By Region

National	B.C.	Alta.	Sask. Man.	Ont.	Que.	Atlantic
33	16	32	46	25	33	41

By Age

18–34	35–54	55+
27	31	42

By Gender

Female	Male
28	36

By Church Attendance

National	Weekly	Monthly	Occasional	Never
33	68	43	29	9

By Denomination

R.C.	Angl.	United	Luth. Presby.	Conserv.	World Rel.	No Rel.
32	25	19	31	73	2	10

Angus Reid Group: July '94. N = 1502

become Christians," three others strongly disagree with the same idea (15% compared to 44%).

Influence without apology

Compared to other Canadians, Christians often have a reputation for trying to convert people. Religious enthusiasts may well deserve the reputation but what is not often acknowledged is that **every** conviction or belief seeks to convert. Consider the effectiveness of the anti-smoking lobby during the past decade. The prevalence of the "blue box" is evidence of environmentalists converting people to their point of view. Social activists continually attempt to influence society. In recent years, feminist, pro-gay, pro-life and pro-choice proponents have all sought to make gains for their particular causes. Liberals regularly seek to convert conservatives and right-wingers seek to win over left-wingers. Rather than denounce the practice of influence without apology, the question is whether it is even "possible not to be a proselytizer of some sort or on some scale if one has deep convictions?"[11]

A pluralistic society, by definition, is a place with many voices. The laws of pluralism require more than one way of thinking. Society becomes a forum for diverse ideas and different ways of conceiving of life. These ways then compete with each other to gain a following. Choosing one's preferences, striving to influence, and lobbying for change are all legitimate forms of expression within pluralism. These dynamics are the essence of pluralism itself.

Pluralism tends to break down, however, when one group in society seeks to shut down another group. In calling for the pursuit of principled pluralism, I have proposed that those who choose to hold to a particular stance must give others the right to articulate and hold positions too. Accordingly, those who want privilege and prerogative must give privilege and prerogative to others. Methodologies and tactics that **seek** to influence without **allowing** influence break the rules of principled pluralism.

Influence without attack

Author and broadcaster Tom Harpur has many right things to say, but in a recent editorial his comments revealed an inconsistency often found within pluralistic arguments. Casting disrepute on the whole gospel of John to make his case, the editorial sought to remove the famous saying from Jesus' lips, "I am the way, the truth and the life; nobody comes to the Father but by me." The point of the column was to counter anyone who "clings to a one-truth ideology." According to Harpur, "The greatest curse of religion as a force in the world is that too many adherents of this or that faith fervently believe theirs is the sole possessor of the fullness of the truth. Nothing bodes more potential for global dissensions and rancor than this. Nothing runs more powerfully counter to the urgent need today for mutual tolerance and societal harmony. It is the enemy of peace."[12]

The paradox of Harpur's attack is that he commits the same sin he accuses his enemies of committing. He clings to the "one-truth ideology" that there cannot be only one truth. Labeling the Pope and Billy Graham as "fundamentalists, ultra-orthodox and conservatives," Harpur reserves his pluralist approval for other like-minded ideological pluralists. Regrettably, in this particular instance, Harpur breaches the rules of principled pluralism and becomes an enemy of the peace he aspires to espouse.

Principled pluralism invites people to affirm who they are without attacking those who disagree with them. Those who give people permission to be who they are find it unnecessary to denigrate others as they stake out their own cultural space. People who accept other people are not pressed to put down the views of others in order to establish their own convictions. Those who live with regard for others are the ones best positioned to be true to themselves.

When Paul the apostle was invited to address the philosophers on Mars Hill in Athens, he practiced principled pluralism (Acts 17:16–34). Paul understood the multi-mindedness that pervaded Athens and he acknowledged the particular religious commitments of the people in his presence (22). He gave them permission to be what they had chosen to be. Rather than attack the philosophers for their beliefs, he expressed appreciation for the truth their teachers taught (28). But Paul was not passive or apologetic. He took permission and spoke with clarity about his own convictions (22–27). He went on to critique what the philosophers believed and stated why he believed that the God he served was more credible (29). With deliberate intent to influence, Paul invited his listeners to reorder their thinking and behavior around Jesus and his teachings (33). Paul treated his audience like God continues to treat people.

As we attempt, as God's people, to do the same today, it will be possible that in "the unfolding of human history there will be significant groups who can, without a sense of superiority, still project their truths and values among others, without manipulating them."[13]

◆ F. Evangelism etiquette in pluralistic times ◆

Paul's missionary mode was effective in his historical context. It can also inform strategic communication in our day. Paul's approach was quite sophisticated; it was much more than a one-way-street message. Before Paul stated "this is what I believe," he acknowledged what the members of his audience believed. Although Paul did not agree with how his listeners viewed their world, he had regard for them.

Because cultural pluralism, by nature, encourages people to "do their own thing" rather than to "consider doing my thing," the current mood of society favors a nonconversion attitude. However, there is another factor that leaves the door ajar for people who believe that God wants them to live evangelistically. Pluralism nurtures open-system living. Instead of one way or one voice being in control, many ways and many voices co-mingle. As a result, people who live in a pluralistic environment are used to getting invitations and making choices. They are subject to influence by voices and alternatives that make a case for their cause. On both the personal and organizational fronts, however, effective evangelistic initiatives will be those tuned into the nuances of the times.

Not all religions mandate evangelism. While some, such as Islam, have engaged in far-reaching missionary activity, others, such as Shinto, do not share the evangelistic impulse. Nor are individual traditions entirely uniform in their practice. For example, the Hare Krishna movement, which does seek converts, evolved out of Hinduism, which generally does not. Conversely, there are Christian denominations that do not actively invite others to believe as they believe, despite Christianity's deeply rooted evangelical tradition.[14]

The very idea of evangelism conjures up a wide range of images and reactions. Some people think evangelism invades other people's privacy and are therefore repulsed by the notion. Those who have had negative experiences or who have made personal attempts to evangelize that have failed, tend to lapse into silence and avoidance. The mere notion of evangelism engenders guilt or fear for many people. But for others, the thought of evangelism encourages them to invite people to know the same God they enjoy and desire to serve.

Stated simply, Christian evangelism involves making sense out of who God is and what Christ has done. It means helping people to personally check out God's ways, and to decide whether or not they want to buy in or opt out.

Scholars and practitioners have numerous ways of defining and describing evangelism. William Abraham defines evangelism as, "that set of intentional activities which is governed by the goal of initiating people into the kingdom of God for the first time."[15] William Willimon more graphically sees "evangelism as a gracious, unmanageable, messy by-product of the intrusions of God.[16] Walter Brueggemann says that evangelism means inviting people into the gospel as the definitional story of our life, and thereby authorizing them to give up, abandon, and renounce other stories that have shaped their lives in false or distorting ways.[17]

According to Willimon, using the story motif for the divine-human encounter, the question then is, "When did the story of Jesus come to illumine and make sense of my story in such a way that my little life became part of the larger adventure called the gospel?"[20]

Christians living amid today's cultural pluralism who have a concern for evangelism can learn not only from Paul's strategy in Athens but also from Peter's encounter with Cornelius. God nudged Peter to change some of his assumptions about other people. As a result, he also had to alter how he perceived himself. In Peter's case, he became a bigger person as he expanded his view of God's family to include Gentiles. Peter also adjusted his understanding of God. Before the encounter, Peter's view of God was small and culturally contained. But from that time on, Peter left room for God to work in surprising ways. Christians who seek to convert non-Christians to Christianity will be helped as they reflect on how they view themselves in relationship with others. Leaving room for God to work in new ways is nothing more than letting God be God.

Start with acceptance and appreciation

People active in evangelistic efforts often start with themselves and their message of truth. They know who they are, what they believe, and what they think others should believe too. In a pluralistic society, people who start with themselves and stick to predetermined scripts will most often fail.

The problem is that evangelists who start with their own story send the wrong message and push people away from potential influence. Rather than communicating the assumption that we live in a world where there are many ways to think and believe, they convey the message, "I'm right and you are wrong." In former times, when most people both inside and outside of God's family believed that truth existed as an objective reality, "right" and "wrong" categories made sense. In this age, the categories of "right" and "wrong" have been replaced with attitudes that assume "You have your opinions" and "I have my opinions." The one thing that is certain is that "my opinions are just as valid as your opinions."

Even the golden rule has been amended from, "Do unto others as you would have them do unto you," to "Let others do what they want to do so you can do what you want to do." A judgmental spirit breaks the accepted code of conduct in a pluralistic society. Morality is a private matter. Values are sorted according to individual tastes.[19] Starting a conversation or beginning a relationship on any other terms will simply shut down communication.

Accepting people as they are and where they are in their journey with life and God is the starting point for evangelism today. Unless people are given permission to be what they have chosen to be, they will never be influenced by others to consider Christ or anything else significant. "Rather than nurturing a mentality that categorizes people as those who have either accepted or rejected Christ" the more appropriate attitude is to relax with people and embrace them as they are.[20] It may help those who feel compromised when they accept people to remember that, except for a few occasions when Jesus confronted the religious and the righteous, he consistently accepted people. When he met people, his pattern was to give people permission to be what they had chosen to be.

Appreciating people extends beyond acceptance. Even though appreciating people who put their lives together in different ways than we do can involve emotional tension, the effort is right. Appreciation sends a positive signal to others. Instead of conveying judgment, appreciation is an act of surrender to others. It says, "I am ready to see life from your point of view." Appreciation of others projects value and communicates legitimacy.

Caution! When appreciation is contrived as a means to convert people, it emits a foul odor. But as an authentic perspective toward others, it can be the bridge upon which we exchange real life.

Stop labeling people

There is an experience imbedded in my mind that illustrates the negative effects of labeling people. The setting was in a downtown hotel in Vancouver, British Columbia. The room was packed with radio and television station owners and managers who were bidding for a rare FM radio license on an open frequency. I was present as a consultant to a radio station that had invested heavily in its presentation. Members of the communications regulatory board (the CRTC—Canadian Radio and Television Commission) sat at the front of the room like queens and kings on their thrones.

Prior to the main proceedings, a group of Christians had been granted a hearing to make the case that members of the media worked with anti-Christian biases. I was sitting in the middle of the audience listening to the presentation. As the Christian group sought to document their perspective, one of the spokespeople for the group stated that "rather than holding a Christian view of the world, the vast majority of decision-makers in the media were 'pagans.'" Murmurs of dissent and disgust swept through the audience. People were offended. If there was any sympathy in the room for the Christian cause, it ended with that statement. It was also at that moment that I vowed to stop labeling and defining others from my particular point of view.

Labeling people is destructive because it stereotypes them. Although we know that not all men are alike and neither are all women alike, sexual stereotyping continues. In the religious realm, labeling flourishes even though we realize that just as Christians differ, so do people who build their lives on other assumptions and other beliefs.

Stereotyping and labeling demeans people. Unfortunately, evangelists are often guilty of this offense. Although the terms they use may make sense when viewed through a Christian lens, labeling people as either "sinners" or "pagans" degrades them. Describing people as "heathen" is similarly derogatory. Even the designation "non-Christian," which I have used in a research-related question in this book, is ultimately unhelpful. The practice defines others negatively. From the lips of Christians, the designation says "you are not like me." In communication, it can send the message, "I'm better than you are." It is comparable to white people describing visible minorities as "non-whites." There are difficulties in finding adequate ways to describe others who are different from ourselves, but I'm-better-than-you signals push people away from those who send them. Rather than encouraging people to seriously consider Christ and his ways, labels often push them away from Christ and the restoring power of the cross.

The December edition of *Christianity Today* illustrates the type of communication to be avoided. "Let the pagans have the holiday," proclaimed the article title. Acknowledging that the spirit of secularism and material consumption challenges the real meaning of Christmas, the writer of the article makes a case for Easter as the central Christian holiday. The idea was to preserve Easter as a genuine Christian celebration, but to surrender Christmas to "the pagans."[21] Although the article was credible, the title was a derogatory put-down of all those worldly "pagans" who spend money and give presents to the special people in their lives!

The better way is to identify people as they identify themselves. In Canadian society, three out of four people are comfortable with their Christian identities. Understanding others from their own point of view instead of labeling them as "non-Christian" is an important place to begin. When visible Christians and those who have privatized their beliefs engage each other in spiritual discussion and explore the place of God in their lives, faith will flourish.

More than one way

In today's world, adversarial evangelism leads to social isolation and evangelistic failure. The strategy already articulated is worth restating. Without compromising personal beliefs or surrendering spiritual convictions, evangelists can continue to have a place if they give people the same permission God gives people to construct their lives as they choose. The attitude necessary to gain a hearing is embodied in a spirit that says, "We both have the same right to decide for ourselves what to believe. Let's look at each other's ways of building our lives and then discuss what is valid and credible."

A positive example which illustrates that "there is more than one way to construct your life" happened recently on a university campus. The event centered around the emotionally explosive issue of abortion. Early in the school term, a coalition of Christian groups sponsored a debate on the question, "Does God Exist?" The event followed the typical debate protocol wherein both sides of the question were addressed and then the debaters engaged each other. The event attracted hundreds of students and stimulated healthy reflection and discussion.

Later that term, the leaders of the students' union sponsored an evening on the subject of abortion and invited Dr. Henry Morgentaler to be the featured speaker. The students who had sponsored the "Does God Exist?" debate looked at the agenda and wondered why both sides of the issue weren't going to be addressed. Citing their own model for handling both sides of an issue, the Christian students went to their campus leaders and asked if the pro-life alternative could also be voiced. The student leaders concluded that the request was fair and turned to the delegation before them and asked, "We don't know anyone on the pro-life side, can you find someone for us?" The abortion debate proceeded in an orderly manner and, again, constructive interaction ensued.

On matters such as abortion where Christians and those who believe otherwise stand on both sides of the debate, one-way thinking is destructive. Acknowledging the legitimacy of more than one way to view such matters is constructive.

In order for any society to retain its substance and strength, it needs to commend people who have the courage to live out their convictions. In pluralistic societies, encouraging a cross section of participants to affirm their convictions is imperative. Otherwise, collective life will either tumble into a state of undefined nothingness, or be overtaken by the wishes of the loudest and strongest voices in control of the cultural moment.

Offer clarity without superiority

I believe that, as well as expressing appropriate sensitivity toward others, Christians need to speak out clearly in their multi-voiced society. While defending the right of other people to hold to their views, God's people need to hold firmly to their commitments too. And Christians are people with a slate of convictions and commitments.

For example, theologian Helmut Thielicke contends, "When

the drama of history is over, Jesus Christ will stand alone on the stage. All the great figures of history—Pharaoh, Alexander the Great, Charlemagne, Churchill, Stalin, Johnson, Mao Tse-tung—will realize that they have been but actors in a drama produced by another."[22]

The doctrine of the second coming of Jesus Christ and the hope of life after death are long-affirmed assumptions of Christian orthodoxy. The scriptures specifically state that Jesus will be the one seated on the throne, saying, "See, I am making all things new... for these words are trustworthy and true." (Revelation 21:5) Whether they fully understand God's revelation or not, committed Christians aspire to remain faithful to the tenets of the faith. They are encouraged to see themselves as shafts of light in an increasingly dark world. Biblical metaphors such as "you are the salt of the earth" and the "yeast and leaven" of life represent a call for clarity and decisiveness for many Christians. But it would be a miscalculation to offer clarity without the balance of humility.

The balance to aim for is clarity without superiority. Giving the gift of clarity in the current climate of ambiguity is like handing an official road map to people lost in a large metropolitan city. Offering lost people a map and pointing them in the direction they desire to go is courteous and helpful. Suggestions about the routes they might take to get to their destination will be appreciated. That kind of clarity will instill peace of mind.

Drawing people a personal map and telling them where they need to go is another matter. This is especially so when people are not even sure they are lost. Instead of being grateful for direction, people will bristle and think to themselves, "Where does this know-it-all get the right to tell me where to go?"

When we **impose** maps on people and prescribe how they should believe, we step across the line. Rather than offering clarity, we convey superiority. Although our intentions may be honorable, anything that says "I am better than you are" will simply cause people to disregard the recommended direction.

Still, Christians have every right to live with confidence about the rightness of their beliefs. Although it would be preposterous to contend that Christianity is the only game in town, it is still desirable to champion Christianity as the best game in town.

Because, on the surface, this sounds like simply another statement of superiority, it is important to ask ourselves in what sense Christianity is "best." Simply talking about the goodness of the faith will not convince anyone that it's the best game in town. Neither is it defensible simply to reduce evangelism to the proclamation of truth and the invitation to embrace theoretical claims. If ever there was a time for evangelistically concerned Christians to **practice** the faith they treasure, the time is now. Words without deeds are not be-lievable. Seeking to save souls without also wanting to feed hungry bodies misrepresents the faith. Worship without works amounts to collective selfishness. Bible study to the neglect of compassionate service is narcissistic. Prayer as an end in itself is virtuous but inadequate. Applauding the merits of personal faith without applying the truth of the gospel to social justice concerns is fraudulent.

However, a **holistic** gospel will be good news in these times. The faith—affirmed as both word and deed, as both personal experience and social action—will make sense to people. The holistic invitation to love God with heart, soul, mind, and strength, and our neighbors as themselves, will still hold appeal.

In the February 6, 1994 issue of the *Toronto Star*, Tom Harpur presents a challenging and instructive perspective. "The world is begging for transformation. We need the moral strength to match the advances of a technology that has outpaced our wisdom; we need the courage to make the global village a just and livable reality. We can only do this together."[23]

The golden rule resolve

In the coming decade, the pursuit of principled pluralism will be fraught with progress and setbacks, successes and failures. Whatever the circumstances, however, we have a code of conduct which can offer stability. In the midst of ambiguity, when dazed by the maze of options or confused by unresolved complexity, opt for the golden rule. In situations where questions outnumber answers, when standing with a sense of confidence seems impossible, God has provided a reliable touchstone: "In everything do to others as you would have them do to you." (Matthew 7:22)

◆ Demonstrating a Believable Alternative ◆

Chapter Seven

Introduction

Can a divided church have anything to say to a culture committed to diversity? Can a segment of society which claims a shared spiritual identity, but informally has difficulty getting along, contribute to the well-being of the society as a whole?

During Jesus' final hours on earth with his disciples, he prayed that his followers would work out their relationship with the world and be unified among themselves. (John 17:1–26) In Jesus' mind, the question of unity among his followers had enormous implications. He likened the relationship he had with God in heaven to what he hoped and prayed would exist between his followers on earth. Jesus prayed, "As you are in me and I am in you, may they also be in us." (21) He then linked the issue of how his followers related to each other, with whether or not "the world would believe" that he was sent from heaven to earth. (21, 23)

Just as it is crucial for Canadians to affirm their core culture, the time has come for Canadian Christians to affirm their common life in Christ. Affirming our common life in Christ should not entail disregarding doctrinal distinctives or minimizing the differences that form our various spiritual styles. Neither should it invite an innocuous oneness that blends and blurs deeply held convictions into lusterless faith. Affirming and even celebrating our common life in Christ does not mean working toward sameness. Rather, it means showing the world that our differences do not need to divide us. At the very least, it involves surrendering attitudes of spiritual superiority that engender judgment, and living with positive regard for each other's claim to be followers of Jesus. Affirming our common life in Christ requires linking arms across denominational lines and our Christian religious traditions. It means looking at creation with a sense of wonder while standing close to the cross with genuine humility. Affirming our common life in Christ includes embracing shared values, turning from sin, overcoming evil with good, celebrating the sacraments, and pursuing justice on earth. And in these pluralistic times, it also involves giving permission and taking permission. Celebrating our life in Christ includes dealing with diversity across our denominational and Christian religious traditions.

Continuing to promote a divided church nurtures Christian competition and diverts energy from the common mission of the church. Accepting a diverse church extends the church's ability to incorporate a wider range of people and to reach the world. Affirming the diversity of the church is the better way. Then all God's people are free to carve out space for their own beliefs while making sure there is room for the beliefs of other visible Christians who also love God and desire to live faithfully in today's world. Only then will all members of God's family have the personal and organizational space they need to be true to God and themselves.

◆ A. Smorgasbord spirituality ◆

While churches continue to wrestle with each other and disrupt life in society around them, spiritual searching and experimentation abound. Citing a "massive search for meaning in life," and profiling types of New Age Spirituality, the cover of *Maclean's* proclaimed the appearance of "The New Spirituality."[1] *Newsweek*'s cover championed the same pursuit under the banner, "The Search for the Sacred."[2] In another expression of spiritual interest, after decades of quiet existence on the fringes of audio culture, recordings of Gregorian chant burst onto the pop charts. One disc featuring monks from Catalonia recently sold over five million copies.[3]

Since January 20, 1994, the Airport Vineyard Church has been "host to a renewing move of God that has brought a long-awaited revival of faith, hope and love... There has been a most notable release of freedom and healing, joy and power—every night but Mondays. By the first of September, 1994, conservative estimates count a cumulative attendance total of 90,000; 30,000 first-time attenders." Over 4,000 pastors, spouses and leaders from the United States, Britain, South America, Asia, Africa, New Zealand and Australia have experienced what the British press labels "The Toronto Blessing." An account of the Canadian spiritual hot spot is reported in a book, ironically published in England, entitled *Catch the Fire*.[4]

Author Guy Chevreau describes the current happenings: "The various physical and emotional manifestations that literally thousands upon thousands have experienced—uncontrollable laughter, 'drunkenness' in the Spirit, intense weeping, falling on the floor, physical convulsions or 'jerks,' pogoing and bouncing, shouting and roaring, visions, prophetic words and announcements."[5] Although some of the manifestations extend beyond the reach of my spiritual comfort zone, a visit to the Vineyard and discussions with others makes one conclude that God is obviously present in the phenomena.

Reflecting on the current interest in spirituality generally, Roman Catholic bishop Remi de Roo of Victoria observes that "while the physical membership of churches is collapsing all around us, that doesn't mean people are less religious. It's fascinating how words like 'values,' 'soul,' and 'spirit' are coming back into discourse."[6]

The current spiritual smorgasbord is consistent with the postmodern mood that is emerging throughout today's society. People have hungry hearts anxious to taste a spiritual reality that transcends the rational. But when reason is dethroned and experience rules the day, other forms of excess can invade the void. One can only wonder if the corrective to past rational control needs to be going on unreflective spiritual binge. The present need for spiritual discernment is self-evident.

While there is interest and openness to spirituality in society, the country's historic churches are struggling. Front-page newspaper coverage declared that the United Church of Canada, the country's largest Protestant church, "should focus its spiritual energies on God and talk less about politics and global issues if it wants to reverse a continuing and rather drastic decline in membership." In a report based on a survey of 2,400 members, Reginald Bibby predicts an attendance free-fall to less than one-third the church's present size by the year 2015.[7]

While Catholics and mainline Protestant churches are figuring out how to deal with their declines, the country's conservative evangelical churches are either holding their own or showing modest growth. Proclaiming the enduring truth of the scriptures, inviting people to experience Jesus, and calling for clear commitment, evangelical churches are finding ways to attract and retain members.

But it is the country's ethnic churches that are experiencing rapid expansion. During the past 30 years, the Chinese community has started a new church every 45 days. Fueled by immigration and because they offer people places to know God and enjoy each other, the future looks promising for a broad range of ethnic churches.

No thoughtful Christian would dispute the right of different churches to exist. Diversity within the Christian family is a celebrated point of strength. But if we are going to call for discernment on other matters, we must also observe that, although all churches are equally valid, they are not all equally effective. There are differences, especially if one criterion for effectiveness is the importance of faith in day-to-day living. (*See Fig. 7.1*)

The differences are not limited to just denominational affiliation. Regional variations are significant. Those over 55 years of age value the link between their faith and their daily living far more than younger Canadians. The gap between males and females is illuminating, if not startling. The fact that eight out of ten who attend church weekly also ascribe importance to implementing the theory of their faith into the practice of their lives is a statement of coherence for those who worship frequently.

A casual approach to spirituality will not be enough to establish a coherent faith in the complexity of these times. Churches and individual members will be wise to beware of a weightless God. Reducing God to a junior partner in the religious enterprise will be a mistake. Scaling down the gospel to accommodate the spirit of

Fig. 7.1

"My religious faith is very important to me in my day-to-day life."

Percent who "Agree strongly" or "Moderately agree"

By Region

National	B.C.	Alta.	Sask. Man.	Ont.	Que.	Atlantic
33	25	31	31	33	36	42

By Age

18–34	35–54	55+
22	32	49

By Gender

Female	Male
40	26

By Church Attendance

National	Weekly	Monthly	Occasional	Never
33	79	38	22	12

By Denomination

R.C.	Angl.	United	Luth. Presby.	Conserv.	World Rel.	No Rel.
40	29	22	33	63	30	14

Angus Reid Group: July '94. N = 1502

the age will not give the church much of a future. A clear commitment to a consequential God and a substantial gospel will nurture an adequate faith capable of meeting the demands of the age.

Whatever the organizational label, however, unless God orchestrates a genuine spiritual turnaround, it will be as difficult for the organized church to maintain its following as it was for TSN (The Sports Network) to maintain its audience without Major League Baseball and The National Hockey League. Missiologist Lesslie Newbigin rightly contends that, when a society enters a stage following "the rejection of Christianity, [the society] is far more resistant to the gospel than the pre-Christian paganism with which cross-cultural missions have been familiar."[8] "Christianity will once again need to prove itself deliberately as a faith which is not self-evident; it will be forced to distinguish itself more sharply" from the dominant cultural ethos.[9]

In the coming years, both the socialization of faith and the simple invitation to believe will be inadequate to nurture a strong church and a believing society. Even in the family, the transmission of faith from parents to children will be intercepted by the culture. As a result, children will not necessarily appropriate the faith of their parents. Explaining the intent of the Creator and the purpose of the cross, and then inviting belief, will not be enough. The church and its people must reestablish the plausibility of Christian belief. The credibility of the faith will again have to become a common assumption if the majority of the nation is to be inspired to believe deeply.

◆ B. Cultural contributors in the past ◆

In the past, the church served the culture in the same way lighthouses served ships making their way to their destinations. They provided direction and protection. The collective voice of the church warned of danger and helped followers navigate through life.

If it were possible to abolish evil and do away with sin, we could also eliminate the need for lighthouses. A revolution of goodness is a splendid thought, but the atrocities and aberrations of modern life preclude such optimism. Citing the reality of evil does not deny the reality of goodness that also pervades the world. But it does acknowledge, in the words of James Q. Wilson, that the underlying human "moral sense is not a strong beacon of light radiating outward to illuminate in sharp outline all that it touches. It is rather, a small candle flame, casting vague and multiple shadows, flickering and sputtering in the strong winds of power and passion, greed and ideology. Brought close to the heart and cupped in one's hands, it dispels the darkness and warms the soul,"[10] but it does not stem the tide of evil in today's world.

Although the following comment by Larry L. Rasmussen was originally aimed at the United States, in this case, it also applies to Canada: "Our society currently lives from moral fragments and

Fig. 7.2
Cherished Social Values
Percent viewing as "Very Important"

	Honesty	Forgiveness	Generosity
Frequent Attenders	76	75	51
Non-Attenders	61	48	33

Bibby & Posterski: Project Teen Canada '92[12]

community fragments only, and both are being destroyed faster than they are being replenished...Ours is a season of moral sprawl and breakdown, moral homelessness and drift."[11]

The research conclusions from studies on Canada's youth reveal moral sprawl and drift inside our own borders. Reasoning that the church has been a significant source of influence for social values in the past, the studies confirm that participation in church life affirms our cherished social values while absence from involvement in the church contributes to the erosion of these same values. Clearly, compared to those who separate themselves from the influence of the church, young people who attend church regularly value more highly the virtues of honesty, forgiveness, and generosity. (*See Fig. 7.2*)

Conceding to the marginalization of formal religion in the culture is inescapable. Finding a means, other than the church, for bringing the positive good the church brought to the culture is another matter. The intent of contrasting those who attend church with those who absent themselves from church life is not to portray the church as the only source of positive social values. However, it does raise the concern that, while we as a society have pushed the church to the sidelines of culture, there is no evidence we have been intentional about proposing effective alternatives. Other analysis has resulted in the conclusion that television not only serves as a source of entertainment but also stands as the dominant cultural lighthouse in modern society.[13] Alas, the importance of defining and affirming Canada's core commitments and values emerge again as a critical task.

Those of us who continue to live as visible church-attending

Christians can still have confidence in our source of light. We also have every reason to continue to communicate with those in the culture who may be open to taking another look at what they have disregarded or discarded.

◆ C. Coherence in complexity ◆

We are better at taking life apart than we are at putting it back together again. Increasing numbers of people seem to specialize as critics. Critiquing what is wrong comes naturally to them. Just as tearing apart a malfunctioning lawnmower is easier than repairing and reassembling the pieces into a clean cutting machine, it is simpler to diagnose what is wrong in Canadian society than it is to advance solutions.

Modern life is complex and often confusing. Applauding the pluralistic privilege of having many choices is admirable, but it can also be exhausting. When there seem to be no right answers and very few fixed points of reference, finding one's way is difficult. The idea of limitless alternatives sounds inviting, but it is also a script for endless unresolved questioning. A world in which "personal preference is principle" and "principle is personal preference" contains little hope for stability. When everything is possible and nothing is certain, life feels as if it is spinning on the edge of chaos. No wonder maneuvering through the modern world can seem like paddling a canoe in perpetual white water.

One aspect of the Christian faith that makes it plausible is that it holds the potential to make sense out of life. Credible Christianity does not shrink the complexities of modern existence to simplistic equations and answers. Questions continue to outnumber answers. Ambiguities remain and some pieces of life refuse to fit together. Still, the gift of coherence can be one benefit for people who take Christ and his teachings seriously. Coherence in the midst of complexity is available to those who pursue the goal of spiritual integration. At the same time, people who are able to articulate and demonstrate spiritual integration contribute to both the plausibility and credibility of the faith.

Scholar Diogenes Allen asserts that in this pluralistic and postmodern world, "Christianity is intellectually relevant. It is relevant to the fundamental questions, Why does the world exist?

and Why does it have its present order, rather than another? It is relevant to the discussion of the foundations of morality and society, especially on the significance of human beings."[14]

The relevance of the faith is not simply an intellectual matter. God's redemptive reach touches the whole person and extends to the renewing of an evil and broken world. While God's revelation feeds the mind, encountering Christ and experiencing the inner presence of God's spirit touches the heart. Teaching and preaching offer clear guidance for godly decision making and behavior that translate theory into practice. In the faith, Christian scholarship and visionary leaders find a solid framework within which they can think deeply and plan boldly to transform unjust structures into equitable forces for good.

In the coming years, all Christians will need to use this framework of faith to interpret and cope with the changes which will be made to the Canadian social fabric. For example, Canada's enormous public debt is compromising the country's long-term future. Governments at every level are scrambling to control costs and reduce spending. One major area of social spending, and of future spending cuts, is our nationally-cherished universal health care system, which has an annual cost for every Canadian citizen in excess of $2,000.[15]

This profoundly humane but technologically expensive approach to enhancing and extending life is a marvelous benefit. Yet, an examination of the escalating costs reveals what one would expect. An astonishing amount of the monies expended on health care are spent on people in the latter stages of life.[16] As Christians we must ask some probing and perhaps disturbing questions: for example, "Can our Christian faith contribute anything to our perspective on where and how future cutbacks might happen?"

Christians believe that death is not the end of the journey; the reality of death is always interwoven with the promise of life after death. The questions which emerge from this realization are even harder. If God's people really believe what they claim to believe, should this affect how we use medical services in the final stages of life? Can we as Christians not only choose to die with dignity, but also to intentionally minimize the expenses we incur as we die?

Admittedly, the complexities of modern medical technology

defy our ability to even propose consistent guidelines. And the medical oath dictates the preservation of life. These are complicated and delicate concerns, but the faith is given to inform our decision-making on all matters of life and death.

It is highly unlikely that anyone will find personal spiritual coherence in the maze of the modern world without involvement in a church. While solitary, personal experiences of God are valid, the movement toward spiritual wholeness requires the wisdom and support of a faith community. So too, if churches hope to transform, in any significant way, the structures of the world, they will have to unite or form coalitions to express their social vision and influence.

People do not expect to govern themselves without political institutions; they cannot earn their livelihoods without economic institutions; they cannot even participate in their "private" leisure activities—reading books, playing golf, watching television—without the benefit of social institutions. Religious life is no different. Those who pursue spirituality apart from involvement in specific churches or synagogues nevertheless depend heavily on the fact that these institutions exist.[17] Peter Berger agrees: "Religious institutions are necessary to provide a plausibility structure for religious beliefs. In this, once more, religion is not unique; every belief requires such social support."[18] For those who take faith seriously, the role of the organized church becomes especially important at a time when fewer people in the society embrace religious commitment.

◆ D. Distinctive in the midst of multi-mindedness ◆

In the midst of cultural and Christian complexity, God's people, who confirm the credibility of the faith, will not only struggle with cultural dilemmas, they will also figure out how to live with distinctiveness. Instead of climbing into the cultural blender, they will carve out places to stand. They will be different. While living in the maze of alternatives, their attitudes, ambitions and behaviors will be identifiable.

As much as Christianity may be about belief, and as much as it may be about experience, it is also about how to live.[19] The gospel is not just a set of interesting ideas about which we are supposed to make up our minds. The gospel is **intrusive** news that evokes a

Fig. 7.3

Attitudes toward God and faith

Percent responding "agree strongly"

	Committed Participants	**Conditional** Participants	**Cultural** Christians	**No** Religion
I feel God is the source and sustainer of everything.	72	71	36	17
God is understanding and forgiving.	88	84	56	27
I have felt God's presence in my life.	68	64	29	16
I feel God is looking out for me personally.	65	68	31	14
I have an intense personal relationship with God.	49	40	13	7
My religious faith is very important to me in my day-to-day life.	68	63	24	14

Angus Reid Group: July '94. N = 1253

new set of principles, a complex of habits, and a way of living in the world.[20] Particularly in the midst of multi-mindedness, the invitation to place one's faith in Christ not only offers direction for decision making, but also an enhanced ability to live differently.

A comparison of the attitudes Canadians hold toward God, the way they respond to forgiveness issues, and their views on ethical matters is revealing. Using the four categories of Canadians discussed in chapter one—committed and conditional participants, cultural Christians, and those who claim no religious affiliation—the following data documents significant differences between those groups of people. *(See Fig. 7.3)*

The line of distinction is clear. Those who attend church regularly hold different attitudes and perceptions than those who absent themselves from involvement in church life. The "committed" and "conditional participants" hold highly positive views of God, and for two out of three, their faith is important in their day-to-day life.

Fig. 7.4

Forgiveness and compassion issues

Percent responding "agree strongly" and "agree moderately"

	Committed Participants	**Conditional** Participants	**Cultural** Christians	**No** Religion
If I had a spouse who was unfaithful, I would be committed to reconcile the relationship.	63	59	53	56
If someone harms me I will try to get even.	17	21	24	31
If the actions of a drunk driver resulted in the death of a member of my family, I would eventually forgive that person.	53	52	33	36
If a guest in my home stole something from my house, I would forbid that person from entering my home again.	55	71	70	70
I feel I personally have an important responsibility to help people in poor countries around the world.	78	77	60	64

Angus Reid Group: July '94. N = 1253

As expected, those in the "no religion" category have the lowest views of God and faith. As for the vast majority of "cultural Christians"—those who identify themselves as either Catholics or Protestants but who are not active in church life—they are more similar to the "no religion" sector than to the active participants. On the bright side, approximately one out of three of the cultural Christians retain positive views about the nature of God.

When it comes to forgivness, the pattern prevails. (*See Fig. 7.4*) Church participation makes a difference. Although it could be argued that those who are formally taught "to forgive in order to be forgiven," should be higher on the forgiveness and compassion scale than they are, the differences are still both real and consistent. Whether the issue involves marital reconciliation, forgiveness for a drunk driver, or compassion for the world's poor, active church-goers are more ready to offer people a fresh start than those who

Fig. 7.5
Ethical Issues

	Committed Participants	**Conditional** Participants	**Cultural** Christians	**No** Religion
What is right and wrong is a matter of personal opinion.* **Percent responding "agree strongly" and "agree moderately."**	43	56	58	65
I would likely tell Canada Customs that I spent less money than I did on my U.S. shopping trip in order to avoid paying duty. **Percent responding "agree strongly" and "agree moderately."**	39	43	50	52
Some people think there is always a right and wrong, regardless of the situation. Other people think that sometimes choice depends on the situation. **Percent responding: "Always a right and wrong choice."**	33	31	22	20
Gambling Issues				
The social costs of legalized gambling outweigh the benefits to society (some people becoming problem gamblers and the values gambling promotes). **Percent responding: "Yes."**	68	72	58	56
Do you believe that gambling is right or wrong? (It is simply a form of entertainment; it promotes an "easy money" philosophy). **Percent responding: "Wrong."**	46	45	26	26
In an average month, how much do you yourself spend on gaming and gambling. **Percent responding: "None."**	49	50	27	39

Angus Reid Group: October '94. N = 1412 *July '94. N = 1253

distance themselves from church participation.

Canadians who regularly take time to worship and receive formal Christian teaching also live with a sense of moral oughtness. (*See Fig. 7.5*) They continue to have categories for "right" and "wrong." Compared to Canadians who detach themselves from organized religion, they are more inclined to look outside themselves for their moral standards. The views of church attenders affect their perceptions. They are more inclined to see gambling as morally wrong behavior and they resist being situational in their ethics. They also perceive that gambling is a social detriment to society, and accordingly, they spend less time standing in line to buy lottery tickets.

Isolating one particular item, such as gambling, from the three preceding charts may not be all that significant. And while one could legitimately ask, "Why aren't church-attending Christians more distinct in what they think and how they behave?" the other question you have to ask is, "What will Canadian society look like if the Christian presence continues to erode and we do not find alternate delivery systems for our collective morals and ethics?"

The data drives the conclusion that positive views of God motivate people to implement their religious faith into their day-to-day living. Consequently, the religiously committed indicate a greater willingness to exhibit forgiveness and compassion than the uncommitted. What would life be like without the virtues of compassion, forgiveness, and reconciliation? On questions of honesty, those who participate in church life are pulled toward doing the right thing. On perceptions and concerns related to gambling, it is the attenders who raise warning flags. What kind of values and lifestyles do we want to encourage in our future?

The most alarming projections from the data are linked to the contradictions exhibited by the "cultural Christians." Although these Canadians continue to say they believe God exists, although they hold orthodox views of Jesus, and self-identify as "Christians," the vast majority are spiritually indifferent. God is a marginal influence in their lives. Whether the focus is on God, forgiveness, compassion, ethics, or gambling, "cultural Christians" consistently align themselves with those Canadians who profess to have "no religion." Although cultural Christians will continue to knock on church doors and expect to receive the sacred rites of passage, although they will continue to use the church to enhance their spiritual moments, there is little evidence of active faith in their lives.

To those who now see themselves as spiritual but who are no longer actively religious, a caution must be made. Spirituality that remains only an inner affair, an adventure of the self without some form of supportive community and structure for action, quickly becomes spiritual self-indulgence or detached narcissism. The tree of true spirituality is known by its "fruits." It needs the fertilizing, pruning, and caring concern of others to develop its full potential.[21]

It is also sobering to realize that, at this stage of our history, cultural Christians make up the majority of Canada's population. They are now the group that increasingly defines society's norms. Not surprisingly, they also make up the majority of the "cocooner" segment in society. They shovel the snow to their property line and pretty much live within the boundaries of their self-interest.

"Without examples, without imitation," historian Robert Wilken writes, "there can be no human life or civilization, no art or culture, no virtue or holiness. The elementary activities of... learning to speak or sculpting a statue, have their beginning in the imitation of what others do." A society benefits from the saints among us in a similar way. "By observing the lives of holy men and women and imitating their deeds we become virtuous. Before we can become doers, we must first become spectators."[22] Is it possible that the spiritual indifference of cultural Christians has been fostered because the church has produced so few saints?

Affirming the positive influence of human modeling is not intended to create a religion without any need for God. Rather, it is to affirm the principle that the attraction of saints "is their power to lure us beyond virtue to virtue's source."[23] The scriptures concur: "You are our letter, to be known and read by all. You show that you are a letter of Christ... written not with ink but with the Spirit of the living God." (2 Corinthians 3:2–3)

God is not only the creator of all human life, but also the plus sign in people who intentionally open themselves to divine presence and power. In an ideal portrait of the Christian life, God's people, touched by God's Spirit...

Think more clearly
Feel more deeply
Speak more truthfully
Love more extravagantly
Serve more creatively
Give more lavishly.

God's people, touched by God's Spirit... live more fully. And as they do so, the faith they believe becomes more believable.

◆ E. Transcendence in life and death ◆

Transcendence is another dimension of the gospel that can make faith believable for both Christian believers and those who believe otherwise. Transcendence is the word we use to describe the fact that we can live in the here and now, and at the same time, participate with God in a reality that extends beyond ordinary experience. Transcendence is what empowers us to live with hope in the face of death; it allows us to embrace the promise that an earthly grave is not our final resting place.

For visible Christians, worship is an obvious invitation into transcendence. In worship, God steps out of divine mystery into our history, and **we** move from our history, into divine mystery.[24] What happens when we break the bread and lift the cup cannot be adequately explained. The invitation to, "Eat this in remembrance of me," and "Drink this in remembrance of me" represents more than mere ceremony or Christian duty. The sacrament is infused with mystery. The eating and the drinking transcends the rational. As a moment when the divine reaches and touches the human spirit, the sacrament reinforces the reality of God.

Many people can name books that have profoundly influenced their lives. Years ago, a book enthusiast gave me a copy of Harry Blamires', *The Christian Mind*. At the time, the main message I gleaned was that I should construct my mind out of Christian presuppositions so that I could think Christianly, and consequently behave Christianly. Sometime later, the deeper message of distinguishing between secular thinking and Christian thinking became meaningful. For Blamires, secular thinking "is to think within a frame of reference bounded by the limits of our life on earth; it is to keep one's calculations rooted in this worldly criteria." In contrast, those who practice Christian thinking will "cultivate the eternal perspective." The Christian thinker will be "supernaturally oriented and bring to bear upon earthly considerations the fact of Heaven." The Christian mind sees the "natural order as dependent upon the supernatural order."[25]

Simply stated, the Christian mind, according to Blamires, believes in miracles. Christians expect God to enter into the present. Christians are not surprised when prayers are answered. What appear to be chance meetings with people are understood as divine appointments. Impromptu telephone calls are made to people in need because of a supernatural nudge. For the Christian, God's intervention is normal. Transcendence enters the present tense.

The experience of spiritual transcendence spans the circumstances of life to the reality of death. The statement that flowed from the inner spirit of Father Sean O'Sullivan is potent. O'Sullivan served his church as a priest, and his country as a member of parliament. Even while dying of cancer, his faith transcended pain and the fear:

> I have paid the price of serious illness. Even with that pain and suffering, however, I am not afraid to live. Nor am I afraid to die. For I have the comfort of friends and the strength of my faith.
>
> I may be summoned home. But sing no sad songs for me; for I am a Christian. Without merit of my own and trusting only in [God's] abundant mercy, I go gently toward that glorious goal. To other cancer victims and their families, to Catholics and all people of goodwill, I say: Remain steadfast, keep stout hearts and hold unwavering hope. Fear not, our God is still at work. However dark the coming days, [God] will triumph and be with us always, even until the end of time.[26]

Faith becomes believable when the reality of transcendence empowers people to deal meaningfully with the obstacles of life. Faith becomes credible when the people who claim to be in touch with God are able to cling to hope in the presence of death.

◆ F. Courage to change ◆

Presenting and promoting the ideals of faith is one way to call God's people to full-fledged faith. However, we must also acknowledge that many who have taken God seriously have not been as virtuous as they think. Too often, God's committed people have been racist, sexist, elitist, or blithely uncaring about the environment or distant neighbors. A conscientious churchgoer is as susceptible as any other member of the public to interests that opportunistically work both sides of the street. "I wrestled all night with my conscience," Swiss historian Jakob Burkhardt is reputed to have announced to friends one morning, "but I won!"

When we "win" in this way, we avoid, in the first place, our responsibility to carefully form moral convictions, and in the second place, to judge those convictions we **do** form. As a community of moral conviction, whatever other tasks the church has, exercising self-criticism and throwing open the windows to hear from the unchurched should be among them.[27]

As part of this task of self-criticism, some of God's people will need to summon the courage to change how they view diversity in today's world. At this point, however, the experience of Fuller Seminary President, Richard Mouw serves as a caution. Mouw was attending a meeting at which Peter Berger was present. In the enthusiasm of his youth, Mouw made the statement that "every Christian is called to engage in radical obedience to God's program of justice, righteousness and peace." Berger, apparently, thought that Mouw was operating with a rather grandiose notion of "radical obedience." Somewhere in a retirement home, Berger replied, there is a Christian woman whose greatest fear in life is that she will humiliate herself in the cafeteria line because she is unable to control her bladder. For this woman, the greatest act of radical obedience to Jesus Christ is to place herself in the hands of a loving God every time she goes off for a meal.[28]

We do not have the right to legislate what we believe Christian obedience should be for others. We must be modest in what we expect of other people. However, because our spiritual obligation is not just to God but also to each other, we also must lift up what we believe is the best way to be faithful in these times.

Throughout this book, I have contended that people respond, or in some cases react, to diversity in different ways. The five distinct types—tribalizers, reclaimers, accommodators, cocooners, and collaborators—have repeatedly made their entrance into the text. Although the stimuli of specific issues and situations prompt us to embrace and be embraced by more than one type, each of us has a dominant way in which we view the diversity that swirls around us.

Tribalizers highly resist expressions of diversity that counter their strong views. They are instinctively judgmental. Other people's views are inherently invalid.

Reclaimers also live with strong convictions that can prevent them from understanding other people's perspectives. Their "objective" view of truth generates a confidence of conviction that can set

Fig. 7.5
An invitation to change

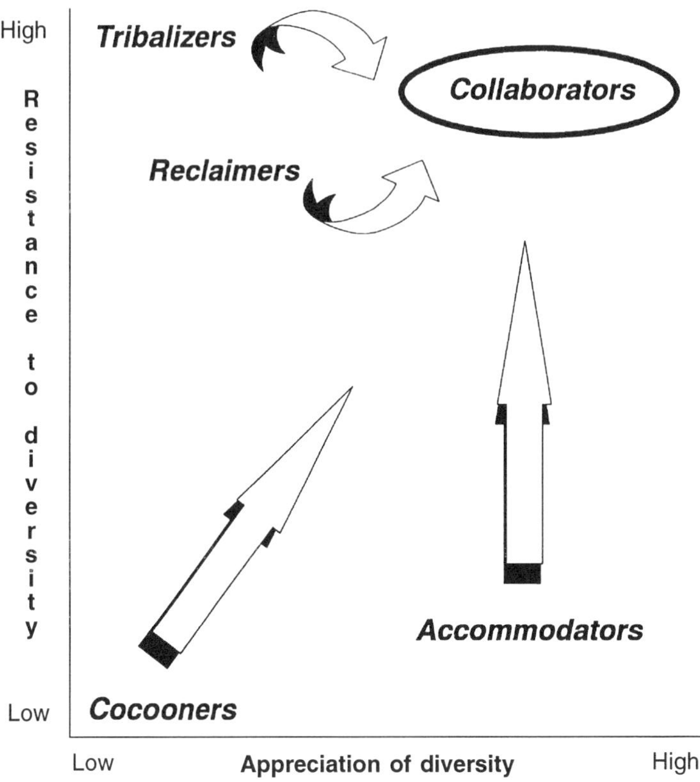

them up to alienate others who disagree with them.

Accommodators can hold fast to clear convictions, but their appreciation of diversity prompts them to be inclusive and non-judgmental. Their subjective shading of truth invites them to lean toward being permissive.

Cocooners are the spectators in society. Their focus on personal interests keeps them on the sidelines of life. If they have opinions, they pretty much keep them to themselves.

Collaborators live with a double focus. They are unapologetic about their personal convictions. At the same time, they make room in the world for the convictions of others too. They are neither permissive with themselves nor judgmental toward others.

The five cultural types are not offered as a way of pigeonholing or stereotyping people. Different situations could well push any of us from one type to another. But eventually, a pattern of responses will identify our dominant way of perceiving and responding to diversity.

At this point, then, we need to ask several key questions. Which cultural type best explains my dominant style? Am I content with how I view and respond to the diversity swirling around me? In particular, how do I treat people who are different from me? When I think about specific issues such as religion in public schools, world religions, gender equality, immigration policy, homosexuality, abortion, euthanasia, and evangelism, am I at peace with my own views? How do I think about the views of others? If I were to consider altering my views, what would hinder me from making changes? What practical things can I do to step back and take a fresh look?

Identify and evaluate your dominant type

The first step is to identify one's dominant type. When someone different enters your world, or when a group in society presses for rights that are contrary to your preferences, do you respond as a reclaimer, tribalizer, cocooner, accommodator, or collaborator? Do you think it is right to handle diversity and treat people the way you do? When the church or group you normally identify with publicly responds to controversial issues, do you sometimes disagree with the stated position? As we are able to identify and evaluate our personal patterns of response to diversity, we will be more able to be true to the self God desires us to be.

Distinguish attitudes from beliefs

Part of the good news about life and the gospel is that it is possible to alter one's attitudes without changing one's beliefs. The distinct beliefs we establish help to shape our self-definition. They are the building blocks of conscience. Attitudes are the dispositions we cultivate in our inner selves that determine how we express our beliefs outwardly. For example, I may believe that truth exists, and accordingly, I may conclude that being a father or mother of a child outside of a committed relationship is morally wrong. Holding tenaciously to that truth, however, is a separate matter from how I choose to treat a father or a mother who have no intention of living in a committed relationship. When attitudes drain the compassion out of beliefs, they produce harshness and foster alienation. When attitudes develop conviction but also engender empathy, they foster relationships and open the door to interpersonal influence.

Identify the points of control

All of us who manage to cope with the basic demands of life are subject to controls. Very few people are laws unto themselves. We have internal monitoring systems. Our beliefs and values, our ethics and morals frame the decisions we make and the behaviors we express. Society also sets limits and imposes consequences for behavior outside its limits.

One of the controls for visible Christians may be the influence and standards of the church they attend. Many Christians behave as their churches either formally or informally require. This is the case for those who lean toward the conservative or liberal side of the faith, or for others who think they are balanced between the two poles. Other followers of Jesus may be primarily influenced by what their parents taught them, what their friends think is right, by the biases of their minister's preaching, or by what they sincerely believe the Bible teaches. Those who live with closed systems and exclusive views of truth will be controlled by those systems and their convictions of truth.

Whatever the sources of control, it is impossible to think insightfully about making changes in the future until there is clarity about who or what influences determine the present.

Consider the people in your life

Resistance to change is almost automatic for many people. When invited to alter how we perceive the world around us, we often put up stop signs. When we reflect on shifts we have made in the past, however, we usually find a correlation between the people in our lives and the changes we have adopted. This is particularly true when members of our families, or other people who are close to us, expose us to expressions of diversity we have previously disputed.

Until recently, people who got divorced faced both social stigma and formal exclusion from many churches. As divorce has become more frequent, it has also become more accepted in society and in many churches. In the future, those churches that continue to exclude divorced people from full-fledged status will likely alter their positions too. Particularly as family members and people in close relationships with the church decision-makers experience divorce, those in charge will be influenced to be more inclusive.

The power of the personal profoundly affects us. When we know people by name who are different from us, and they know us by name, perceptions start to shift. When accommodators have close contact with reclaimers, and collaborators share personal experiences with tribalizers, influence will flow.

Take time to reflect with God

Ironically, many Christians have reputations for being rigid. One would think that growth in one's faith would inspire a continual series of Spirit-led changes. A few years ago, a common slogan stated, "God isn't finished with me yet." God is a change agent. The divine agenda is to fashion newness. God's history includes new songs, new covenants, new commandments, new wineskins, new births, a new earth, and eventually a new heaven. God is a re-creation specialist. God's promises ring with hope, "A new heart I will give you and a new spirit I will put within you." (Ezekiel 36:26) "Therefore we will not fear, though the earth should change, though the mountains shake in the heart of the sea, though its waters roar and foam, though the mountains tremble with its tumult." (Psalm 46:2–3)

Does this mean a shift from one cultural type to another is on God's agenda for everyone? Obviously not. Praying and taking time with God will reveal what God desires. We can be assured that if God wishes us to change how we think and feel about people and the diversity around us, the courage to change can be there too.

God is more like a dynamic verb than a static noun. Just as it is impossible to know what it is like to take a train trip by simply studying the timetables, so it is impossible to experience the reality of God without taking the journey of faith.[29] In dealing with the dynamics of diversity, from which there is no escape in today's world, the journey of faith may involve moving into new cultural space. My hope is that increasing numbers of God's people will be convinced that living faithfully on this earth, at this time, involves a commitment to collaborate with others, whether we agree with them or not.

In the future, there will always be room in society and in God's family for the five specified types. The present cultural mood may even favor churches whose spiritual style rings with reclaimer and tribalizer tones. When times are uncertain and the social environment is easily polarized, many people find voices of certainty and a strong measure of dogmatism reassuring. But we must ask ourselves, how many people will be pushed away from the faith because of the alienation dogmatism engenders in this multiminded age? In contrast, churches that place themselves in the accommodator category will render themselves ineffective if they run so far from anything sounding dogmatic that they end up being convinced about almost nothing. Ambiguity in the midst of uncertainly does not and will not incite commitment.

In the long term, it will be Christians and churches who are ready to deal constructively with the differences surrounding them that will demonstrate the kind of faith that will engage a pluralistic society. They will be neither judgmental nor permissive. Instead of alienating people who are different from themselves, they will lift the level of life and relationships to a point where mutual respect can be genuinely exchanged. In the future, it will be "collaborator" churches and individuals who will most effectively and redemptively reach those who today resist the reign of God in their lives.

◆ G. Communities of diversity ◆

This chapter began with the question, "Can a divided church have anything to say to a culture committed to diversity?" A second series of questions addressed the plausibility and credibility of the faith in the modern world. In response, the preceding pages have acknowledged the smorgasbord of spirituality that pervades today's world. Although in the past, the role of the church had greater prominence in society, the faith still stands with strength and viability.

As local churches across the land increasingly become communities of diversity, God's people will have more to say to the culture. When church leaders and denominational spokespeople more gracefully affirm leaders from other churches and faith communities, people in the culture will see another reason to believe that the faith is credible in this age.

Community welcomes diversity: Like other groups, whenever people come together to participate in church life, they bring their differences with them. They only become a community as they develop regard for each other and begin to function productively together. Healthy churches have a clear sense of the common beliefs and commitments that frame their identity. They also know that excessive sameness reduces people to clone-like robots. In order to keep healthy, they welcome a measure of diversity. Images of church and community include people like ourselves; but they also conjure up pictures of people of all colors and shapes and ages, of women, men, and children speaking different languages, following different customs, practicing different habits, but all worshiping the same Lord.[30]

Community balances individualism: Communities are made up of individuals. In community, individuals are protected from the vices of excessive individualism. In churches, different people with unique gifts gather together in the name of Christ. They do not surrender their individuality, but neither do they parade their individual prowess. Particularly in today's world, when individualism so often pushes aside the value of collective life, a commitment to community serves as a check and balance. Communities of faith are places where people bring their contributions of ministry, as gifts to each other. And everyone involved benefits.

Community authenticates privatized spirituality: Community "is God's visible sign of salvation" in the world.[31] That statement is not a judgment against those who claim to love God but who choose to absent themselves from organized church life. It does, however, posit a preference. While privatized spirituality has value, it is a precarious way to make the journey of faith. Ideally, those who are now finding their own way spiritually would bring their enthusiasm and insight into their respective churches to help the renewal that is needed there. Failing that, those who value faith will be wise to at least become a part of a small group of like-minded believers.[32]

Creating heaven on earth

One of the common expressions of faith that transcends all Christian differences, everywhere, is the Lord's Prayer. Across the country and around the world, again and again God's people pray, "Thy will be done... on earth as it is in heaven." C. S. Lewis rightly reminds us that, in the end, there are only two kinds of people: those who say to God, "Thy will be done," and those to whom God says, in the end, "Thy will be done."[33]

Accordingly, a central commitment of the church must be to participate in the work of creating heaven on earth. The church must work to bring the ways of God into both the beauty and twistedness of life. Pope John Paul II states, "The truth about God the Creator of the world, about Christ the Redeemer, is a powerful force which inspires a positive attitude toward creation and provides a constant impetus to strive for its transformation and perfection."[34]

Although, because we are human, we will always live with less than perfection, God's impetus can motivate us to reach for the reality of heaven on earth. The Creator's presence in us can energize us to re-create what God intended in the first place. The Redeemer's vision can inspire us to transform brokenness into wholeness.

Can there be anything more godly than to live this side of heaven with a vision for reconciliation? The life of Jesus and the purpose of the cross centers on reconciliation. Instead of alienation, the cross proposes peace. Is there anything more beautiful than to watch forgiveness replace hate, justice overwhelm injustice, and love chase away prejudice? Rather than splintering and fracturing and tearing life apart, reconciliation seeks to heal and restore. In the face of racism or classism or sexism, reconciliation spawns understanding and solicits mutuality. When the spirit of reconciliation is set free, differences between people are not just tolerated. The reconciling presence of Christ resolves those differences so that diverse people can treat each other with respect.

"Thy will be done... on earth as it is in heaven."

◆ Conclusion ◆

Paradigm for living in cultural pluralism

In the beginning, God created the heavens and the earth... and ever since that time, people who have lived with a commitment to serve the God of the universe have sought to figure out what to believe and how to behave. As every age in history is unique, so too the circumstances in our current culture are unique. And just as others who have gone before us have found their ways to be faithful, we can live in the pluralistic multi-mindedness of the modern world and find our ways too.

Trust God and follow Christ

The Christian way begins with God. Those who are created not only acknowledge the Creator, they allow the God who conceived and shaped the world to shape their lives too. They are convinced that God is good and fair and just. In quiet moments, they sometimes deal with doubts and wonder if the whole Christian scheme can be trusted. Still, Christians in the modern world continue to count on the uniqueness of Christ and the drama of the cross. They keep saying "yes" to Jesus' invitation to "Come unto me."

Be true to yourself

People who are in touch with God also have inside information about themselves. They can know what is healthy and strong and good. Followers of Jesus also know what is weak and wrong. They seek to discern God's truth about themselves as well as about issues in the world. Those who take the time to do so carve out convictions concerning what is important to them. They self-define. Because of their connectedness to God, they know what they believe, who they are, and how they aspire to behave. They are true to themselves. Without apology, they speak with a clear voice in a multi-voiced society.

Give regard to others

Although Christians are ready to take a stand, they are also committed to stand with others. The scriptures press them "not only to look out for their own interests, but also the interests of others." (Philippians 2:4) Rooted in the security of their own convictions, God's people extend compassion to others who are different from themselves. They know that the world God created belongs to everyone. They make room for others whose views differ from their own. Diversity is valued. Committed Christians are neither permissive toward themselves nor judgmental toward others. They realize that, rather than coercing creation, God gives people choices; they aim to treat people like God treats people.

Relinquish rights for the common good

Although Christians believe their way of understanding life is right and best, for the sake of the common good, they also believe in relinquishing rights. God's people reject the notion that one particular voice can speak for everyone. In a democratic and pluralistic society, no single sector has the divine right to rule. But neither can a society be built exclusively on diversity. Individual and group autonomy must surrender to the collective good. Personal preferences need to bow to measures of community control. Beyond the requirement to live within the boundaries of the criminal code, all citizens must be willing to sacrifice private desires for shared public goals.

Fly your flag in the pluralism parade

A democratic society invites its citizens to participate. Consequently, one prerogative of life in Canada is the freedom to influence public policy. A pluralistic culture provides social structures for cradling diversity. Accordingly, people who are different from each other can live together in the same society.

Christians and those who believe otherwise have the same privilege to self-define. As we live together in the midst of our multi-mindedness, pursuing “principled pluralism” will help us live peaceably and productively with our increasing diversity. As all members of society both **take** permission to be true to themselves and **give** permission to others to be true to themselves, we will stand together on level cultural ground. Only then will we be free to unabashedly fly our multi-colored flags in the pluralism parade.

Love and lobby

Christian flags are multi-colored too. Although members of God’s family believe in the same Creator and Redeemer, differences mark their lives. Even though they are embraced by the same Spirit and nurtured by the truth of the same faith, God’s extended family is profoundly diverse. It is multi-colored. But Christians are also marked with some common colors. Their shared life in Christ generates common commitments. In these pluralistic and multi-minded times, people of faith are called to live a life of love and to lobby for the ways of God. How else can “thy will be done... on earth as it is in heaven...”?

◆ Notes ◆

Preface

1. Katherine Paterson, *Gates of Excellence* (New York: E.P. Dutton, 1988), 63.
2. Jacques Ellul, *The Presence of the Kingdom* (Colorado Springs: Helmers and Howard, 1989), 35.

Introduction

1. Leszek Kolakowski, *Modernity on Endless Trial* (Chicago: University of Chicago Press, 1990), 70.
2. Jeffrey Simpson, *Faultlines: Struggling for a Canadian Vision* (Toronto: HarperCollins Publishers Ltd, 1992), x.

Chapter One

1. Michel Foucault, "Two Lectures," *Power Knowledge, Selected Interviews and Other Writings 1972–77*, C. Gordon, ed. (New York: Pantheon Books, 1980), 80.
2. From the *King James Bible* © 1977, Thomas Nelson, Inc. Publishers.
3. Charles H. Long, "Worlds, and Other: The Search of Utopian Unities," *Pushing the Faith: Proselytism and Civility in a Pluralistic World*, Martin E. Marty and Frederick E. Greenspahn, eds. (New York: Crossroad, 1988), 3.
4. Angus Reid Group, July 1994. A survey sample of a representative cross-section of 1502 (N = 1502) Canadian adults, providing an overall margin of error of plus or minus 2.5 percentage points, statistically reliable in each major region of Canada. Within each province, the sample is stratified by census division, and households are selected from a computer-based sample using a modified random digit dialing procedure. The survey data are statistically weighted to adjust for the slight intentional over-sampling in Quebec and B.C., and to ensure the sample's age and gender composition reflects that of the actual adult Canadian population according to the 1991 Census.
5. This designation was first defined by Donald C. Posterski and Irwin Barker in *Where's a Good Church?* (Winfield, B.C.: Wood Lake Books, 1993), 15.
6. Statistics Canada, *The Daily*, 1991 Census of Canada, 5.
7. Stephen L. Carter, *The Culture of Disbelief* (New York: BasicBooks, 1993), 22.

8. Larry L. Rasmussen, *Moral Fragments and Moral Community* (Minneapolis: Fortress Press, 1993), 28.
9. Gordon W. Allport, "The Religious Context of Prejudice," *Journal for the Scientific Study of Religion* 5 (1966), 434.
10. Reginald W. Bibby, *Unknown Gods* (Stoddart: Toronto, 1993), 132.
11. Elton Trueblood, *The Predicament of Modern Man* (New York and London: Harper and Brothers, 1944), 59–60.
12. Bryan Wilson, *Religion in Secular Society* (London: Penguin, 1969), 14.
13. Philip E. Johnson, "Nihilism and the End of Law," *First Things* (March 1993), 20.
14. Donald C. Posterski, from a paper entitled, "Affirming the Truth of the Gospel: Anglicans in Pluralist Canada," presented at the ESSENTIALS '94 conference in Montreal, June 1994.
15. Peter L. Berger, *A Far Glory: The Quest for Faith in an Age of Credulity* (New York: Doubleday, 1992), 28.
16. Berger, *Far Glory*, 125.
17. Berger, *Far Glory*, 67.
18. Berger, *Far Glory*, 125.
19. Berger, *The Heretical Imperative* (Garden City, New York: Anchor Press, 1979), 16.
20. Albert Borgmann, *Technology and the Character of Contemporary Life: A Philosophical Inquiry* (Chicago: University of Chicago Press, 1984), 35, 41.
21. Benton Johnson, "Modernity and Pluralism," in *Pushing the Faith*, 17.
22. One of the assumptions postmodernists do not accept is the validity of "meta-narratives," the use of grand-scale stories such as creation and redemption to explain history and reality.
23. Foucault, *Power Knowledge*, 80.
24. Cited by Richard Gwyn, "Managing the world's new 'tribalism,'" *Regina Leader Post*, August 3, 1994.
25. Lesslie Newbigin, *Truth to Tell: The Gospel as Public Truth* (Grand Rapids: Eerdmans, 1991), 68.
26. Richard Niebuhr, *Christ and Culture* (New York: Harper & Row, 1951), 39–44.
27. The term "cocooning" was recently popularized by Faith Popcorn in the book, *The Popcorn Report*.
28. David J. Garrow, *Bearing the Cross* (New York: Vintage Books, 1988), 71.
29. Glenn A. Watson, "The Report of the Ministerial Inquiry on Religious Education in Ontario Public Elementary Schools," January 1990, 62.
30. "Religion in the Public School Curriculum: Questions and Answers, National Council on Religion and Public Education," Springfield, Missouri, n.d.

31. Watson, "The Report," 69.
32. Watson, "The Report," 2–3.
33. Watson, "The Report," 91.
34. Allan Thompson, "Ottawa takes Jesus out of daily prayer," *Toronto Star*, February 19, 1994.
35. From a birthday card received from World Vision Canada staff colleagues John and Dorothy Howat.

Chapter Two

1. Donald C. Posterski and Irwin Barker, *Where's a Good Church?* (Winfield, B.C.: Wood Lake Books, 1993), 103.
2. *Webster's Ninth New Collegiate Dictionary* (Toronto: Thomas Allen & Son, 1991), 1061.
3. J.I. Packer, *Hot Tub Religion* (Wheaton: Tyndale House Publishers, 1988), 13.
4. David F. Wells, *No Place for Truth or Whatever Happened to Evangelical Theology* (*Grand Rapids*: Eerdmans, 1993), cited in *Current Thoughts and Trends*, Special Report #18, July 1994.
5. Frederick Buechner, *Telling Secrets* (San Francisco: HarperCollins, 1991), 105.
6. Lesslie Newbigin, *The Gospel in a Pluralistic Society* (Grand Rapids: Eerdmans, 1989), 13.
7. —, *Truth to Tell: The Gospel as Public Truth* (Grand Rapids: Eerdmans, 1991), 32.
8. Richard J. Mouw, *Distorted Truth: What Every Christian Needs to Know About the Battle for the Mind* (San Francisco: Harper & Row, 1989), 145.
9. Newbigin, *The Gospel*, 9.
10. Alister E. McGrath, "The Challenge of Pluralism for the Contemporary Christian Church," proceedings of the Wheaton Theology Conference (1992), 233.
11. Peter L. Berger, *A Far Glory: The Quest for Faith in an Age of Continuity* (New York: Free Press, 1992), 45.
12. S.D. Gaede, *When Tolerance Is No Virtue* (Downers Grove: InterVarsity Press, 1993), 46.
13. Reginald Bibby, *Mosaic Madness* (Toronto: Stoddart, 1990), 9.
14. Lesslie Newbigin, *Foolishness to the Greeks* (Grand Rapids: Eerdmans, 1986), 16.
15. McGrath, "The Challenge of Pluralism," 230.
16. Newbigin, *The Gospel*, 1.
17. Gaede, *When Tolerance Is No Virtue*, 27.
18. Cited by J. I. Packer in *Freedom, Authority and Scripture* (Downers Grove: InterVarsity Press), 31.
19. Dallas Willard, "No Pluralism in Moral Matters?" *Discernment* (Winter 1994), 2.
20. His Holiness John Paul II, *Crossing the Threshold of Hope* (Toronto:

Alfred A. Knopf, 1994), 78.

21. James Q. Wilson, *The Moral Sense* (Toronto: The Free Press, 1993), 199.
22. John Paul II, *Crossing the Threshold*, 81–82.
23. Morris Ginsberg, *Reason and Unreason in Society* (London: Longmans, Green, 1947), 308.
24. McGrath, "The Challenge of Pluralism," 239.
25. John Hick, *Truth and Dialogue* (London: Sheldon Press, 1974), 148.
26. McGrath, "The Challenge of Pluralism," 256.
27. John Paul II, *Crossing the Threshold*, 80–81.
28. C. Glock and E. Stark, *Religion and Society in Tension* (Chicago: Rand McNally, 1965), 120–121.
29. Newbigin, *Foolishness to the Greeks*, 144.
30. Richard F. Lovelace, *Dynamics of Spiritual Life* (Downers Grove: InterVarsity Press, 1979), 16–17.
31. Frederick Buechner, *Whistling in the Dark: An ABC Theologized* (San Francisco: Harper & Row, 1988), 33–35.
32. Descriptions 1–5 were compiled from notes attributed to Richard Foster.
33. Gaede, *When Tolerance is No Virtue*, 62.
34. Stephen L. Carter, *The Culture of Disbelief* (New York: BasicBooks, 1993), 25.
35. Posterski and Barker, *Where's a Good Church?*, 65.
36. Naomi Wolf, "A 'new' feminist fires back," *Toronto Star*, September 18, 1994.

Chapter Three

1. Ron Graham, *God's Dominion* (Toronto: McClelland & Stewart, 1990), 11–12.
2. Michael Bliss, "The death of God hurts us most at this time of year," *Toronto Star*, December 16, 1994, A29.
3. Gordon Moir, "A Christian in a post-Christian age," *Globe and Mail*, November 16, 1994.
4. Elizabeth Renzetti, "Fifth Column," *Globe and Mail*, March 29, 1994.
5. Cited in Neil Bissoondath, *Selling Illusions: The Cult of Multiculturalism in Canada* (Toronto: Penguin Books, 1994), 192, in conversation with Michael Ignatieff, December 1, 1993.
6. Paul Marshall, "True pluralism is grounded in God's patience," *Christian Week*, April 27, 1993, 3.
7. Quoted in Russell Kirk, *The Conservative Mind From Burke to Eliot* (Chicago: Regnery, 1986), 17.
8. Michael Novak, *Free Persons and the Common Good* (New York: Madison Books, 1989), 9.
9. Oliver F. Williams, "To Enhance the Common Good: An Introduction," in *The Common Good and U.S.Capitalism*, Williams and Houck, eds. (Lanham, MD: University Press of America, 1987), 3.

10. Vatican Council II, The Church in the Modern World (1965) *Graudium et Spes*, 26. Cited in Michael Novak, *Free Persons*, 17.
11. Cardinal Joseph Hoeffner, S.J., *Fundamentals of Christian Sociology*, cited in Michael Novak, *Free Persons*, 17.
12. Debra Fieguth, "Wilkinson to serve sentence at home," *Christian Week*, August 2, 1994.
13. "Tenured Radicals," *New Criterion*, January 1991, 13. Cited in Charles Taylor, *Multiculturalism: Examining the Politics of Recognition* (New Jersey: Princeton University Press, 1994), 72.
14. J.M.S. Careless, *The Canadiana Encyclopedia*, Volume I, (Edmonton: Hurtig Publishers, 1985), 232.
15. Philip Resnick, *Thinking English Canada* (Toronto: Stoddart, 1994), 32.
16. The Constitution Act, 1982, amended by Constitution Amendment Proclamation, 1983, Government of Canada.
17. Cited in Kevin J. Christiano, "Federalism as a Canadian National Ideal: The Civic Rationalism of Pierre Elliott Trudeau," (Unpublished paper, 1990), 21.
18. Resnick, *English Canada*, 29.
19. Northrop Frye, 1953. Cited in Pierre Berton, *Why We Act Like Canadians: A Personal Exploration of Our National Character* (Toronto: McClelland and Stewart, 1982), 43.
20. Pierre Berton, *Why We Act Like Canadians: A Personal Exploration of Our National Character* (Toronto: McClelland and Stewart, 1982), 85.
21. Berton, *Why We Act*, 58.
22. Cited by Reginald Bibby, *Mosaic Madness* (Toronto: Stoddart, 1990), 95.
23. Cited by Rosemary Speirs, "Canadians know who they are, PM says," *Toronto Star*, July 2, 1994.
24. Bissoondath, *Selling Illusions*, 192.
25. Talcott Parsons, "Polarization of the World and International Order," *Sociological Theory and Modern Society* (New York: Free Press, 1967), 484.
26. Don E. Eberly, *Restoring the Good Society* (Grand Rapids: Baker Books, 1994), 107.
27. Sandro Contenta, "Quebec and the politics of diversity," *Toronto Star*, January 15, 1995.
28. Cited by Seymour Martin Lipset, *Continental Divide* (Toronto: C.D. Howe Institute, 1989), 180.
29. Charles Taylor, *Multiculturalism*, 38, 41.
30. Gad Horowitz, "Mosaics and Identity," in *Making It: The Canadian Dream,* Bryan Finnigan and Cy Gonick, eds. (Toronto: McClelland and Stewart, 1972), 465–473.
31. Cited by Bissoondath, *Selling Illusions*, 46.
32. Cited by Bissoondath, *Selling Illusions*, 50.

33. Sandro Contenta, "Politics of Diversity."
34. *The Reid Report* (Vol. 8, No. 4), 1–10.
35. Bissoondath, *Selling Illusions*, 177.
36. Angus E. Reid and Margaret M. Burns, *Canada and the World: An International Perspective on Canada and Canadians* (Winnipeg: Angus Reid Group, 1992), 86.
37. Angus Reid Group, July 1994, N=1502.
38. Caleb Rosado, "America the Brutal," *Christianity Today*, August 15, 1994, 20.
39. Peter C. Newman, "New Age Dreams in Hard Times," cited in *Maclean's*, October 10, 1994, 38.
40. Douglas Coupland, *Life After God* (New York: Pocket Books, 1994), 273–274.
41. "The myth of Canadian diversity," editorial, *Globe and Mail*, June 13, 1994.
42. Gerald Vandezande, *Let Justice Flow* (CJL Foundation, 1994), 21.
43. Mark Kingwell, "Citizenship and Civility," *University of Toronto Magazine* (Winter 1994).
44. Robert Bellah, *Habits of the Heart* (New York: Harper & Row, 1985), 15.
45. Eberly, *Good Society*, 16.
46. St. Augustine, *City of God*, Vernon Bourke, ed. (Garden City, NY: Image Books, 1958), 27–29.
47. S. D. Gaede, *When Tolerance Is No Virtue* (Downers Grove: InterVarsity Press, 1993), 55.
48. Quotation attributed to John Henry Jowett, contained in a fax received by D. Miller Alloway, November 23, 1994.

Chapter Four

1. Brian C. Stiller, letter from EFC, February 14, 1994.
2. Nicolaas Van Rijn, "Catholics told: fight same-sex benefits," *Toronto Star*, May 29, 1994.
3. Michael McAteer, "Church seeks tax change to help same-sex couples," *Toronto Star*, November 25, 1993.
4. —"Anglican cleric urges blessing of gay unions," *Toronto Star*, November 24, 1993.
5. "'Repressive' traditional family not worth saving, Hite says," *Toronto Star*, February 19, 1994.
6. Rita Zekas, "Bible belter out to out Bert & Ernie," *Toronto Star*, January 30, 1994.
7. Cited in a National Film Board of Canada marketing brochure with a covering letter from Peggy Fothergill, Professional Programs. The offer expired December 31, 1994.
8. Stephen Strauss, "Homosexual fantasies not unusual, study finds," *Globe and Mail*, August 18, 1994.
9. *MacLean's*, June 20, 1994.

10. Kelvin Browne, "Gay pride: too much of a good thing?" *Toronto Star*, July 25, 1994.
11. Bernard Bass, *Leadership, Psychology and Organizational Behavior* (New York: Harper Brothers, 1960), 362.
12. Sidney Mead, cited in Lesslie Newbigin, *Foolishness to the Greeks* (Grand Rapids: Eerdmans, 1986), 144.
13. Stephen Kliewer, *How to Live With Diversity in the Local Church* (New York: The Alban Institute, 1987), 10.
14. Gordon W. Allport, *Personality and Social Encounter: Selected Essays* (Boston: Beacon, 1960), 210.
15. Larry L. Rasmussen, *Moral Fragments and Moral Community* (Minneapolis: Fortress Press, 1993), 17.
16. Cited at the United Church General Council Meeting, Sudbury, Ontario, 1986. Quoted in *Nation to Nation: Aboriginal Sovereignty and the Future of Canada* (Concord: House of Anansi Press Limited, 1992), 33. Used by permission of the United Church of Canada.
17. Cited in the *Globe and Mail*, June 20, 1994.
18. Lois Sweet, "Gay love gets special blessing," *Toronto Star*, February 14, 1994.
19. Doug Koop, "Presbyterians adopt human sexuality statement," *Christian Week*, June 21, 1994.
20. Cited by Patrick Doyle, "Chrétien rebuffs right-to-life backers in emotional debate," *Toronto Star*, February 23, 1992.
21. Allan Thompson, "Liberals split on benefit plan for gay couples," *Toronto Star*, March 17, 1994.
22. Tim Harper, "PM clamps lid on anti-gay talk," *Toronto Star*, September 29, 1994.
23. Lois Sweet, "Pulpit Power," *Toronto Star*, June 4, 1994.
24. Newbigin, *Foolishness to the Greeks*, 137.
25. William Walker, "55% of Ontarians want new same-sex bill," *Toronto Star*, August 15, 1994.
26. Sean Fine, "Two men seek rights as spouses in court," *Globe and Mail*, November 1, 1994.
27. Recorded from a television interview on CTV's *Canada AM*, November 1, 1994.
28. "Anti-gay protesters warn MP's of 'demoralization,'" *Royal Gazette*, February 15, 1994.
29. Nancy Gibbs, "Why? The Killing Fields of Rwanda," *Time*, May 16, 1994.
30. Andre Picard, "World stands accused," *Globe and Mail*, July 25, 1994. Reprinted with permission from the *Globe and Mail*.
31. Richard J. Barnet and John Cavanagh, *Global Dreams: Imperial Corporations and the New World Order* (Simon & Schuster, 1994.) Cited in a review by Ann Shortell, *Globe and Mail*, May 14, 1994.

32. Newbigin, *Foolishness to the Greeks*, 129.
33. Angus Reid Group, July 1994.
34. Elias Chacour, *Blood Brothers* (Tarrytown, NY: Fleming H. Revell Co., 1984)

Chapter Five

1. Cited by John Allemang, "Why Isaiah Berlin matters," *Globe and Mail*, November 25, 1994.
2. Milton Rokeach, ed., *The Open and Closed Mind: Investigations Into the Nature of Belief Systems and Personality Systems* (New York: BasicBooks, 1960), 33.
3. Myron and Jan Chartier, "Clergy Self Care," *The Clergy Journal* (Vol. LXX, No. 9), 3.
4. William H. Willimon, *The Intrusive Word: Preaching to the Unbaptized* (Grand Rapids: Eerdmans, 1994), 9.
5. Rita Daly, "Teacher's win called threat to Catholic education," *Toronto Star*, September 11, 1994.
6. —"Barred religion teacher back on job today," *Toronto Star*, September 14, 1994.
7. Stephen Kliewer, *How to Live With Diversity in the Local Church* (New York: The Alban Institute, 1987), 12.
8. Gordon W. Allport, *Personality and Social Encounter: Selected Essays* (Botson: Beacon, 1960), 210.
9. Rod Mickleburgh, "Prohibit surrogate mothers, report says," *Globe and Mail*, November 30, 1993.
10. *Maclean's*, November 28, 1994.
11. James Davison Hunter, *Culture Wars: The Struggle to Define America* (New York: BasicBooks, 1991), 13, 18.
12. Editorial, The Toronto Star, July 19, 1994.
13. Robert Sheppard, "A solid vote against assisted suicide," *Globe and Mail*, May 30, 1994.
14. Lisa Priest, "Assisted suicide supported in poll," *Toronto Star*, March 3, 1994.
15. Brian Stiller, "The temptations of sympathy," *Toronto Star*, February 24, 1994.
16. "I'll support assisted suicide: Manning," *Toronto Star*, April 23, 1994.
17. Frank Jones, "Let's not view suicide as a solution," *Toronto Star*, October 24, 1994.
18. Andrew Coyne, "The slippery slope that leads to death," *Globe and Mail*, November 21, 1994.
19. S.D. Gaede, *When Tolerance Is No Virtue* (Downers Grove: InterVarsity Press, 1993), 27.
20. Paul and Jennifer Brink, "The Tolerant Personality: A Review of Psychological Theory," (unpublished paper, June 1994), 1.
21. Gaede, *When Tolerance Is No Virtue*, 27–28.
22. Maureen Lennon, "Home Alone," *Globe and Mail*, October 28, 1994.

23. Willimon, *The Intrusive Word*, 80.
24. Douglas John Hall, *The Future of the Church: Where Are We Headed?* (Toronto: The United Church Publishing House, 1989), 57.
25. Robert J. Schreiter, "Changes in Roman Catholic Attitudes toward Proselytism and Mission," in *Pushing the Faith: Proselytism and Civility in a Pluralistic World*, Martin E. Marty and Frederick E. Greenspahn, eds., (New York: Crossroad, 1988), 93.
26. Salvatore R. Maddi, *Personality Theories: A Comparative Analysis* (Homewood, Ill.: Dorsey, 1980), 518.
27. T. W. Adorno, Else Frenkel-Brunswik, Daniel J. Levinson, and R. Nevitt Sandord, *The Authoritarian Personality* (New York: Norton, 1982), 147.
28. Brink, "The Tolerant Personality," 15.
29. Adorno, Frenkel-Brunswik, Levinson, and Sandord, *The Authoritarian Personality*, 150.
30. Harry A. Van Belle, *Basic Intent and Therapeutic Approach of Carl R. Rogers* (Toronto: Wedge, 1980), 60–61.
31. Rokeach, *The Open and Closed Mind*, 63.
32. Gaede, *When Tolerance Is No Virtue*, 37–38.
33. Rokeach, *The Open and Closed Mind*, 10.
34. Hunter, *Culture Wars*, 298.
35. Cited by Don E. Eberly, *Restoring the Good Society* (Grand Rapids: Baker Books, 1994), 74.
36. Richard J. Mouw, *Uncommon Decency: Christian Civility in an Uncivil World* (Downers Grove: InterVarsity Press, 1992), 21.
37. Christopher Lasch, *The True and Only Heaven: Progress and Its Critics* (New York: W. W. Norton, 1991), 32.
38. David Tracy, *Plurality and Ambiguity: Hermeneutics, Religion, Hope* (Chicago: University of Chicago, 1987), 83.
39. Stephen L. Carter, *The Culture of Disbelief* (New York: BasicBooks, 1993), 41.
40. James MacDougall, "Murder of child with disabilities can't be excused," *Toronto Star*, December 9, 1994.
41. Lois Sweet, "Face to Face," *Toronto Star*, July 16, 1994.
42. The inscription printed on the placemats at The Globe Restaurant, Rosemont, Ontario.
43. I. Howard Marshall, from an article "Towards Maturity" (source unknown)
44. A. Van Kaam and S. Muto, *Am I Living a Spiritual Life?* (Denville, NJ: Dimension Books, 1978).
45. Marshall, "Towards Maturity"
46. John B. Cobb Jr., "Being a transformationist in a pluralistic world," *The Christian Century*, August 10–17, 1994, 749.

Chapter Six

1. Alister E. McGrath, "The Challenge of Pluralism for the Contemporary Christian Church," Proceedings of the Wheaton Theology Conference (1992), 229.
2. Frederick Buechner, *Telling Secrets* (San Francisco: HarperCollins, 1991), 63–64.
3. Paul Marshall, "Religion and Canadian Culture," in "Shaping a Christian Vision for Canada: Discussion Papers on Canada's Future," Aileen Van Ginkel, ed., The Task Force on Canada's Future, Evangelical Fellowship of Canada (Markham: Faith Today Publications, 1992), 20–21.
4. Southamstar Network, "He returns lost $1,400," *Toronto Star*, December 16, 1994.
5. Reginald Bibby, *Mosaic Madness* (Toronto: Stoddart, 1990), 98.
6. Richard J. Mouw, *Uncommon Decency: Christian Civility in an Uncivil World* (Downers Grove: InterVarsity Press, 1992), 20
7. Paul Watson, "Death by stoning on a hot afternoon in Somalia," *Toronto Star*, December 10, 1994.
8. Ovide Mercredi and Mary Ellen Turpel, *In The Rapids: Navigating the Future of First Nations* (Toronto: Penguin Group, 1993), 2.
9. Lorrie Goldstein, *Toronto Sun*, April 9, 1993. Reprinted with the permission of Canada Wide, a Division of the Toronto Sun Publishing Corporation.
10. Martin E. Marty, "Religious Power in America: A Contemporary Map," *Criterion* (21:1, Winter 1982), 31.
11. Martin E. Marty and Frederick E. Greenspahn, eds. *Pushing the Faith: Proselytism and Civility in a Pluralistic World*, (New York: Crossroad, 1988), 158.
12. Tom Harpur, "Historically, Jesus never claimed to be the 'only' way," *Toronto Star*, December 18, 1994.
13. Marty, *Pushing the Faith*, 158.
14. Marty, *Pushing the Faith*, xii.
15. William J. Abraham, *The Logic of Evangelism* (Grand Rapids: Eerdmans, 1989), 95.
16. Willimon, *The Intrusive Word: Preaching to the Unbaptized* (Grand Rapids: Eerdmans, 1994), 4.
17. Walter Brueggemann, *Biblical Perspectives on Evangelism* (Nashville: Abingdon Press, 1993), 10.
18. Willimon, *The Intrusive Word*, 135.
19. Donald C. Posterski, *Reinventing Evangelism* (Downers Grove: InterVarsity Press, 1989), 67.
20. —"Awakening the Spiritually Indifferent," *Decision Magazine* (November 1992), 10.
21. Rodney Clapp, "Let the pagans have the holiday," *Christianity Today*, December 13, 1993, 31.
22. Helmut Thielicke, *The Waiting Father* (New York: James Clarke,

1966). Cited in Rowland Croucher, *Still Waters, Deep Water* (Australia: Albatross Books, 1987), 207.
23. Tom Harpur, "New growth of spirituality can't flourish in isolation," *Toronto Star*, February 6, 1994.

Chapter Seven

1. *Maclean's* cover, October 10, 1994.
2. *Newsweek* cover, November 28, 1994.
3. Robert Everett-Green, "Signs of the sacred in an age of disenchantment," *Globe and Mail*, December 24, 1994.
4. Guy Chevreau, *Catch the Fire: The Toronto Blessing* (Great Britain: Marshall Pickering, 1994), 17.
5. Chevreau, *Catch the Fire*, 27.
6. Cited by Peter C. Newman, "New Age dreams in hard times," *Maclean's*, October 10, 1994, 38.
7. David Roberts, "Get back to God, study tells church," *Globe and Mail*, December 10, 1994.
8. Lesslie Newbigin, *Foolishness to the Greeks* (Grand Rapids: Eerdmans, 1986), 20.
9. Romano Guardini, *The End of the Modern World*, 128–29.
10. James Q. Wilson, *The Moral Sense* (Toronto: The Free Press, 1993), 251.
11. Larry L. Rasmussen, *Moral Fragments and Moral Community* (Minneapolis: Fortress Press, 1993), 11.
12. Reginald W. Bibby and Donald C. Posterski, *Teen Trends: A Nation In Motion* (Toronto: Stoddart, 1992), 248.
13. Bibby and Posterski, *Teen Trends*, 272–299. Also Posterski and Barker, *Where's a Good Church?* (Winfield, B.C.: Wood Lake Books, 1993), 103–105.
14. Diogenes Allen, *Christian Belief in a Postmodern World* (Louisville: Westminster/John Knox Press, 1989), 5–6.
15. Mark Novak, *Aging and Society: A Canadian Perspective* (Toronto: Nelson Canada, 1993), 192.
16. C. David Naylor, Geoffrey M. Anderson, and Vivek Goel, eds., *Patterns of Health Care in Ontario* (Toronto: The Institute for Clinical Evaluative Sciences in Ontario), 22–36.
17. Robert Wuthnow, *Christianity in the Twenty-first Century* (New York: Oxford University Press, 1993), 5–6.
18. Peter L. Berger, *A Far Glory: The Quest for Faith in an Age of Credulity* (New York: Doubleday, 1992), 172.
19. Wuthnow, *Christianity*, 7.
20. William H. Willimon, *The Intrusive Word: Preaching to the Unbaptized* (Grand Rapids: Eerdmans, 1994), 39.
21. Tom Harpur, "New growth of spirituality can't flourish in isolation," *Toronto Star*, February 6, 1994.
22. Robert Wilken, "The Lives of the Saints and the Pursuit of Virtue,"

First Things (December 1990), 45.

23. Kenneth L. Woodward, *Making Saints* (New York: Simon and Schuster, 1990), 403.
24. Cited in Rowland Croucher and Grace Thomlinson, *High Mountains Deep Valleys* (Australia: Albatross Books, 1990), 23–24.
25. Harry Blamires, *The Christian Mind* (London: SPCK, 1963), 44, 67.
26. Sean O'Sullivan, *Both My Houses: From Politics to Priesthood* (Toronto: Key Porter Books, 1986), 234–235.
27. Rasmussen, *Moral Fragments*, 15.
28. Richard J. Mouw, *Uncommon Decency: Christian Civility in an Uncivil World* (Downers Grove: InterVarsity Press, 1992), 168.
29. Croucher and Thomlinson, *High Mountains*, 14.
30. S.D. Gaede, *When Tolerance Is No Virtue* (Downers Grove: InterVarsity Press, 1993), 63.
31. Karl Rahner, *Theological Investigations* Vol. XXII (New York: Crossroad, 1991), 123.
32. Harpur, "New growth of spirituality can't flourish in isolation," *Toronto Star*, February 6, 1994.
33. C.S. Lewis, *The Great Divorce* (London: Geoffrey Bles, 1946), 66–67.
34. His Holiness John Paul II, *Crossing the Threshold of Hope* (Toronto: Alfred A. Knopf, 1994), 88.

Also by Don Posterski
and available from Wood Lake Books...

Where's a Good Church?

Canadians Respond from the Pulpit, Podium, and Pew
by Don Posterski and Irwin Barker

Where's a Good Church? is based on data collected from clergy, academics, and laity, spanning the spectrum of Protestant churches across Canada. The aim is to learn from churches where spiritual vitality is evident, and to assist struggling churches increase effectiveness.

Themes include:

- community and mission outreach
- recruiting and retaining members
- responding to *lifers* and *switchers*
- qualitative and quantitative growth
- balancing relevancy and orthodoxy
- differences in worship styles
- focusing inside or targeting outside

5 1/2 x 8 1/2", 270 pages, softcover, Wood Lake Books
ISBN 0-929032-94-2
929-094 · $17.95

The Emerging Generation

An Inside Look at Canada's Teenagers
by Don Posterski and Reginald W. Bibby
ISBN 0-7725-18181
· $12.95

Teen Trends

New Directions, New Responses
by Don Posterski and Reginald W. Bibby
ISBN 0-7737-55314
· $17.95

To order: Contact your local bookstore or call Wood Lake Books

In Canada phone 1-800-663-2775 Fax: 604-766-2736
Outside Canada phone 604-766-2778 Office hours: 8:00 a.m.–4:30 p.m. Pacific Time